Yugoslavia
Peace, War, and Dissolution

Noam Chomsky
Edited by Davor Džalto

Yugoslavia: Peace, War, and Dissolution
Noam Chomsky. Edited by Davor Džalto
© Valeria Chomsky 2018
Preface © Andrej Grubačić 2018
Introductory chapters © Davor Džalto 2018
This edition © 2018 PM Press

ISBN: 978–1–62963–442–5
Library of Congress Control Number: 2017942916

Cover by John Yates / www.stealworks.com
Interior design by briandesign

10 9 8 7 6 5 4 3

PM Press
PO Box 23912
Oakland, CA 94623
www.pmpress.org

Printed in the USA

Contents

PART III KOSOVO CRISIS

Acknowledgments

This book would have never been completed without the enthusiasm, energy, and support that my dear colleague and friend Marina Sovilj invested in this project over a couple of years. I am deeply grateful for that.

I owe gratitude to my dear colleagues and friends Irene Caratelli, Borut Zidar, Vladimir Veljković, and Emil Džudžević. They gave me many important suggestions and comments that significantly improved the manuscript. My gratitude also extends to Milenko Srećković, who provided me with important materials for documenting and understanding some of the recent developments in the region.

I am grateful to my assistant Ella May Sumner; I cannot imagine the completion of this project without all the time and effort she invested in addressing many practical aspects of the process.

A big "thank you" also goes to Anthony Arnove, who continued to support this project over many years.

Last but certainly not least, I want to thank Noam Chomsky, one of the greatest intellectuals and humanists of our time, for his tireless engagement in the world's affairs and for his struggle against injustice, oppression, and imperial ambitions everywhere, not least in the Balkans.

—Ed.

Remaining Yugoslav

Andrej Grubačić

Sixty years ago, the concrete pier that butts against the Adriatic in the village of Trpanj was strewn with drying fishing nets. Local fishers came into the cannery to empty their bursting nets, and in the summer tourists from the USSR mingled among them. Twenty years ago, it was empty, abandoned because of the Yugoslav civil war. Stone buildings that had housed gathering places and families were transformed into hospitals, the fishing boats long abandoned. I look upon the same pier today, busy with young families and tourists, mostly from the former Soviet republics. A short walk from the harbor, I come upon a magazine stall. The papers report on the most recent attempt to change the name of Marshal Tito Square, five hours north in Zagreb, the capital of Croatia. Despite the passing of decades, the battle for the soul of Croatia, now a member of the European Union, and all of former Yugoslavia rages on. Was Comrade Tito a good Croatian or a pro-Serb dictator? Who inherits modern-day Croatia, antifascists or the heirs of the Ustaše, infamous Nazi-collaborators?

Few in the U.S. have tackled the complexity of the former Yugoslavia the way that Noam Chomsky has. When asked to write this preface, I started reworking my way through Noam's writing. His analysis is ruthless, clinical. His debates with the *Guardian*'s George Monbiot and the new intellectuals of the Bosnian Institute of England are the stuff of legend. Noam's influence on public discourse in the countries of former Yugoslavia remains unparalleled. As I read through his writings, I was struck by what I consider an "Alexievich moment," an absence of what Russian oral historian Svetlana Alexievich called the "interior life of socialism," or "socialism of the soul." (Only a Russian could come up with such a delightful phrase!) Alexievich was referring to everyday life under socialism, a challenge to an oft-repeated falsehood of capitalist historians: that all the world's socialisms were alike. Of course those of us who grew up in the formerly socialist world—ineptly referred to as Eastern Europe, or *where the boogeyman lives*, as a friend from Ohio once told me, only half joking—have certain things in common. But the Soviet man and the Yugoslav woman, for example, were quite different. And they had little in common with a Bulgarian or Romanian socialist citizen.

This preface aspires to be one glimpse of the interior life of former Yugoslavia from the perspective of a Yugoslav, of a Yugoslav exile. And even after multiple exiles—first from Yugoslavia at the end of socialism and later from what was left of the Federal Republic of Yugoslavia after the 1999 NATO bombings—I remain a Yugoslav. My family has lived at the same Belgrade address, first in Socialist Yugoslavia, then the Federal Republic of Yugoslavia, Serbia and Montenegro, and today, Serbia. My story and that of my family are at the same time idiosyncratic and representative of Yugoslav history.

I never met Comrade Tito. But I remember the day he died in May 1980. His funeral procession in Belgrade brought seven hundred thousand to the streets, millions of people wept and mourned throughout Yugoslavia. Many of them were Tito loyalists, pledging their allegiance to our endangered socialist homeland. Many others, like myself, were proud to call themselves Yugoslavs, proud to be from a communist country. A country that hosted the Living Theatre, a country that was home to the music of Laibach and the Black Wave cinema of Dušan Makavejev.

Even as a child, I knew our Yugoslavia was an anomaly. We played Partisans and Germans, not Cowboys and Indians. In the U.S., children *cross their hearts and hope to die* when they make a promise or swear they're telling the truth. As school children in Yugoslavia, we would say *Tita mi!*—I swear on Comrade Tito! For us, there was nothing more sacred. The adults were equally serious. When I was seven, my teacher asked whom I loved more, my mother or Comrade Tito. When I chose my mother—after all, I reasoned, I had never met Tito, while I'd gotten to know my mother quite well—I was called a reactionary and sent home in tears. My mother was fuming; she marched straight to the school, and I was allowed to return the next day.

But my mother could afford to do things like that: her father Rato was one of the most celebrated communists in Yugoslavia. His first family, he once told my mother, was the Communist Party: he was the last secretary of the legendary Communist Youth; a minister in the first post–World

War II Yugoslav state; a member of the Central Committee of the League of Yugoslav Communists; an ambassador to the Non-Aligned Movement; the president of the Socialist Federal Republic of Bosnia; later becoming a member of the rotating Yugoslav presidency after Tito's death. Even before World War II, my grandfather was well known: a professional football player (real football, not that odd thing people do in the U.S.). He used trips to away games to distribute party material. It is even said that he and his cousin Miljenko Cvitković, a fighter in the Spanish Revolution, attempted to assassinate the anti-communist Minister of the Interior of the Kingdom of Yugoslavia. Luckily for the minister (and for my grandfather), they did not find him.

A communist illegalist, Rato also spent time in a Sarajevo prison, then considered a *red university* where young militants were educated. The party, which actively recruited students before the war, later sent him to study law and forestry in Belgrade. After he finished university in 1939 war broke out: my grandfather fought against the fascists, both as a Partisan commander and a political commissar. He helped organize the Sarajevo uprising and took part in the political assemblies of the incipient Yugoslav state, held in the so-called free territories of Užice and Bihać. As Yugoslavs struggled for their liberation, Rato met my grandmother Tatjana, a member of the youth antifascist movement. They were an odd couple. Tatjana, named after the famous Puškin poem, was a well-educated Montenegrin royal exiled after the establishment of the Union of Serbs, Croats, and Slovenes after World War I. Class differences aside, they fell in love. (Tatjana's mother, a royalist taught from an early age that communists were "devils," even came to love my grandfather as one of her own.) Tatjana always held onto a bit of her old elitism, though: she couldn't stand the future communist dissident Milovan Đilas, then a family friend. "The man has never read a single novel in his life," she used to say. One can only assume his penchant for brutally assassinating his wartime comrades was related to this lack of poetic imagination.

After World War II, my grandfather Rato met his counterpart in the Cuban government, the Minister of Light Industry Che Guevara, who was in Yugoslavia seeking arms. My grandfather, who considered Che a bandit incapable of understanding the process of socialist construction, was livid. (According to my anarchist mentor Trivo, who traveled with Che to Latin America, the Argentine was similarly disappointed in the reality of real socialism.) Later, as secretary of the Communist Youth, Rato initiated the organization of youth brigades and work actions in which most of the new country's youth were to participate. In the youth brigades, people fell in love, socialized, and made friends. British Marxist historian E.P. Thompson met his wife Dorothy while they participated in a youth work action brigade. But the brigades were also educational spaces, where people from the country's rural regions learned three important lessons: reading, writing, and living together with fellow Yugoslavs. For these youths, the memory of fratricidal war was still fresh. The youth brigades were convivial laboratories of *Bratstvo* and *Jedinstvo*, or brotherhood (of the nations) and unity (of the working class), as well as an international and international-ist project,

In 1948, the unthinkable happened: the Yugoslav Communist Party, long one of the closest and fiercest allies of the Soviet Union, broke with Stalin. It was a decision as justified as it was courageous. In refuting Stalinism, Yugoslav communists found themselves in a difficult situation. Yugoslavs had long believed a Soviet invasion was imminent. After the break, a need for a new kind of socialism, a new kind of foreign policy, emerged. My grandfather Rato was sent to Egypt and the United Arab Republic as an ambassador of Yugoslavia's new direction. Yugoslav self-management, inspired by revolutionary syndicalism and guild socialism, was built around the notion of social property (everyone owns everything, no one owns anything) and de-bureaucratization (if everyone is a bureau-crat for a while, bureaucracy will become unnecessary), while workers' assemblies served as spaces of direct democracy. (Today, revolutionaries of Rojava approach their popular police forces with a similar logic: the best way to eliminate the need for police is to teach everyone how to do this terrible job.) It was an alternative state socialism, with a market, without a planned economy, and—at least on paper—without bureaucracy.

My anarchist friend Zoran is less sanguine about the Yugoslav experiment. After finishing his studies, he refused the life of the intelligentsia and went to work (and agitate) in a factory. But when a (socialist) worker assassinated the (socialist) boss, Zoran the (anarchist) agitator went to prison. For a long time after, the only work he was allowed was as a leather craftsman; he made beautiful bags. Zoran is one of the gentlest people I know. But we never discuss Marx or Marxism.

De-bureaucratization was complemented by South-South interna-tionalism. For Tito and Yugoslav communists in general, the Non-Aligned Movement was not about neutralism but the refusal and active negation of the tacit agreement between the U.S. and the USSR that created bloc-based politics. The alternative was a South-based anticolonial politics that promoted independence, self-determination, and democratic socialism. It's why my grandfather and his predecessors armed the Algerian revolutionaries with Yugoslav weapons, medication, nurses, doctors, and even theater troupes. (The French, with the exception of Sartre, were not happy.)

My parents met in Sarajevo. My father came from a family of communist revolutionaries as well, but of a different shade of red. My paternal grandfather Kosta, one of fifteen children born to a family in the mountains of Herzegovina, was a lifelong communist. He defended his thesis on Marxist education in Prague in 1937, his communist organizing got him fired after a stint at the University of Belgrade, after which he went underground. In these days of illegal activity, he met my grandmother Emilia, a German communist from the Serbian town of Vrsac, where her parents had moved when it was still part of the Austro-Hungarian Empire. After World War II, she would witness the forced exodus of her neighbors, when German civilians, or *Volksdeutsche*, were deported from Yugoslavia en masse.

During World War II, my grandfather Kosta was a Partisan commander in Herzegovina. As one of the more educated communists of his time, Kosta became the first president of the liberated university in the free territory of Bihać. It was here that he received news of my grandmother's capture by Serbian collaborators, known as Četniks. Emilia was delivered to the Germans and ended up in a concentration camp in Bileća, Herzegovina, where she gave birth to my father. His name is Slobodan, meaning "freedom," and he ate powdery slaked lime, calcium hydroxide, from the walls, which my grandmother was forced to feed him in the camp. Soon after the camp was liberated, my three-year-old father became ill and needed penicillin. There was enough medicine to save only a single life, but in addition to the child a Partisan soldier lay dying. The Partisan insisted the penicillin be given to the child. My father was saved, the young Partisan died soon after.

In 1948, my grandfather Kosta was taken to a gulag on the Adriatic Sea. Goli Otok Island housed thousands of sincere communists who disagreed with Tito's decision to cut ties with Stalin, enraged Yugoslavia had been formally expelled from the socialist world. Kosta spent seven years surrounded by comrades as stubborn and loyal to their beliefs as he was. He survived the camp and the beatings, before eventually succumbing to the consequences of torture. Before he died, he created the scholarly foundations for the disciplines of library science, psychology, and pedagogy in socialist Yugoslavia. He was formally pardoned for his "crimes" in 2017, at long last no longer an "enemy of the people." It is a cruel irony that as my grandfather received his pardon, the same Serbian Četniks who had captured and tortured his pregnant wife posthumously underwent the same official "rehabilitation" process.

While my grandfather was "away on business"—code for being held captive at the Goli Otok camp, and the title of the famous Emir Kusturica film—my grandmother Emilia received her PhD in linguistics and supported the family by teaching at the universities of Sarajevo and Zagreb. She lived long enough to receive news of her daughter's untimely death: my aunt Slobodanka was killed by a sniper's bullet during the siege of Sarajevo in the 1990s.

My grandmother Emilia, a materialist, was terrified by the possibility of my becoming a philosophical idealist, so she fed me a constant stream of works by Feuerbach—ambitious reading for a twelve-year-old. As a child, I once asked her if she still believed in communism. "I will always be a communist," she told me, "despite all the disappointments. But the path to communism my generation has chosen is wrong." The task of your generation, she later said, is to find a different path. This conversation— along with Alexander Herzen's memoir *My Past and Thoughts*, a gift from my maternal grandmother Tatjana—led me to anarchism. Not much later, along with many of my comrades, I discovered the work of Noam Chomsky.

I joined the anarchist movement when I was in my teens. Early on, I encountered the Belgrade Libertarian Group, a left-libertarian offshoot of the Yugoslav Praxis group. Praxis was among the most important examples of Yugoslav Marxist thought: a humanist attempt at rescuing libertarian Marx from positivist Marxism, a left communist vision built on the insights of Karel Kosík, Karl Korsch, Rosa Luxemburg, and others. Praxis summer meetings were held on Korčula Island, and brought together Yugoslavs and Western Marxists. (The group included many young people who would go on to play a major role in Yugoslav politics, including Kropotkin's translator Zoran Đinđić, who became the first neoliberal prime minister of Serbia after the transition to capitalism. He was murdered in 2003.)

Among other indispensable texts, *Yugoslavia: Peace, War, and Dissolution* includes letters Noam wrote about the student movement and the remarkable intellectual movement that influenced it. Some members of Praxis felt the Yugoslav model justified an anarchist criticism of the Bolshevik concepts of state-socialism, democratic centralism, and vanguardism. Noam's influence on the group was considerable.

I first met Noam in the 1990s, during my earliest visits to the United States. Like anarcho-syndicalist thinker Daniel Guérin, Noam was keenly interested in Yugoslav self-management. He was patient with its contradictions and aware of its limitations, while also cognizant of its directly democratic and libertarian socialist elements. Noam signed countless petitions on behalf of Serbian workers resisting the neoliberal destruction of Yugoslavia in the 1990s. My comrades and I, for our part, translated and wrote about his work, while at the same time resisting Serbian nationalist attempts to co-opt his analysis, which included the publication of a doctored public correspondence between Noam and former Yugoslav President Dobrica Ćosić. In 2004, when I got into rather unpleasant trouble concerning my organizing in an occupied factory struggling against privatization, I immediately contacted Noam. He advised me to leave Yugoslavia and helped me come to the United States, where he supervised my doctoral dissertation.

The question remains: Where is Yugoslavia today? Yugoslavia, the socialist Yugoslavia of my youth, no longer exists. The country of my birth is now confined to the glass cases and archives of the Museum of Yugoslav History, near the resting place of Comrade Tito in Belgrade. During a recent visit to the city, I tried to get a taxi to take us to the Museum; the driver refused. "Tito was godless," he said, "not a Serb, and certainly not a democrat—why would you want to go anywhere near his grave?" The experience in the taxi sparked another memory: one day, a year earlier, Bosnian Prime Minister Bevanda appeared in our Croatian seaside village, surrounded by bodyguards. They started kicking people off the beach, and I tried to intervene, telling them the beach is still public property. I was thrown off guard when I realized that his bodyguards recognized me. "When your grandfather Rato was alive," one of them said, "during communism, anyone could use the beach. But now we live in a democracy." A valuable lesson in what political scientists call transition. Old communist bureaucrats are the new

European liberals. Former secret police agents have become gangsters. Ex-dissidents work as police spies. Bodyguards are political theorists. The world, our Yugoslav world, has been turned upside down.

Most of my former compatriots no longer call themselves Yugoslavs. In fact, the word is now often used as an insult. So why do I insist on calling myself one? To an extent, Yugoslav is a negative (and provocative) declaration, a nonidentity that negates ethnic identity. Yugoslav is a refusal of what exists now: six (or is it seven?) miniature ethnic states. Yugoslav is a refusal of new borders, new protectorate-states, six (or is it seven?) national languages carved out of a single tongue. Yugoslav is a homage to people like my grandparents, antifascist revolutionaries who spent their lives building socialist Yugoslavia. And perhaps most certainly, Yugoslav is a result of existential confusion: I was born a Yugoslav in a country called Yugoslavia. I was raised a Yugoslav. Why should I choose an ethnic identity now?

But it is not enough to be sensitive to the socialism of the soul. Remaining a Yugoslav is more than mere sentiment: Yugoslavia was and remains a political project. It was the strength and success of this project—not its weakness—that made its demise inevitable. Socialist Yugoslavia was a dangerous alternative economic model in the anti-utopian age of neoliberalism, an important experiment in an era of so-called humanitarian interventions and state building. Yugoslav multiethnicity was genuine and far-reaching, not an artificial construction. It was, it is, an expression of a collective commitment of the Yugoslav and Balkan peoples, and it took the combined power of banks and tanks to destroy it.

When I first moved to the United States, I discovered the absence of any serious interest in Yugoslavia. Yugoslavia, as it turns out, doesn't translate well. I went from one activist meeting to another, trying to get younger people interested in the history of self-management and to open up discussions on the lessons its destruction offered. Surely, an alternative model of socialism—however imperfect—could be worthy of consideration, particularly as we are repeatedly told there is no alternative. The neglect of the Yugoslav experiment in self-management and non-aligned politics is one of the most startling oversights of the U.S. Left. To be fair, Yugoslavia is a difficult experience to explain. I was invited to give a talk in San Francisco on Yugoslav non-alignment and my experiences with it, and I tried with little success to explain that geographically European Yugoslavia was one of the leading forces of the Third World movement and anticolonial politics. I grew up on a street named after Patrice Lumumba, I told the audience, and had friends who were Algerian students (we used to meet in front of the Palestinian embassy). A discussion of my favorite elementary school classes (Marxism and Esperanto, the latter in the Japanese tradition) and high school subjects (Frantz Fanon was required reading) were greeted with confused faces. I tried to temper the disbelief with a humorous anecdote: Haile Selassie, emperor of Ethiopia, upon a visit to Yugoslavia in the 1950s, was received with the greeting: "Welcome, comrade-tsar!" I tried my best, but seriously, how can you explain a country like that?

Yugoslavia was never a silent country. It was always full of music, poetry, theatre, and intellectual duels in coffee shops. Nor did it ascribe to strict traditions. A visiting friend, confused by the sight of a Christmas tree in a Yugoslav home, asked the inevitable: What kind of communists are you, anyway? My response only added to his confusion: the display of Christmas trees in Yugoslav homes, I said, was an invention of the Women's Antifascist Front. After World War II, the organization set out to reinvent domestic life, deciding to minimize the Christian significance of Christmas without abolishing it (religious holidays were tolerated under Yugoslav socialism). Instead, antifascist women appropriated the tree as a symbol of the secular New Year. Many of us never particularly enjoyed state-sponsored May Day marches or ostentatious celebrations of Comrade Tito's birthday. But New Year's—with its socialist Christmas trees—was the most important family and public holiday in the country.

I am often asked if I believe another Yugoslavia is possible. I believe it is inevitable: the idea of Yugoslavia, in one form or another, reappears with every generation. Yugoslavia, after all, was just one historical manifestation of the larger project of a Balkan federation. I hope the next attempt to construct a transethnic community in the Balkans will draw from the ideas of the nineteenth-century Serbian socialist Svetozar Marković, who believed in a stateless, horizontally organized region, a directly democratic society based on workers' associations and agricultural cooperatives. These ideas could be part of an exciting dialogue with the rich tradition of libertarian socialism, best represented by Noam Chomsky.

In Yugoslavia we have a saying that it is impossible to be born and die in the same country. It is probably also true that despite our shared experience as Yugoslavs, no two families share the same story. My story, which I shared above, is admittedly idiosyncratic. Montenegrin royals, Titoists, Stalinists, royal, communist, and anarchist exiles—perhaps we aren't an ordinary family. But then Yugoslavia wasn't an ordinary country. I hope my personal story of what it meant to grow up Yugoslav—and to refuse to become anything else—offers readers a sense of a remarkable country and a singular experience in the history of state socialism.

As I write, overlooking the sea from the village of Trpanj, I also commemorate my grandfather Rato's one-hundredth birthday. Much has changed. But in Yugoslavia we do not easily forget. On June 27, hundreds of people gathered around my grandfather's grave in the cemetery in Sarajevo. Most of them were his Partisans and fellow communists. But some were young people, inspired, perhaps, by the antinationalist Bosnian uprising of 2016. Socialist Yugoslavia may have been consigned to a museum, but the memory of the Yugoslav political project endures, as do our memories of the antifascist struggle, the heroism of Gavrilo Princip and Young Bosnians, and the tradition of multiethnic coexistence. Another Yugoslavia, in some different, and hopefully more developed form, is inevitable. I am sure of it.

Introduction

Davor Džalto

In 2017, we commemorated twenty-five years since the beginning of the war in Bosnia and Herzegovina, once upon a time the central Yugoslav republic. It was an opportunity to reflect on the devastating policies of both the "international community" and the local political elites—the policies that led to the breakup of Yugoslavia and the bloodiest conflict in Europe since World War II. It is also an opportunity to revisit the Yugoslav story, the events surrounding the formation of Yugoslavia, and its growth and disappearance.

Given its specific position and role within the Cold War world, the significance of Yugoslavia overcomes local boundaries. Faced with the Cold War, Yugoslavia responded actively and creatively. With its "no" to Stalin's USSR, its experiment in self-governing socialism, and its role in the Non-Aligned Movement, Yugoslavia was the place where some of the most important political processes and ideas of the post–World War II world were reflected.

Just as the international context had made a significant impact on the formation and the character of post–World War II Yugoslavia, the changed international context after the fall of the Berlin Wall influenced—some would claim decisively—the fate of Yugoslavia in 1990s and the fate of the region in the first decades of the new century.

This book aspires to show the complexity of these processes. It also aspires to present their interpretation from the point of view of Noam Chomsky's political philosophy. The book presents Chomsky's works on the Yugoslav region—that span over forty years—for the first time in a single volume. Chomsky's approach to the manifold issues surrounding the Balkan crisis clarifies the complex interplay between international politics and the internal forces within Yugoslav society that finally led to the breakup of Yugoslavia and its tragic aftermath.

As an important subject in international affairs over the past decades, Yugoslavia could not escape Chomsky's radar. His engagements with Yugoslav regional affairs go back to Tito's era. He closely followed the events surrounding the Yugoslav regime's repressive measures against dissident thinkers. The Yugoslav crisis, its dissolution, and the wars of the 1990s made Yugoslavia one of the central topics in Chomsky's reflections on international affairs in the 1990s and early 2000s. His articles, interviews, talks, and letters focusing on the (ex-) Yugoslav territories represent an important body of work for understanding the international interests in the region, the domestic dynamics, and the way the mainstream media have reported on these issues, which does not only distort but often contradicts the reality.

This book contains lessons from Yugoslav history, but its relevance goes beyond that. It is also a guide to understanding the broader political processes and interests that continue to have a decisive impact on international affairs in many parts of the world. Issues such as unresolved hostilities, nationalistic rhetoric, the perpetual deterioration of democratic potentials, mafia-style political leaderships, widespread corruption, neoliberal policies, broken economies, and a humiliated working class are by no means the exclusive property of most of the ex-Yugoslav societies. These "blessings" can be found in many other parts of the world and are increasingly becoming features of developed countries in the Western hemisphere as well.

The lessons from Yugoslavia can thus be instructive for all of those who aspire to understand the complex processes that have been defining the fate of the Balkans over the past couple of decades, as well as for those who aspire to change them.

Structure

The book is divided into three chapters, following the chronology of Noam Chomsky's engagements with the region's affairs.

The first chapter covers the period of Yugoslavia under Josip Broz Tito's leadership. It includes Chomsky texts addressing a variety of issues, from self-managing socialism to the activities of Yugoslav dissidents.

The second chapter is related to the crisis of the late 1980s and early 1990s and the dissolution of Yugoslavia. In the texts in this chapter, Chomsky deals with the broader European and international background of the Yugoslav crisis, the process of dissolution, and the wars in Croatia and Bosnia and Herzegovina.

The third chapter focuses on the Kosovo issue, starting with the events that led to the NATO bombing of 1999, the course of the bombing, and its aftermath.

The book concludes with Chomsky's brief reflections on the future of the region in the changed international context.

Every chapter begins with an introductory text by the editor, the purpose of which is to situate the concepts, events, and personalities discussed in each of the chapters in their broader social and historical context, to provide a more solid background to the complex Yugoslav mosaic, against which readers who may not be experts in the region can understand the specific issues that each of the texts addresses. Since Chomsky's analyses are primarily focused on the international factors and the international context of the Yugoslav crisis, the introductions mainly explore the internal factors of the Yugoslav drama, thereby complementing the main body of text.

All of the texts, including previously published articles and interviews, have been edited for the sake of consistency and clarity. All local names, concepts, and toponyms are given in their original form, except when quoted from other sources. With the exception of Albanian names, other names and concepts from the region follow their standard Serbo-Croatian form, written in Latin script.

Glossary of Acronyms

AVNOJ   Antifascist Council for the National Liberation of Yugoslavia, (Antifašističko V[ij]eće Narodnog Oslobođenja Jugoslavije)
KFOR   Kosovo Force (NATO-led)
FNRJ   Federal Peoples Republic of Yugoslavia (Federativna Narodna Republika Jugoslavija)
FRY   Federal Republic of Yugoslavia (Savezna Republika Jugoslavija)
ICTY   International Criminal Tribunal for the Former Yugoslavia
JNA   Yugoslav People's Army (Jugoslovenska Narodna Armija)
KLA   Kosovo Liberation Army (a.k.a. Ushtria Çlirimtare e Kosovës, UÇK)
KVM   OSCE Kosovo Verification Mission
NDH   Independent State of Croatia (Nezavisna Država Hrvatska)
OSCE   Organization for Security and Cooperation in Europe
SFRJ   Socialist Federal Republic of Yugoslavia (Socijalistička Federativna Republika Jugoslavija)
TDF   Yugoslav Territorial Defense Forces
UNHCR   United Nations High Commissioner for Refugees
VJ   Yugoslav Army (Vojska Jugoslavije)

PART I
YUGOSLAVIA

Yugoslavia: Dreams and Realities

Davor Džalto

"Yugoslavia" ("Jugoslavija") refers to the state of South Slavs. The term is derived from the word describing the South Slavic population.[1] In reality, there was more than one Yugoslav state.

"First" Yugoslavia was born out of the Kingdom of the Serbs, Croats, and Slovenians, which was formed in 1918.[2] Prior to World War I, in the territory that would become the Yugoslav state, only Serbia and Montenegro existed as independent kingdoms. The war brought about the collapse of the Austro-Hungarian monarchy, which created the opportunity for the "liberation of the Slavic population" from the centuries-long rule of various empires over the region. The newly liberated territories would join Serbia and Montenegro to form the first modern multinational State of South Slavs. The Kingdom of the Serbs, Croats, and Slovenians was renamed in 1929, becoming the Kingdom of Yugoslavia, ruled by the Karađorđević Serbian royal dynasty.

The "second" Yugoslavia was a child of World War II. After Hitler's Germany invaded the Kingdom of Yugoslavia (on April 6, 1941), two anti-fascist movements were formed—the "Četniks" of Colonel (later General) Dragoljub (nicknamed Draža) Mihailović, loyal to the exiled Yugoslav government, and the Yugoslav Partisans, led by the secretary general of the Communist Party of Yugoslavia, Josip Broz, nicknamed "Tito." Hitler's invasion resulted in the immediate partition of Yugoslavia into smaller units controlled either directly by Germany or its allies. It also resulted in the formation of the fascist Independent State of Croatia ("Nezavisna Država Hrvatska," hereafter NDH), subordinated to Hitler's Germany. The fascist "Ustaša" regime of the NDH would expand and radicalize atrocities in the region, primarily targeting the Serbian, Jewish, and Roma populations.[3]

This complex war landscape of the 1940s meant that World War II in the Yugoslav territories was not only a war of the local, predominantly Slavic population against Nazi Germany and its allies (and, with various degrees of cooperation, between the Slavic resistance movements and the global anti-Nazi coalition) but also a civil war between two different camps, one royalist (the Četniks) and the communist-led Partisans, for control over the future state, its system, and internal organization.

The foundations for the new Federal Yugoslavia were laid in the middle of the war, in the second session of the Antifascist Council for the National Liberation of Yugoslavia (AVNOJ) in 1943.[4] This meeting and its decisions would be the basis for the formation of the postwar Yugoslav state that would encompass more or less the same territories previously occupied by the Kingdom of Yugoslavia (with the later addition of Istria). The meeting was also important as it laid down the basis for the future demarcation lines between the Yugoslav republics. The internal Yugoslav borders, drawn in 1946,[5] would be criticized later on, primarily in Serbia, as arbitrary, lacking legitimacy, and being drawn against the Serbs' interests. One reason for these claims was that the new internal borders meant that Serbs lived in four different republics—apart from Serbia, a significant Serbian population also lived in Croatia, Bosnia and Herzegovina, and Montenegro. Another reason was that only Serbia, among all the other Yugoslav republics, was further split into the Autonomous Province of Vojvodina and the Autonomous Region of Kosovo-Metohija (from 1963 the Autonomous Province of Kosovo and Metohija), as defined by the 1946 Yugoslav Constitution. The reason for this probably lies in the attempts of the new Yugoslav leadership to balance out the predominant number of Serbs among the Yugoslav nations and to prevent Serbia occupying a dominant position as the biggest of the republics.[6]

The first elections took place immediately after the war on November 11, 1945. Although nominally free, only the communist National Front participated, which led to its triumph and the establishment of the one-party system. The Constitutional Assembly, formed after the elections, officially abolished the monarchy and proclaimed the Federal Peoples Republic of Yugoslavia ("Federativna Narodna Republika Jugoslavija," hereafter FNRJ) on November 29.

The first constitution of the FNRJ was approved on January 31, 1946. This constitution is important not only for its definition of the internal political and economic organization but also because of its treatment of

Socialist Federal Republic of Yugoslavia (with the internal borders of the Yugoslav Republics and the neighboring countries).

the ethnicities that lived in the newly formed state. In this document, we find a subtle (and still not consistent) terminological distinction between "nations" ("narodi") and "nationalities" ("narodnosti"). I will briefly address the complex issue of the national, ethnic, and religious landscape of communist Yugoslavia. Understanding this landscape, at least in its main features, is important since it is this diversity and the many ethnic tensions that had existed before and during World War II that played an important role in the later history of Yugoslavia and its dissolution in the 1990s.

The Yugoslav state would change its name two more times. With the constitutional amendments of 1963 the name of the country was changed to the Socialist Federal Republic of Yugoslavia ("Socijalistička Federativna Republika Jugoslavija," hereafter SFRJ). This state would continue to exist until the Yugoslav Wars of the last decade of the twentieth century. The new, and the last, Yugoslavia was proclaimed in 1992 under the name of the Federal Republic of Yugoslavia ("Savezna Republika Jugoslavija," hereafter FRY), consisting at that point of only Serbia and Montenegro.[7]

The "Brotherhood-Unity" of the Yugoslav People(s)

From the above description of Yugoslav history up to 1946, one can obtain a sense of the complexity of the ethnic, national, and religious landscape of Yugoslavia. The Kingdom of Yugoslavia was multiethnic, composed of three main South Slavic ethnic/national groups—Serbs, Croats, and Slovenians. In addition to these three, the communist Yugoslav government would also recognize Macedonians and Montenegrins as "nations."[8] This means that post–World War II Yugoslavia, in its early years, was composed of five "constitutive nations."

The political vocabulary of communist Yugoslavia requires a little bit of decoding at this point. What was meant by (constitutive) "nations" is that these peoples were political entities, equal in their rights, which also included the right to self-determination.[9] The common interpretation of the political rights of the constitutive nations and the right to self-determination was that all these nations freely decided to come together and form the Yugoslav state during their joint fight against fascism.[10] This would have important consequences regarding the way self-determination would be interpreted in Yugoslavia later on.[11] Drawing of the borders of the Yugoslav republics and specifying the concept of the Yugoslav "nations" was probably an attempt to find a balance between recognizing the existence of particular national identities (i.e., Serbs, Croats, Muslims, etc.), an attempt to make these nations "free" in the new communist Yugoslavia,[12] and an effort to preserve the unity of Yugoslavia.

The 1946 Yugoslav Constitution also mentions the existence of "nationalities" ("narodnosti")[13] and "national minorities" ("nacionalne manjine").[14] These concepts also require an explanation because of the way they were used in later Yugoslav political vocabulary. The concept of "nationalities" referred to the ethnic/national groups who lived in Yugoslavia, but whose state of origin (the state where they were a constitutive nation) was outside of Yugoslavia.[15] For instance, the Yugoslav nationalities, according to this criterion, were Albanians, Hungarians, Romanians, Bulgarians, etc. Finally, "national minorities" (later incorporated into the concept of "nationalities") were all those minority groups that did not fall into any of the above categories, meaning those that were not constitutive nations, but who also did not have their own "home" country outside of Yugoslavia (such as the Roma population, for instance).[16]

An additional complication was religion. Yugoslavia was home to three large religious groups—Orthodox Christians (to which most of the

Serbs, Montenegrins, and Macedonians belonged), Roman Catholics (mostly Croats and Slovenians), and Muslims (predominantly inhabiting the regions of Bosnia and Herzegovina, southwestern Serbia, and the AP of Kosovo and Metohija [ethnically mostly Albanian]).[17] The case of the Muslim population is especially interesting.

Prior to World War II, and also in the first decades of the new post–World War II Yugoslavia, the Muslim population of Bosnia and Herzegovina was generally considered, in terms of its national belonging, either Serbian or Croatian. This was based on the understanding that segments of the South Slavic population (usually interpreted as premodern Serbs and/or Croats) converted to Islam during the centuries of Ottoman rule in the region. Thus just as parts of the South Slavic population remained Orthodox or Roman Catholic, other parts converted to Islam. That means that there was a sense of distinction between the national and religious identities, while nonetheless a specific ethnic identity in the case of the Bosnian Muslim population was recognized.[18] This, however, would slowly change in communist Yugoslavia.

In 1968, in a session of the Central Committee of the League of Communists of Bosnia and Herzegovina, the committee recognized Muslims in this Yugoslav republic as a separate Muslim nation. This was formalized on the federal level in 1971, when the census allowed for members of the Muslim population to also choose the option "Muslim, in the sense of nationality." This meant the recognition of the Bosnian Muslim population as a constitutive nation of Bosnia and Herzegovina. It also created a strange situation in which the word "Muslim" meant two different things at the same time: a nation, in the case of south Slavic Muslims (living primarily in Bosnia and Herzegovina); and a religious group, which was by no means limited to the Bosnian South Slavic population but also included segments of, for instance, the Albanian or Roma populations.[19] This concept of Bosnian Muslims as having a separate national identity would become the basis for the later concept of "Bosniaks" ("Bošnjaci"), which became, toward the end of the twentieth century, the standard term for describing the ethnicity/nationality of the Bosnian Muslim population.[20]

What one can conclude, based on this picture, is that post–World War II Yugoslavia was ethnically and religiously an extremely diverse country. It was composed of six federal republics, two autonomous provinces, six nations, three major religious groups, and many more nationalities and ethnic groups. In addition to that, except for Slovenia, which was inhabited almost exclusively by Slovenians (they comprised over 90 percent of the total population), all other Yugoslav republics had much more diverse national and religious landscapes. These facts would also have important repercussions for later events in the SFRJ, as well as during its breakup.

In spite of the official doctrine of "brotherhood and unity" ("bratstvo-jedinstvo") among the Yugoslav "nations and nationalities" advocated by the Yugoslav leadership and promoted by official state propaganda, national tensions did not cease to exist. Here we come across one of the many contradictory elements of the complex Yugoslav puzzle.

On the one hand, Yugoslavia was the incarnation of the "South Slavic dream" to form a unified state that would gather together South Slavs and enable them to resist various imperial aspirations.[21] On the other hand, from the very beginning, there was a perception of Yugoslavia (especially among segments of the Croatian population) as an oppressive state in which the biggest population, Serbian, dominated the other nations.[22] The drive toward independence in Slovenia and Croatia would continue to be one of the major elements of the Yugoslav story, and some interpretations even hold the initial desire among the Slovenians and Croats to join Yugoslavia to have been primarily opportunistic—to avoid their integration into other neighboring countries (primarily Austria, Hungary, and Italy).[23] The situation, in this respect, was different among the Serbs as the most "scattered" of all the Yugoslav nations across the borders of the republics. In various Serbian national programs there had been a drive toward a more unified and centralized state—a state in which "all Serbs" would live.[24]

These two opposing drives would significantly contribute to the fate of Yugoslavia toward the end of the twentieth century.

Yugoslav People(s) and National Tensions

The national tensions in post–World War II Yugoslavia have a couple of sources.

The first one has to do with World War II memories, as well as with different perceptions of the character and meaning of the Kingdom of Yugoslavia for the different Yugoslav ethnicities and their intellectual elites. The perception of pre-war and World War II history defined to a significant extent the way in which segments of the national body politic in each of the Yugoslav republics would interpret their own position, meaning, and objectives within communist Yugoslavia.

Apart from the Serbian-Croatian tensions caused by the genocide committed against the Serbian (as well as Jewish and Roma) population in the NDH during World War II, there were other conflicts along the national or ethnic lines that contributed to the tensions caused or magnified by the war.

The Četnik formations, for instance, massacred Bosnian Muslims, especially during the first years of World War II, usually rationalized as revenge for the atrocities committed against Bosnian Serbs.[25] Unlike the Serb population, the Muslims in Bosnia and Herzegovina were perceived by the Ustaša regime as "Croatian nobility" and the "purest race,"[26] and thus were not subjected to the oppression that many non-Croats and non-Roman-Catholics experienced.[27] Moreover, a separate SS division was created in Bosnia, the infamous "Handžar" division, which fought mostly against the Orthodox Serbian population in Bosnia.[28]

Since Albania was also an ally of the Axis powers, Albanian fascist leaders and the military forces applied a policy of ethnic cleansing in Kosovo against the Serbs and Montenegrins. A special division of the Wehrmacht, the Albanian SS Waffengebirgs Skenderbeg, fought against the Partisans and the Četniks in 1944.[29] But tensions also existed along the lines of different ethnic and religious identities—Albanians do not belong to the South Slavs, and the majority of the Albanian population in Kosovo and Metohija are Muslims, as opposed to Orthodox Serbs. These tensions existed in the pre–World War II period and would continue after the war. The inhabitants of Kosovo and Metohija experienced Serbian oppression immediately after the Turkish Empire had been defeated (in the Balkan Wars of 1912 and 1913), and the region had been incorporated into the modern Serbian state. Occasional violence between Kosovo Albanians and Serbs in post–World War II Yugoslavia continued,[30] which provoked Yugoslav police oppression against Albanians. The situation was further complicated by the aspirations of some Kosovo Albanians, advanced very early on, to proclaim independence and to join Great(er) Albania.[31]

These factors played an important role in later developments in the Balkans. As already noted, war memories made many Serbs afraid of any potential *independent* Croatian state, given the scale and character of extermination the Serbs experienced in Croatia during World War II. Given the massacres committed in Bosnia, a certain level of mistrust between the Muslim and Serbian populations also existed. Many Muslims perceived the Partisan (and later communist) regime as its protector; once the communist regime started collapsing, it has been claimed, many Muslims feared possible Serbian revenge.[32] Finally, as noted above, the secessionist ideas among Kosovo Albanians predate the Yugoslav crisis of the 1990s, and conflicts with the local Serbs and state police only escalated the mistrust and hostilities.

The second source of the national tensions in the post–World War II period has to do with Croatian and Serbian postwar emigration. Toward the end of the war, many Croats and Serbs associated with the Ustaše and the (predominantly Serb) Četniks left the region, escaping the revenge of the communist Partisans.[33] In the last years of the war and in the postwar period many Croatian nationalists emigrated to Western Europe, North and South America, and Australia, and the same goes for many of the Serbian nationalists and royalists who had sympathies for the Četnik movement. Radicals from both groups would take responsibility for organizing multiple terrorist attacks on Yugoslav officials abroad, as well as within Yugoslavia in the 1960s and 1970s.[34] Segments of this emigration would also represent a major source of support to the Croatian and Serbian nationalists of the 1980s and 1990s.

The third source of the tensions has to do with the national tensions among the Yugoslav communists. The turbulence among the Croatian political and intellectual elites of the late 1960s and early 1970s, known as the "Croatian Spring,"[35] was one manifestation of these tensions that attracted broad public attention and provoked concern across Yugoslavia, causing even Marshal Tito to react and warn against the rising nationalism that had "gone wild."[36]

Given the national, ethnic, and religious complexity, communist Yugoslavia can be seen as an attempt to relax those tensions by appealing to 1) the shared antifascist (Partisan) fight in which the members of all the major ethnicities/nations took part, 2) the supranational communist ideology and the unity of the working-class people, and 3) the decision supposedly made by the representatives of all the Yugoslav nations to live together, expressed in the second session of the AVNOJ.

The most vocal advocates of Yugoslav unity could be found among Serbs and Bosnian Muslims, although for different reasons. Yet some of the events of the 1960s and 1970s would make many Serbian communists doubt the honesty and purpose of the Yugoslav project. The turning point for many of them was the removal of Aleksandar Ranković, Tito's close friend and collaborator.

Ethnically Serbian, Ranković was arguably the second most influential figure in Yugoslavia in the post–World War II years. He was perceived by many conservative Serbian communists as their defender and their voice at the very top of the federal and party hierarchy (although Serbian nationalists would accuse him of being bitterly anti-Serbian for affirming his [nation-less] communist and Yugoslav party position). Following the controversial case in 1966, in which Ranković had been accused of conducting secret surveillance of Tito's residence, Ranković resigned and was expelled from the League of Communists of Yugoslavia. This disappointed many "hard-liners" among the Serbian communists and made some of them suspicious about Tito's position vis-à-vis the Serbs.

An additional problem was that following the crisis of the 1970s (first in Croatia, and then in Serbia, in the conflict with the so-called liberals), the regime would either marginalize or remove the most progressive among the Serbian communists, thus effectively stopping the democratic and, in some cases, clearly pro-West oriented tendencies within the Communist Party (embodied in the figures of Koča Popović, and, among the "liberals," Marko Nikezić and Latinka Perović). The elimination or marginalization of this faction within the Communist Party establishment also meant the marginalization of progressive, open-minded intellectuals more generally. This resulted in the promotion of many conservative, lower-level opportunistic bureaucrats in Serbia, who would take the leading positions. This course of events would become one of the major problems for Serbia in the following decade.

It has been pointed out more than once that one of the crucial factors of the unity of Yugoslavia was its president, Marshal Tito. In the context of Noam Chomsky's interest in the Yugoslav region, the figure of Tito is relevant primarily for two reasons. Chomsky was very much interested in the activities of Yugoslav dissidents during the 1960s and 1970s (see below), their opposition to some of Tito's policies, and their criticism of the dogmatic aspects of Yugoslav ideology. Through his texts and letters (published in this chapter), Chomsky supported students and dissident scholars on multiple occasions in their right to freely express their thoughts and disagreements. Thus, in the letter that Chomsky signed together with nine other prominent intellectuals, Tito was called upon to stop the oppression against Yugoslav scholars and scientists and to not abolish self-management and the autonomy of the Yugoslav universities, which had become "a pride of the nation and a model for the world at large."

In what follows, I will briefly address Tito's presidency as an important piece of the Yugoslav puzzle and as an introduction to two other significant aspects of the post–World War II Yugoslav policies: the Non-Aligned Movement and the Yugoslav self-managing system, both of which attracted Chomsky's attention.

Tito

Josip Broz Tito (1892–1980) performed many official roles in Yugoslavia, from being the secretary of the Communist Party of Yugoslavia in the prewar period and the leader of the Yugoslav Partisans and marshal of the Yugoslav army during the war to being the president of postwar Yugoslavia and president of the League of Communists of Yugoslavia.

Just as the character of the Yugoslav federation has been disputed and painted both in the academic literature and in the popular discourse with a variety of colors, from pure white to pure black, the same is true of Tito's personality and his role in the World War II resistance movement and in the postwar Yugoslav state. The overall assessment of Tito's historical role lies way beyond the scope of this introduction—or this book as a whole. In this context, Tito is interesting primarily as the chief Yugoslav authority, who had the power to influence, often decisively, the course of many political, economic, and cultural processes of Yugoslav society, as well as to influence the course of events vis-à-vis important international issues of that time.

The image of Tito as one of the key figures on the post–World War II international stage, and of Tito's Yugoslavia as a major international player, was advanced not only internally through the Yugoslav state and party propaganda but also by influential international (especially U.S.) political figures. Thus Zbigniew Brzezinski claimed that "Yugoslavia was, together with [the] USA and [the] USSR the only country which had managed to position itself as a factor in the global arena."[37] Jimmy Carter's descriptions of Tito as "a great world leader" and "a remarkable man," who deserves "respect and admiration,"[38] reflect the more general U.S. support that Tito enjoyed most of the time.

Tito exhibited the characteristics of both a ruthless pragmatist and a Yugoslav communist idealist. As a pragmatist, he was capable of recognizing and utilizing opportunities to seize and expend his personal influence and of eliminating enemies that would stand in the way of ideas he perceived as important or in the way of his personal power. But as a Yugoslav and communist idealist, it seems that he believed in the possibility of creating a new, different, and more just society that could serve as a model for other countries in different parts of the world. He was also internationally recognized as one of the chief postwar promoters of independence of nations and countries (from the colonial rule) and one of the most vocal advocates of anti-imperialism in the world. This is what secured Tito and Yugoslavia an unprecedented prestige in the world, much bigger than the previous history of the country, its size, and its geostrategic position would normally permit.[39]

This also translates into the character of Tito's policies. On the one hand he was dogmatic about Yugoslav socialism and the need to fight against all the "heretics" within the Communist Party, as well as all other (real or imaginary) enemies of the state and its official ideology, both internally and externally. On the other hand, however, he showed, more than once, flexibility in regard to changing the political course in order to respond to the changing economic and political situation. He was open to hearing different opinions (as long as they did not question the general ideological framework or his personal power) and was ready to change his mind when presented with new facts or views he took to be credible.[40]

This ambivalent character of his personality and his policies is probably the reason why Tito can be seen as one of the most important factors of Yugoslav unity, its domestic and international successes, and, at the same time, as one of the major Yugoslav problems. The system of personal loyalties, the party ideology, and the state apparatus he presided over, which were becoming more and more rigid, resisting reforms, and the cult of personality that was created (not necessarily because of his own intentions or decisions) became obstacles to developing functioning mechanisms that could sustain the prosperity of the Yugoslav state. Merging the very idea of Yugoslavia and Yugoslav unity with Tito's personality turned out to be a problematic equation, since it was not clear how such a complex state should continue to function after Tito's death. Already during Tito's lifetime there was a concern about the future of Yugoslavia after Tito,[41] and many expressed their disbelief that Yugoslavia would be able to survive without him.[42] Just a decade after Tito's death, the SFRJ would disappear in the bloodiest conflict that Europe had seen since the end of World War II.

Dissidents

The one-party system of Yugoslavia (with a party and state leader who was exhibiting many elements of authoritarian rule) did not normally appreciate diversity of opinions or public criticism of the highest leadership or the official ideology. Although nominally affirming democracy, freedom, and socialism, the system ceased to develop instruments to constructively deal with the plurality of approaches to public policy and their interpretations. This made many, including some of the most prominent Yugoslav dissidents, accuse Tito's regime of never departing from its Stalinist roots.

Of course, the oppressive state system functioned differently in different periods. The most brutal oppression against those perceived as the enemies of the state, party, or ideology took place in the first years following the war. Many of those who were not sympathetic to the Partisans and the new communist ideology, or who were simply labeled as "class enemies," were killed without due process.

The fight against "internal enemies" continued and was intensified after 1948, this time directed primarily against fellow communists. The turning point was the famous "Cominform Resolution" of 1948, which came as a result of a series of confrontations between Stalin and Tito, in particular Tito's refusal to turn Yugoslavia into another satellite state of the Soviet Union. By advocating an independent course for Yugoslavia and the Yugoslav Communist Party (independent of Stalin, at least), Tito was laying the ground for his own role as the undisputed leader of Yugoslavia. The Soviet Resolution accused the Yugoslav Party leadership[43] of ideological "mistakes," of "braking with the Marxist theory," and an "unfriendly policy" toward the Soviet Union. It condemned the Yugoslav Party leadership and excommunicated the Yugoslav Communist Party from "the family of the fraternal communist parties" and the Cominform.

The immediate effect this had in Yugoslavia was that Stalin became a "bad guy" overnight and the Soviet Union a major foreign threat to the survival of Yugoslavia. Tito was determined to resist Stalin, even if it resulted in a military conflict with the (much more powerful) Soviet Union. As we will see, Tito's "no" to Stalin would have enormous consequences for both the character of Yugoslav communism[44] and for the international position of Yugoslavia in the decades to come.

From 1948, and over the next couple of years, faced with the economic and political sanctions imposed by the Soviet Union and the threat of a possible invasion by the Soviet army, Tito's regime tried to consolidate its power and fight against all real, potential, or fictional enemies within Yugoslavia. The strongly anti-Stalin and anti-Soviet position that Tito and his companions took was, however, remarkably "Stalinist" in its application. The regime initiated a series of "purges" ("čistke") of the state and the party against "anti-revolutionary elements." One of the first institutions established for this purpose was the Goli Otok prison,[45] where primarily political prisoners accused of conspiring against Tito and Yugoslavia were subjected to heavy mental and physical torture.[46] After Stalin's death and Nikita Khrushchev's repenting visit to Yugoslavia, which normalized the bilateral relations, the measures would become less brutal.

This was the beginning of the Yugoslav party leadership and the government's crusade against the "infidels." In most of the cases, the rebels were communists and even close former collaborators of Tito, who at some point started to be critical of the course that the party was taking, or who were advocating changes in order to further develop Yugoslav socialism. Many of them criticized authoritarian tendencies within Yugoslav society, calling for an authentic socialism/communism against the "red bourgeoisie" and the new ("communist") power structures that were being constructed.

The example of Milovan Đilas (1911–1995) was paradigmatic, since he was one of the most prominent personalities in the party and in the Yugoslav leadership and was a close collaborator of Tito during the war and in the first postwar years. As the "patron saint" of Yugoslav dissidents, he came into conflict with the party leadership for criticizing, in the early 1950s, what he perceived as various anomalies of Yugoslav society and its leadership, including "bureaucratization" and "dogmatism," and for advocating "socialist democracy" and the competition of ideas in the political realm. Some claim that the primary target of this criticism was Tito, and that the reason for the political elimination of Đilas was his increasing popularity, which threatened the more conservative segments of the party.[47] Đilas's views and actions would soon be criticized as "antiparty," "counterrevolutionary," even as "anarchism" and "bourgeois liberalism."[48] He was expelled from the Central Committee in the famous Third Plenum of the Central Committee of the League of Communists of Yugoslavia, in 1954. When he continued with his criticism and characterized the Yugoslav system under Tito as "totalitarian," he was arrested. He would later serve multiple prison sentences.

Another famous dissident figure, who would later become Chomsky's friend and collaborator, was Vladimir Dedijer (1914–1990). Unlike many other dissidents coming to the West from communist countries, Dedijer was, in Chomsky's view, a "serious kind of dissident":

Dedijer was an amazing person. I learned a lot from him about Yugoslavia, just by talking to him, but then we were also involved in all kinds of other things together. He was very active in the international antiwar movement in the 1960s. He was a very serious kind of dissident. He understood the complications of the situation that he was protesting. He wasn't just trying to make friends with powerful people in the West. He had a very sensible critical analysis and was very engaged till the very end. He and his wife experienced many difficulties in their lives. They were both seriously wounded in the war. He had many later problems as well—one of his sons was murdered, probably by Tito, but I don't think they ever proved anything. However, he just kept at it, straight to the last minute.[49]

Dedijer served as a Partisan officer in World War II and became a member of the Central Committee of the Communist Party in 1952. But two years later he was expelled from the party for his support of Milovan Đilas in the Third Plenum. He left Yugoslavia in 1959 and devoted his career to history, activism, and teaching.

Some dissidents, however, were attacking the regime because of its breakup with the Soviet Union and the dismissal of the Yugoslav Communist Party from the international (Soviet-controlled) communist family. Vladimir (Vlado) Dapčević (1917–2001) was a famous Yugoslav dissident who attacked Tito (but also the post-Stalin Soviet leadership) for deviating from authentic Marxism and for flirting with capitalism. He was arrested and imprisoned, serving a part of his sentence on Goli Otok, exposed to heavy torture.[50]

Not only isolated individuals but entire groups of intellectuals were subjected to various types of oppression. Chomsky closely followed the case of dissident students and professors at the University of Belgrade, most of them at the Faculty of Philosophy. In his 1974 article (coauthored with Robert S. Cohen) "The Repression at Belgrade University," Chomsky gives a detailed analysis of the government's repressive measures against students and professors of the University of Belgrade that suppressed academic and civil freedoms.

Chomsky also raised his voice in the case of one of the leaders of the student protests of the 1960s, a philosophy student named Vladimir Mijanović (nicknamed "Vlada the Revolution"). The conflicts between students and the police started in 1966, when students of Belgrade University (associated primarily with the Faculty of Philosophy) organized protests against the Vietnam War. The position of the regime vis-à-vis this war was ambivalent, since Tito supported North Vietnam against the U.S. aggression on principle but at the same cultivated time good relations with the U.S. government. Students organized a protest walk to the U.S. embassy in Yugoslavia, which was stopped by the police. The conflicts between the students and the police forces continued over the upcoming years. The 1968 student protests against the "red bourgeoisie" (that, in the end, Tito publicly endorsed) were followed by a series of repressive measures by the regime, which finally led to Mijanović's imprisonment. Oppression and arrests against students and their supporters provoked further series of protests in other university centers, in the early 1970s.[51]

The case of the Yugoslav government suppressing not only the protests advocating for more freedom and more socialism but also the protests that were directed against the U.S. military interventions is particularly interesting. It speaks to the general "in between" policy of the Yugoslav leadership, but even more to Yugoslav foreign policy in the times of the "Brezhnev doctrine" and the renewed conflict between Yugoslavia and the Soviet Union (which escalated during the Czechoslovakia crisis).

From both the official statements of the U.S. administration and from declassified internal documents, one can see that U.S. support for Tito and Yugoslavia was more or less consistent after Tito's break with Stalin[52] (although relations between the two states were not without serious disturbances on multiple occasions). Yugoslavia was one of two communist countries (together with Poland) that enjoyed "most favored nation" treatment of its goods, as well as a U.S. military equipment supply.[53] There were, however, also voices within the U.S. establishment (such as George F. Kennan) who were warning against the "powerful enemies" that Yugoslavia had among American right-wing groups.[54]

In spite of the very high level of U.S. support (both military and economic, strengthened through U.S. presidents' public endorsements), two aspects of Yugoslav policies were not necessarily in accordance with U.S. interests. One was Tito's dedication to the Non-Aligned Movement and his consistent critique of all imperialisms (including U.S. imperialism) and military interventions in sovereign countries. The other was the Yugoslav economic experiment in self-management. The idea of self-management was in direct contradiction with the state capitalism that the U.S. had cultivated and was especially irreconcilable with the "neoliberal" ideology that was slowly replacing the regulatory U.S. state mechanisms over the 1970s and 1980s. I will briefly discuss both of these aspects of Yugoslav policies.

The Non-Aligned Movement

The role of Yugoslavia and Tito in the Non-Aligned Movement tells us much about the international position of Yugoslavia under Tito's leadership and about the internal issues that Tito was indirectly addressing by promoting the Yugoslav leadership within the movement.

The fate of the Yugoslav nations and the fate of Yugoslavia as a whole have always depended to a significant extent on the balance between major European and world powers. The will of the great powers manifested itself in the formation of the first Yugoslavia, which coincided with the aspirations of the South Slavic population at that time and with Serbia emerging out of the Balkan Wars and World War I as a victor. The will of another great European power—Hitler's Germany—ended the Kingdom of Yugoslavia. As we have seen, Tito's Yugoslavia appeared out of the antifascist struggle of the Yugoslav people, but its formation and survival were also highly dependent on the support of the anti-Hitler coalition (the Soviet Union, Great Britain, and the U.S., although not always simultaneously) for Tito and his Partisans during the war.

The obvious problem that threatened the very existence of the Yugoslav state in the first post–World War II years was twofold. On the one hand, the Western powers (primarily the U.S.) would take a strong anti-Soviet and more generally anti-communist position. In other words, the primary enemy in the West in the post–World War II period would become the Soviet Union, its client states, and the entire ideological corpus that was broadly (and vaguely) called "communism." On the other hand, the break with the Soviet Union put Yugoslavia in an extremely weak position, exposing it to the very real possibility of a Soviet invasion in the moment when Yugoslavia did not have any trustworthy allies in the West it could confidently count on. In spite of the many changes, internally and externally, this position "in between" the two worlds would, to a significant extent, define the official ideological profile of Yugoslavia and its policies during the entire period of Tito's rule.

One expression of this "third way" that Yugoslavia took was the Non-Aligned Movement. Gathering together the non-aligned ("Third World" or "third block") countries, and leading the Non-Aligned Movement was a way for Tito and Yugoslavia to avoid isolation and to open new avenues for Yugoslavia's prosperity and prestige.[55]

The Yugoslav "third way" would thus come to symbolize the opposition to imperial ambitions both from the East (Soviet-style centralist communism) and from the West (representing the bourgeoisie, colonial rule, the exploitation of the poor, etc.).

Another factor in building the Non-Aligned Movement was Tito's quest for personal prestige, both internally and internationally. Taking on the role of leader of the Non-Aligned Movement served both purposes. The Non-Aligned Movement represented (and still does) the majority of the world's population. It helped Tito and Yugoslavia become very visible on the international scene, advocating the principles of justice, freedom (primarily freedom from colonial rule and American-style neo-imperialism), and self-determination, as well as self-management.[56] This, in turn, strengthened the Yugoslav position in the West as well.

The first conference of the Non-Aligned Movement took place in Belgrade, in September 1961, after Tito's long visit to Africa earlier that year. The support of Indian Prime Minister Jawaharlal Nehru and Egyptian president Gamal Abdel Nasser was crucial in securing the consent of other (Asian and African) countries and the success of the initiative. Tito became the first secretary general, which formalized his leadership role within the movement.

The Yugoslav role in the Non-Aligned Movement has also been perceived as important vis-à-vis Yugoslav internal issues. Since the Muslim population was dominant in many of the non-aligned countries, this had an effect on policies concerning Yugoslav Muslims. One aspect of this can be seen in the promotion of the Bosnian Muslim population to the rank of Yugoslav constitutive nations, as well as in the nomination of Bosnian Muslims to ambassadorial positions in Islamic countries.[57] In turn, applying more favorable policies toward the Muslim population internally had a positive effect externally—Tito and Yugoslavia were perceived as friends of the Muslim nations across the world and supporters of their political rights and claims.

The Non-Aligned Movement would continue to exist and, as a collective effort its first generation of leaders, Tito, Nasser, and Nehru, would be one of the longest-lasting achievements of the post-colonial Cold War era.

It seems that the U.S. was ready to support Yugoslavia, and even to a certain extent the Non-Aligned Movement itself, as long as the movement kept the non-aligned countries outside the zone of immediate Soviet influence. But the basic ideas and values that Tito and the rest of the non-aligned leaders advocated were in contradiction with long-term U.S. interests and policies.

Self-Managing Socialism

Many of the contradictions and inconsistencies that we find in the political and ideological spheres, narrowly taken, naturally apply to the economic sphere as well. During the first postwar years, the Yugoslav regime started to implement Soviet-style economic policies that advanced public ownership, nationalization, a centrally planned economy, and the forced collectivization of agriculture.[58] By 1950, it became clear that this economic model was not working. In addition to the inefficiency of the centrally planned economy, the (often inconsistent and violent) application of these policies provoked much resentment among the peasant population. On top of the difficulties with the economic model itself, there was the serious impact of the Soviet sanctions put in force immediately after the resolution, as well as an enormous increase in defense spending because of the imminent threat of a Soviet invasion.[59]

The years 1950 and 1952 would become crucial for establishing the new economic model. According to Milovan Đilas, it was he and Edvard Kardelj, chief ideologist and high Party official, who conceived the idea of self-managing socialism, with the help of Boris Kidrič. Đilas described the introduction of self-management in Yugoslavia in his book *The Unperfect Society* as follows:

> The idea of self-management was conceived by Kardelj and me, with some help from our comrade Kidrič. Soon after the outbreak of the quarrel with Stalin, in 1949, as far as I remember, I began to reread Marx's *Capital*, this time with much greater care, to see if I could find the answer to the riddle of why, to put it in simplistic terms, Stalinism was bad and Yugoslavia was good. I discovered many new ideas and, most interesting of all, ideas about a future society in which the immediate producers, through free association, would themselves make the decisions regarding production and distribution—would, in effect, run their own lives and their own future. The country was in the stranglehold of bureaucracy, and the party leaders were in the grip of rage and horror over the incorrigibly arbitrary

nature of the party machine they had set up and that kept them in power. One day—it must have been in the spring of 1950—it occurred to me that we Yugoslav Communists were now in a position to start creating Marx's free association of producers. The factories would be left in their hands, with the sole proviso that they should pay a tax for military and other state needs "still remaining essential." With all this, I felt a twinge of reservation: Is not this a way for us Communists, I asked myself, to shift the responsibility for failures and difficulties in the economy onto the shoulders of the working class, or to compel the working class to take a share of such responsibilities from us? I soon explained my idea to Kardelj and Kidrič while we sat in a car parked in front of the villa where I lived. They felt no such reservation, and I was able all too easily to convince them of the indisputable harmony between my ideas and Marx's teaching. Without leaving the car, we thrashed it out for little more than half an hour. Kardelj thought it was a good idea, but one that should not be put into effect for another five or six years, and Kidrič agreed with him. A couple of days later, however, Kidrič telephoned me to say that we were ready to go ahead at once with the first steps. . . . A little later, a meeting was held in Kardelj's cabinet office with the trade-union leaders, and they proposed the abolition of the workers councils, which up to that time had functioned only as consultative bodies for the management. . . . Tito, busy with other duties and absent from Belgrade, took no part in this and knew nothing of the proposal soon to introduce a workers council bill in the parliament until he was informed by Kardelj and me in the government lobby room during a session of the National Assembly. His first reaction was: our workers are not ready for that yet! But Kardelj and I, convinced that this was an important step, pressed him hard, and he began to unbend as he paid more attention to our explanations. The most important part of our case was that this would be the beginning of democracy, something that socialism had not yet achieved; further, it could be plainly seen by the world and the international workers' movement as a radical departure from Stalinism. Tito paced up and down, as though completely wrapped in his own thoughts. Suddenly he stopped and exclaimed: "Factories belonging to the workers—something that has never yet been achieved!" . . . A few months later, Tito explained the Workers' Self-Management Bill to the National Assembly.[60]

The party and Yugoslav leadership openly admitted the mistakes of the previous model, and turned from promoting it, as they had done in the previous years, to openly criticizing it.

However, apart from the very real need for different economic policies, the new model of "self-management" also had a very clear political and ideological meaning: it allowed the Yugoslav leadership to advance a different approach compared to the one implemented in the Soviet Union, and thus put into practice something that would strengthen the new position of Yugoslavia, which continued to reject the "old" capitalist system but also rejected the Soviet model. The new system was meant to be the expression of the "authentic" (Yugoslav) socialism that would oppose the capitalist exploitation of the working class in the West, as well as the Soviet centralist state-communism in the East. Self-managing socialism would thus become the conceptual expression of the Yugoslav "third way," the justification and a practical-ideological consequence of the reality that Yugoslavia found itself in after the break with Soviet communism.

The Workers' Self-Management Act was passed the same year (1950) and additional legislation followed in 1952, which allowed broader rights to the workers' councils.[61] This led to the Yugoslav type of "self-managing (socialist) system" ("samoupravni sistem").

There have been various assessments of the Yugoslav self-management experiment. For Hans Dieter Seibel and Ukandi G. Damachi, Yugoslavia was "the only large-scale experiment in self-management."[62] They held the view that it was precisely under the system of self-management that "Yugoslavia made the transition from an underdeveloped to a developed country."[63] Others perceived self-management as a capricious, inefficient system that served only the eccentric and unsustainable policies of the communist regime.[64] One dimension of the problem of how to assess the overall (in)efficiency of Yugoslav self-management is that the proclaimed principles of self-management that (according to chief ideologist Edvard Kardelj) should have been applied to all segments of society and the state were only partially applied. An additional problem is that it is not clear how much of the relative economic success during the 1950s and 1960s should be attributed to self-management and how much to other factors, such as foreign aid.[65]

The Yugoslav application of self-management was another area that Chomsky closely followed. He recognized the ambivalences of Yugoslav self-management and the tensions between its theory and the practical application in Tito's Yugoslavia:

> I was very interested in Yugoslav self-management. I was in close touch with a group of Belgrade intellectuals at that time, the Praxis group. Of course, they have changed a lot since. I read a lot of material on the self-management experiments, which were pretty interesting to me. There were problems with them. They were in the framework of the authoritarian structure, but if you abstract from the structure that should have been dismantled, in many ways I think they were doing important things.[66]

Yugoslav self-managing socialism started as an attempt toward a radical democratization of the society (not only of the means and conditions of production) and the de-bureaucratization of the state.[67] Yet, at the same time, it was paralleled by the rigid authoritarian and pyramidal party system (with the party leader as the primary source of power), which prevented all the processes that had the potential to take away its power. Verbal (and only to a limited extent actual) affirmations of democratic socialism were accompanied by ideological dogmatism or oppression.

In spite of that, the Yugoslav experiment in self-management remains an important chapter in the history of socialist, democratic, and anarchist ideas. It was also an "export" product of Tito's Yugoslavia. Yugoslav support to the countries that were fighting against colonial rule was also used to spread ideas about Yugoslav-style socialism and secure in that way strong relations (including business relations) between these countries and Yugoslavia. This can be seen in the example of Algeria. Tito was a strong supporter of Algeria's independence, against the colonial French rule.[68] The Algerian War left the country devastated and in a desperate need for educated administrators who would start rebuilding it. Tito provided both legal and economic advisors, which influenced the formation of the self-managing Algerian system, shaped on its Yugoslav prototype.[69]

A reflection on Yugoslav self-management is also important because of the radically different economic policies that would be implemented in Yugoslavia following Tito's death. The so-called neoliberal policies that Yugoslavia started to implement in the 1980s were, in the view of many, one of the most significant reasons for the Yugoslav crisis and the breakup.

The fact that self-management did not seem to have been an important obstacle in U.S.-Yugoslav relations during Tito's time, in spite of a clear ideological contradiction between Yugoslav self-management and the U.S. state capitalist (and neoliberal) system, can, perhaps, tell us something about the way the U.S. administration perceived the seriousness and the long-term impact of the whole experiment. It seems that this aspect of Yugoslav ideology could have been tolerated as another expression of the differences (and distance) between *communist* Yugoslavia and the Soviet Union and as an experiment with only limited application. Probably the only real "danger" of self-management lay in the possibility that it would spread to other countries, primarily those that belonged to the Non-Aligned Movement, becoming thus a global phenomenon. But the application of neoliberal policies over the decades to come would successfully prevent such developments.

Self-management has, by now, been mostly defamed and uprooted in the ex-Yugoslav territories. Yet as a response to the (largely) unsuccessful privatization of the old industrial complexes—that, together with "foreign investments" doctrine, has been promoted as the only economic policy since 1990s—there have been isolated attempts to restore some aspects of self-management. For instance, in many factories workers protested against the dominant type of privatization, humiliating working conditions, and managerial policies that in many cases ruined what was left of the productive potentials of these industries. In some companies workers' unions tried to organize, establish their own management, and even buy the factories in which they worked (that have been privatized) and run the process of production.[70] This way, workers attempted to exercise some of the core principles of self-management.

Notes

1   In Serbo-Crotian "south" translates as "južni" (hence "jugo-"), and "Sloveni" (or "Slaveni") stands for the "Slavs." "Jugoslovenski" (South Slavic), as a political concept, comes from the German word "Südslavisch," first recorded, according to Gilles Troude, in 1772. The word "Jugoslavija" appears in 1835, in the work of poet Matija Ban. See Žil Trud (Gilles Troude), *Etnički sukobi u Titovoj Jugoslaviji (1960–1980)* (Sremski Karlovci: Izdavačka knjižarnica Zorana Stojanovića, 2010), 14.
2   The idea to form a unified South Slavic state belongs to Romanticist national sentiments typical of nineteenth-century Europe. It goes back to the "Ilirian movement" of Ljudevit Gaj. Other prominent personalities of the nineteenth century, such as Serbian linguist Vuk Stefanović Karadžić (who reformed and standardized the Serbo-Croatian language) and Bishop Josip Štrosmajer, contributed to the further

development of the Yugoslav idea. Before and during World War I, the Yugoslav committee, composed of prominent members of various ethnicities from the region, was lobbying for the formation and international recognition of a new State of South Slavs, to be formed after the war and the collapse of the Austro-Hungarian monarchy.

3   Over the course of World War II, in an attempt to create an ethnically pure Croatian State, the Ustaša regime and its military formations (led by Ante Pavelić) would torture, kill, and expel hundreds of thousands of Serbs. Together with Serbs, tens of thousands of Jews and Roma were also killed in the NDH. Most of the sources estimate that in the concentration camp of Jasenovac alone between 100,000 and 700,000 people were killed (although the latter figure is most probably a gross exaggeration). See Jovan Mirković, "Jasenovac: istorija i istoriografija," *Israeli—Serbian Academic Exchange in Holocaust Research, Collection of Papers from the Academic Conference, Jerusalem—Yad Vashem*, June 2006, 15–20 (Belgrade: Museum of Genocide Victims, 2008), 317–23. The executions were conducted with a brutality that shocked even some of Hitler's generals. Already in 1941, Edmund Glaise von Horstenau, a German general in Zagreb, reported that the Ustaše "have gone raging mad." This report made Hitler intervene and criticize Pavelić for the scale and character of the torture and massacres. See Jonathan Steinberg, *All or Nothing: The Axis and the Holocaust, 1941–43* (London: Routledge, 1990), 28; Trud, *Etnički sukobi*, 26–35. See also Vladimir Dedijer, *Vatikan i Jasenovac* (Belgrade: Rad, 1987), and *Vatikan i Jasenovac—Dokumenti* (Belgrade: Rad, 1987); an English version (although shorter) of these books appeared as *The Yugoslav Auschwitz and the Vatican: The Croatian Massacre of the Serbs during World War II* (Buffalo, NY: Prometheus Books, 1992).

4   The session took place in Jajce, Bosnia and Herzegovina, on November 29–30, 1943, and was theoretically composed of "representatives" of all the Yugoslav ethnicities, although in reality there was no election, and the representatives, even though they belonged to different ethnic and religious groups, were effectively under the control of the Communist-led Partisans.

5   Most (although not all) of these borders were based on the borders of Austro-Hungarian provinces or earlier international borders (such as the border between Bosnia and Herzegovina and Croatia, which mostly followed the border between the Turkish and Austro-Hungarian Empires). See Aleksandar Pavković, *The Fragmentation of Yugoslavia: Nationalism and War in the Balkans* (London: Macmillan, 2000), 48–52; Trud, *Etnički sukobi*, 64–66.

6   Moša Pijade, vice president of the AVNOJ, explained in 1944 that no more could Croatia incorporate all of the Croats than Serbia all of the Serbs; only Yugoslavia as a whole encompasses the "entirety of the Serbian as well as Croatian nation." See Milivoj Bešlin, "Josip Broz Tito i jugoslovenski federalizam (1963–1974)," *Tito—viđenja i tumačenja*, 60.

7   The FRY ceased to exist in 2003, when the state was renamed the State Union of Serbia and Montenegro ("Državna Zajednica Srbije i Crne Gore"). The final step in the disintegration of what was left of Yugoslavia took place in 2006 when Montenegro proclaimed its independence, creating two more independent states—Montenegro and Serbia (with the Autonomous Province of Kosovo and Metohija, under UN Resolution 1244)—on the map of the region.

8   See Pavković, *Fragmentation*, 47.

9   See Article 1 of the 1946 Constitution.

10 See Pavković, *Fragmentation*, 47.

11 The concept of "nation" becomes especially important here, since it refers primarily to the "people" (e.g., Serbs, Croats) not to the institutionalized political structure (state or, e.g., republic). This is the reason why Yugoslavia, as well as its republics, was *de facto one state*, without ever being constituted of *one nation* (in spite of the attempts of the Yugoslav leadership to promote the "Yugoslav nation" in addition to the already recognized Serbian, Croatian, and other nations). The same was true for most of the republics (with the exception of nationally much more homogeneous Slovenia and Macedonia)—they were political entities that did not correspond to a single national identity, as they were normally composed of more than one (constitutive) nation. Different interpretations of national sovereignty and the right to self-determination would become central in the conflicts of 1990s.

12 Here it is important to keep in mind that one of the accusations the Communist Party advanced prior to World War II against the very existence of Yugoslavia in its previous monarchic form was that it was the "dungeon of nations" ("tamnica naroda"), in which the Yugoslav nations were subordinated to the "Serbian bourgeoisie" and the royal dynasty. See Trud, *Etnički sukobi*, 59.

13 As mentioned above, the concepts of "nation" and "nationality" were still not used consistently at this point (compare, for instance, the way "nation" and "nationality" were used in articles 1, 6, 10, and 21). The distinction would become clearer with the Constitutional amendments of 1971 and in the 1974 Constitution, which gives advantage to the concept of "nationalities" as opposed to "national minorities." See "Nationality" in *Pravna Enciklopedija*, vol. 1, ed. Borislav T. Blagojević (Belgrade: Savremena administracija, 1985), 873. An important point that needs to be stressed here is that the reason for introducing the concept of "nationalities" was not to discriminate between the rights of the "nations" and those of the ethnic minorities, but precisely to stress their equality—the equality of all citizens, regardless of their national / ethnic identity. This was to make a clear distinction between the new communist idea of equality, as opposed to the old "bourgeois" understanding of the national/ethnic categories.

14 Article 13.

15 See *Enciklopedija*, 837.

16 See Trud, *Etnički sukobi*, 74.

17 There were also other religious groups, such as Jews and Protestant Christians (especially in the Vojvodina province), but their number was small enough that they did not play a decisive role in determining national identities.

18 For instance, on the census of 1948 in Bosnia, the Muslim population could chose between "Muslim Serbian," "Muslim Croatian," or "Muslim, ethnically neutral." See Trud, *Etnički sukobi*, 128.

19 Bosnian Muslim intellectual and politician Muhamed Filipović (who is also credited with advancing the concept of "Bosniaks" ["Bošnjaci"] in its contemporary meaning) suggested at some point that "muslim" (with a small *m*) be used when describing the religious identity and (big *M*) "Muslim" when referring to the national identity of the Bosnian Muslim population. See Trud, *Etnički sukobi*, 147.

20 Just as other terms describing the national/ethnic identities of the Yugoslav peoples, the term "Bošnjak/Bošnjaci" ("Bosniak/Bosniaks") predates its modern usage. It seems that it had a primarily geographic meaning, describing the regional belonging and even regional identity of those living in Bosnia, and in that sense could be understood as equivalent to the term "Bosanci" (Bosnians—inhabitants of Bosnia,

without any additional, more specific connotations as to the national or religious identity).

21 At various times there were various proposals for organizing this Yugoslav union. Ljudevit Gaj spoke of the entire Balkans as a unified region of "Ilirija," and even Tito contemplated at one point the possibility of including both Bulgaria and Albania into the unified Yugoslav State (see Trud, *Etnički sukobi*, 51).

22 This would be used as a justification of the NHD and Croatian alliance with Hitler, not only at the beginning but also toward the end of the war. As an editorial of the Ohio-based (pro-Ustaše) Croatian journal *Naša nada* explained in 1944: "Four million Croatians . . . who had formerly lived under Hungarian rule, were forced into Yugoslavia to be governed by the Serbs, for whom they had little love. This explains why Croatia did not follow the balance of Yugoslavia into a partnership with the United Nations [antifascist alliance]. It was not because its people loved Hitler or Nazism, but because, like the Hungarians and Austrians, they remembered Versailles too well." *Naša nada*, October 3, 1944. Quoted in "News Notes," [U.S.] Office of Strategic Services, Foreign National Branch, N-59, October 9, 1944.

23 Cf., "One of the reasons that Croatians and Slovenes had been willing to join the Kingdom of the Serbs, Croats, and Slovenes in the first place was the realization that failure to do so would have meant the incorporation of significant portions of their territory into Italy, which had been promised most of Dalmatia and Istria by the allies for its assistance during the Great War. The willingness of Hungary, Italy, and Bulgaria to effectively annex portions of the country during World War II certainly worked to reinforce the idea that Yugoslav unity was necessary to fend off rapacious neighbors." Andrew Wachtel and Christopher Bennett, "The Dissolution of Yugoslavia," in *Confronting the Yugoslav Controversies*, eds. Charles Ingrao and Thomas A. Emmert (West Lafayette, IN: Purdue University Press, 2009), 13–14.

24 This idea does not necessarily imply (an ethnically clean) "Great(er) Serbia," as it would mostly be interpreted during and after the wars of the 1990s—it could also be understood (as in the case of Moša Pijade) in terms of living within a multicultural Yugoslavia, in which "all" of the Serbs lived in one country (together with other nations).

25 This, however, does not mean that there were no Muslims among the Četniks—some estimate that in 1943, about 8 percent of the Četniks were Muslims. See Trud, *Etnički sukobi*, 124.

26 This ideology held that the Bosnian Muslim population was not of Slavic origin but belonged to the Aryan race from the East. See Trud, *Etnički sukobi*, 36–37.

27 There were also Muslim members of the Ustaša formations.

28 The 13th Waffen division of the SS Handschar was formed in 1943 and committed numerous acts of rape, torture, and killing mostly in eastern and northeastern parts of Bosnia.

29 On the other hand, the Yugoslav communists were close with the Albanian communists and would remain in friendly relations with Albania till the 1948 split between Stalin and Tito, in which Albania took the Soviet side.

30 From 1948, Enver Hoxha's Albanian regime was secretly sending arms and militant groups to Yugoslavia in attempts to destabilize the country. In spite of many attempts by the Yugoslav government to improve the economic situation in (the predominantly Albanian inhabited) Kosovo and Metohija, the conflicts continued. The massive and violent protests of Kosovo Albanians in 1968 even advanced the

claims for Kosovo independence. The protests and occasional outbursts of violence would continue in the 1970s and 1980s.

31 This intention still continues to be relevant. According to this idea, all the territories in which the Albanian population represents the majority (Kosovo and Metohija and parts of Macedonia and Montenegro) should eventually join Albania.

32 See Pavković, *The Fragmentation*, 43.

33 Many members of the fascist military formations as well as civilians were killed in their attempts to escape (as, for instance, in the case of the Bleiburg and Kočevski Rog executions). Many were killed later on, once the new regime consolidated its power, often based on loose accusations of cooperation with the enemy or of (in the case of Serbian nationalists) supporting the old regime.

34 The best known cases include the terrorist attack at a cinema in Belgrade, on July 13, 1968, by the "Croatian Liberation Movement"; the assassination of the Yugoslav Ambassador to Sweden, on April 7, 1971, by the "Croatian Peoples Resistance"; and the 1972 attempt to organize an armed conflict in Bosnia and Herzegovina by the nineteen members of the "Croatian Revolutionary Brotherhood." For a more comprehensive analysis of the terrorist activities of Croatian emigration, associated with the Ustaša ideology, see Trud, *Etnički sukobi*, 245–58. Parallel to that, Serbian immigrants in the U.S. planned an assassination of Tito during his official visits to Mexico (in 1965), and the U.S. (in 1963 and 1971).

35 Also known as MASPOK (from "masovni pokret" meaning "mass movement"), or "Zagreb Spring," (as a reference to the "Prague Spring" of 1968).

36 Tito also warned that, because of Croatian and Serbian nationalism, the survival of Yugoslavia might be at stake—in 1971 he asked a rhetorical question "Do you want a new 1941? That would be a disaster!" Trud, *Etnički sukobi*, 299.

37 In Tvrtko Jakovina, "Tito's Yugoslavia as the Pivotal State of the Non-aligned," *Tito—viđenja i tumačenja* (Belgrade: Institut za noviju istoriju Srbije, Arhiv Jugoslavije, 2011), 398.

38 See Carter's welcoming speech during Tito's official visit in 1978: "This morning the people of the United States are honored by the presence of a great world leader, President Tito of Yugoslavia. . . . One of the first actions that I took as President was to ask Vice President Mondale to go to Yugoslavia to present my own respects and admiration to President Tito. He is indeed a remarkable man who has exhibited in his own life tremendous personal courage in battle, in times of severe testing of his strength as a human being and as a patriot. He's a contemporary of great world leaders who survived the crises of world war, a friend and associate of Prime Minister Churchill, President Roosevelt, General de Gaulle. . . . President Tito is a leader who has such great respect that he's able to bridge the gap of communications and understanding between nations and leaders who quite often have difficulty in dealing with one another. . . . Perhaps as much as any other person, he exemplifies in Yugoslavia the eagerness for freedom, independence, and liberty that exists throughout Eastern Europe and indeed throughout the world. He and the people of Yugoslavia are recognized by our own country as worthy of admiration. We understand that the independence and the territorial integrity of Yugoslavia is one of the basic foundations of world peace now and in the future. He's been an inspiration to the people of his own country and to others in his constant insistence on this freedom and independence. The people of Yugoslavia have in a unique way recognized their own willingness to sacrifice to the ultimate degree for the freedom of

their own country. . . . So, President Tito, on behalf of the people of our Nation, we welcome you to our shores, to our country, as a true friend." President Jimmy Carter (on the occasion of Tito's last visit to the U.S.), "Visit of President Josip Broz Tito of Yugoslavia, Remarks at the Welcoming Ceremony, March 7, 1978," *Public Papers of the Presidents of the United States: Jimmy Carter* (January 1–June 30, 1978), 473–74.

39 One indication of this prestige was Tito's funeral. When he died in 1980, at the age of eighty-eight, delegations from virtually all of the world's countries came to Belgrade, in what turned out to be the biggest state funeral in recorded history. Among the attendees of the funeral ceremony, which included over 200 delegations from more than 120 countries, were Margaret Thatcher, Helmut Schmidt, Sandro Pertini, Leonid Brezhnev, Yasser Arafat, Muammar Gaddafi, Saddam Hussein, Indira Gandhi, Kim il-Sung, etc. The American delegation was led by Vice President Walter Mondale and Jimmy Carter's personal representative, his mother Lillian Gordy Carter.

40 This seems to be the case in the economic sphere as well as in the highly sensitive political issues, such as the change of constitution or support to various factions within the Communist Party. For more on the assessment of Tito's political role see Tvrtko Jakovina, *Tito—viđenja i tumačenja.*

41 Already in 1961, a now-declassified NSC document predicted, "The stability of the regime will be in jeopardy when Tito dies because 1. No potential successor is considered able to fill Tito's boots. 2. Dormant nationality problems could arise in an inter-regnum." NSC Background Paper, October 12, 1961, 2, available at https://www.cia.gov/library/readingroom/docs/CIA-RDP80S00003A000100100004-5.pdf.

42 General Charles de Gaulle, for example, held this view (according to A. Peyerefitte), saying that instead of one Yugoslav nation there were just "pieces of wood" held together by a "rope," and that rope was Tito; once Tito was gone these pieces of wood would, de Gaulle felt, fall apart (see Trud, *Etnički konflikti*, 142).

43 The Resolution explicitly names Tito, (Edvard) Kardelj, (Milovan) Đilas, and (Aleksandar) Ranković.

44 After the break with Stalin, the Yugoslav ideological system would more commonly be referred to as "(Yugoslav) self-managing socialism."

45 Goli Otok is an island in the Adriatic Sea, whose name literally translates as "naked (meaning *barren*) island," for the lack of vegetation and animal life.

46 The prisoners were sent to Goli Otok without any legal process, possibility to defend themselves, or the pronouncement of any sentence. The length of their imprisonment was also arbitrary—from a couple of months to many years. Many prisoners ended their lives there, being tortured to death, killed by other prisoners (often collaborators of the secret police), or by committing suicide. The prison was officially closed only in 1988, although after the 1950s the scale of torture would start to decrease. The estimates are that tens of thousands of prisoners went through the camp, while hundreds of people died on the island.

47 See Goran Miloradović, "Ljudi na strateškim mestima. Uzroci, posledice i smisao sukoba Josipa Broza Tita i Milovana Đilasa na Trećem (vanrednom) plenumu CK SKJ 1954. godine," *Tito—viđenja i tumačenja*, 211–28.

48 Miloradović, "Ljudi na strateškim mestima," 216.

49 Noam Chomsky, conversation with Davor Džalto, January 6, 2012, Cambridge, MA.

50 Dapčević escaped Yugoslavia in 1958. He was arrested in Bucharest in 1975 and extradited to the Yugoslav authorities. He was sentenced to death, but the verdict would be changed to twenty years in prison. He was finally released in 1988.

51 For more on the protests of the 1960s and Mijanović's role, see Ralph Pervan, *Tito and the Students: The University and the University Students in Self-Managing Yugoslavia* (Nedlands: University of Western Australia Press, 1978); Nebojša Popov, "Belgrade, June 1968," in *1968 Revisited: 40 Years of Protest Movements*, ed. Nora Farik (Brussels: Heinrich Böll Foundation, 2008), 49–55; *Nebojša Popov, Društveni sukobi—izazov sociologiji. Beogradski jun" 1968* (Belgrade: Službeni glasnik, 2008); Boris Kanzleiter, "1968 in Yugoslavia: Student Revolt between East and West," in *Between Prague Spring and French May: Opposition and Revolt in Europe, 1960–1980*, eds. Martin Klimke, Jacco Pekelder, and Joachim Scharloth (New York: Berghahn, 2013), 84–100.

52 From the available President's Daily Briefs during the relevant period we learn that Tito and Yugoslavia were one of the most important topics of the world's affairs, regularly followed and analyzed.

53 Military cooperation that started with the Tito-Stalin crisis continued in the following decades. See National Security Action Memorandum, no. 212, December 14, 1962 ("U.S. Policy toward Yugoslavia").

54 "Kennan states that US policy toward Yugoslavia has never enjoyed a broad understanding or commitment outside the working level in the Department of State. It has had powerful enemies, moreover, in right wing American and refugee groups, with their religious and Congressional supporters and spokesmen. In addition, the press has failed to provide adequate coverage of Yugoslavia. . . . Short of this, Kennan believes, we had better 'fold out tents' before 'Yugoslavs do it for us.'" Summary of Ambassador Kennan's Views on US Policy Toward Yugoslavia, December 19, 1962 (based on the US Embassy Belgrade Airgram A-543, November 28, 1962).

55 There were many doubts from the very beginning about the Non-Aligned Movement and many criticisms of Tito and Yugoslavia's role in it. "Yugoslavia was quite often regarded as a country not able to understand the urgent needs of the Third World, since it was 'socialist,' and like 'all of you there in Europe,' as the Indonesian press was criticizing in 1964, not attuned with the pressing problems of the Third World." Jakovina, "Tito's Yugoslavia," 390. In addition to that, many Western diplomats and politicians disliked the idea. For more on the reception of the Non-Aligned Movement in the West see Jakovina, "Tito's Yugoslavia," 392–401.

56 "As Budumir Lončar, Yugoslav ambassador to the United States in 1983 said to the members of the *Chicago Council on Foreign Relations*, the Yugoslav foreign policy was one dedicated to the peaceful coexistence, equality of all nations and states, non-interference in others internal development. The Non-Aligned Movement's political doctrine was recognizing freedom and right to self-determination for everyone, it was striving to end all forms of economic and cultural domination." Jakovina, "Tito's Yugoslavia," 389.

57 See Trud, *Etnički sukobi*, 134. Even before the formation of the Non-Aligned Movement, Tito seems to have been laying the ground for special Yugoslav-Islamic world relations. For instance, during Nasser and Sukarno's visits to Yugoslavia in 1956, both met with the Grand Mufti (Reis-ul-ulema) of the Muslim community in Sarajevo.

58 According to Ljubo Sirc, "Public ownership of capital and centralist planning were to be the two main pillars of the new order, as stressed by Marshal Tito when introducing the First Five-Year Plan to the Federal Assembly on 26 April 1947." Ljubo Sirc, *The Yugoslav Economy under Self-Management* (London: Macmillan, 1979), 1.

59 The defense spending went from 6.4 percent of the national income in 1948 to 21.4 percent in 1952. See Sirc, *The Yugoslav Economy*, 3.

60 Milovan Đilas, *The Unperfect Society (Beyond the New Class)*, trans. Dorian Cooke (New York: Harcourt, Brace and World, 1969), 220–23.

61 In reality, self-management predates this legislation—already in 1949 an experiment with introducing a workers' council was made at a select number of large enterprises, possibly to test its efficiency. At the core of the experiment was the attempt (coordinated by Boris Kidrič and Đuro Salaj) to "transform the workers' rights of consultation into a right of decision-making." Hans Dieter Seibel and Ukandi G. Damachi, *Self-Management in Yugoslavia and the Developing World* (London: Macmillan, 1982), 28. The Yugoslav post–World War II self-management builds on a longer tradition of socialist ideas in the Balkans, such as those of Svetozar Marković (1846–75).

62 Siebel and Damachi, *Self-Management*, 1.

63 Siebel and Damachi, 2.

64 See Miroljub Labus, "Uloga ekonomije u raspadu Jugoslavije," *Sociološki pregled* 28 (1994): 225–36; Miodrag Zec, Ognjen Radonjić, "Ekonomski model socijalističke Jugoslavije: saga o autodestrukciji," *Sociologija* 54 (2012): 702.

65 Among other factors that had an important impact on the Yugoslav economy from 1950s onward was U.S. aid, both financial and in goods, as well as the reduction of the unemployment rate due to the emigration of the work force to Western European countries, primarily Germany, beginning in the 1960s. See Susan L. Woodward, *Socialist Unemployment: The Political Economy of Yugoslavia, 1945–1990* (Princeton, NJ: Princeton University Press, 1995).

66 Noam Chomsky, conversation with Davor Džalto, January 6, 2012, Cambridge, MA.

67 Siebel and Damachi recognize three phases in the development of Yugoslav self-management: 1) Paternalistic self-management (ca. 1949–1953), which appeared within the system of state socialism, and where the established workers' council mostly did not have the power of decision-making; 2) Representative self-management (ca. 1953–63), which began with the constitutional amendments of 1953, with which self-management became an "inalienable right" of the working people, and which is characterized by elected workers' councils; 3) Direct self-management grounded in the new Constitution of 1963, where self-management becomes the "direct democratic right to manage production and all public affairs," which the authors hold to be "a new addition to the traditional civil rights proclaimed during the French Revolution." Seibel and Damachi, *Self-Management*, 43–59.

68 This was the primary cause of often-tense relations between France and Yugoslavia at that time.

69 Although Siebel and Damachi consider the development of Algerian self-management spontaneous and the only "method of keeping an economy running" in situations of "total or near-total disaster" (Siebel and Damachi, *Self-Management*, 7), other analyses point to a significant contribution by Yugoslavia and Yugoslav experts in installing self-management as a constitutional category in independent Algeria and in the foundation of the Algerian economy. See Trud, *Etnički sukobi*, 136–39.

70 Some of these protests in Serbia attracted broader media attention, such as those in the Zranjanin-based companies of Jugoremedija and *Šinvoz*. The Freedom Fight movement played an important role in documenting the cases of deindustrialization and oppression against workers. See *Deindustrijalizacija i radnički otpor: borbe i inicijative za očuvanje radnih mesta u periodu tranzicije*, Vladislav Bailović et al., eds. (Belgrade: Pokret za slobodu, 2011).

The Conscience of Yugoslavia

To the Editors:

I should like to call to the attention of readers recent judicial proceedings against a Yugoslavian student, Vladimir Mijanović, the President of the Council of Students of the Philosophical Faculty of Belgrade University, who was sentenced to twenty months in prison. The sentencing on October 23 [1970] set off a two-week student strike of protest. The case now goes to the Court of Appeals of Serbia. Of particular interest is the fact that one of the charges against the students is that on May 7, 1970, they organized demonstrations and published leaflets condemning the U.S. invasion of Cambodia.

Mr. Mijanović and those associated with him are the hope and the conscience of the Yugoslav revolution. In organizing opposition to the American invasion of Cambodia, they joined in a worldwide effort in support of a principle that extends far beyond the Cambodian invasion: the principle that great powers must be restrained from forceful intervention in the internal affairs of other nations. This principle is particularly important for Yugoslavia itself, a country that lies in the grim shadow of the "Brezhnev Doctrine." Not only the demands of justice but also those of practical good sense should impel the Yugoslav leaders to support those forces throughout the world that resist great power intervention.

Noam Chomsky
MIT, Cambridge, Mass.

★ Originally published as: Noam Chomsky, "Letter to the Editors," *New York Review of Books*, January 7, 1971.

The Repression at Belgrade University

A. Background

1949–1950. A new generation of young philosophers and social theorists, many of whom took active part in the liberation war (1941–1945), graduated and assumed teaching positions at the universities of Belgrade and Zagreb. They appeared on the scene during Yugoslavia's resistance to Stalin's attempts to dominate the country. They were mostly Marxists, but from the beginning they opposed Stalinist dogmatism and emphasized freedom of research, humanism, and openness to all important achievements of present-day science and culture.

1950–1960. A decade of discussions on basic theoretical issues, organized by the Yugoslav philosophical association. The debates were quite free; several groups opposed one another on different grounds. By the end of this period they all realigned along two basic lines, the orthodox one, which stayed within the traditional framework of dialectical materialism and considered theory to be essentially a reflection of the objective social situation and material surroundings, and the humanist one, which emphasized the anticipatory and critical character of theory, its unity with praxis, and its great role in the process of humanization of a given society.

1960. At a conference in Bled, the humanist, praxis-oriented trend prevailed and subsequently became dominant in Yugoslav universities, journals, and institutes.

1962. Yugoslav society experienced its first postwar stagnation as a result of an unsuccessful attempt to make its currency convertible. At the biannual meeting of the Yugoslav philosophical association in Skopje, November 1962, the view was expressed for the first time that it is urgent to go beyond abstract theoretical discussion about the nature of man and knowledge, about alienation and freedom, and the relation between philosophy and science—and toward a more concrete, critical study of Yugoslav society, guided by general humanist insights.

1963. A series of conferences and discussions with the attempt to clarify some general social issues: the meaning of technology, of freedom and democracy, of social progress, and of the role of culture in building a socialist society. In August, the Korčula Summer School was founded by Zagreb and Belgrade philosophers and sociologists, with the purpose of organizing free international summer discussions on actual social issues.

1964. The journal *Praxis* was founded by the same group. A new series of discussions, this time about sensitive issues of Yugoslav society: the meaning and perspective of socialism, bureaucratic and authoritarian tendencies in the party and the state apparatus, advantages and weaknesses of the existing forms of self-management and its possibilities for further development, and the right of a minority to continue to defend its views rather than conforming to the views of the majority. Most of these critical views and ideas seemed compatible with the liberal Program of the League of Communists of Yugoslavia (accepted at the Seventh Congress, 1958), but in reality were met with intolerance by alarmed party leaders. The transition from criticism of Stalinism toward a concrete critical analysis of Yugoslav society led to an almost complete break of communication between party officials and leading Marxist social and political philosophers.

1965–1967. While preserving a political system far more elitist and authoritarian than a developed system of participatory democracy could tolerate, the political leadership introduced an economic reform that was to fail: returning to a nineteenth-century model of a laissez-faire economy, leaving the Yugoslav economy at the mercy of big foreign firms in the "free competition" at the international market, causing mass unemployment and huge foreign debts, allowing speculation in real estate and a rapid increase of social differences, and encouraging the growth of autarchic tendencies in the existing six republics of the Yugoslav federation—which later constituted a material basis for strong nationalist movements.

Expression of critical views about these developments (themselves later condemned as manifestations of "liberalism" and "nationalism" by the party itself) was met by growing hostility by the party press. Critical philosophers and sociologists were branded "abstract humanists," "utopians," "revisionists," "anarcho-liberals," "neoleftists," "extreme leftists," and, finally, "political opposition that aspires to political power."

1968. In June, students of the University of Belgrade occupied all university buildings for seven days. They demanded abolition of bureaucratic privileges, further democratization, solution of the problem of mass unemployment, reduction of social differences, university reform. In one of his speeches during the crisis, Tito praised the students, endorsed all their demands, and declared he would resign if he failed to realize them.

Later, when this grave political crisis was over, the political leadership and Tito himself came to the conclusion that philosophers were responsible for it, because through their lectures they had "corrupted their students," "poisoned them with wrong ideas," and thus produced the student movement. The party organization at the Department of Philosophy and Sociology in Belgrade was dissolved. For the first time, Tito expressed the demand that further corruption "of students through their professors must be prevented" and that guilty professors must be ousted from the university.

1969–1972. Growing pressure was exerted by the central party leadership on lower-level political institutions to find a way to eliminate the professors. But this was a difficult task. Yugoslavia had developed a democratic organization of education and culture. All decision-making power in matters of electing, re-electing, and promoting university professors was in the hands of the faculty councils—the autonomous, self-managing bodies composed of professors, assistants, and students themselves. The university law emphasized scholarly qualification as the sole criterion of election. It did not give political authorities any right to interfere.

In the previous period, the officially declared policy of the League of Communists (LC) was that all theoretical controversies should be cleared up through discussion and free exchange of opinion. Therefore the rather democratically minded leadership of the LC in Serbia resisted the use of repressive measures against some of the leading philosophers and sociologists of the country. They were, however, refused access to mass media and mass gatherings, and the possibilities for circulating their ideas became much more limited. Still, they were able to teach, to travel abroad, to have three to four hundred participants from various countries at the Summer School of Korčula, to publish the journals *Praxis* and *Filozofija*, and occasionally to publish a book or two. The time was used to develop a cluster of fairly sophisticated and concrete theories about socialism and social revolution, integral self-management, the phenomenon of bureaucratism, humanization of technology, democratic direction of economy and culture, the problem of nationalism, etc.

Fall 1972. Tito ousted the leader of the League of Communists of Serbia, Marko Nikezić, and a number of his supporters. They were blamed for "liberal" practices and for opposing the new party line. The main feature of this new line was the return to a strong, disciplined, centralized, "monolithic" party that has the right and power directly to control and manage the realization of its policies. This called for complete ideological unity, consequently for a return to a crude form of ideological indoctrination, and for the abandonment of all former sophisticated ideas of creating new socialist consciousness through dialogues or struggles of opinion and patient persuasion.

The Faculty of Philosophy was now exposed to intense pressure. There were rumors of enemies, foreign spies on the teaching faculty; there were threats of stopping further financing, of closing the faculty. The faculty building was equipped with hidden microphones, some of which were found. The University Committee of the League of Communists drew up a list of eight professors to be fired. Passports were confiscated from five of them. Portions of some of their recently published books were banned. Some collaborators of the journal *Praxis* were arrested and sentenced to jail.

At that moment dozens of internationally known philosophers and social scientists from Scandinavia, the U.S., Germany, France, and other countries wrote letters to Tito and the rectors of the universities of Belgrade and Zagreb expressing their concern about those repressive measures and the hope that they would be discontinued in the interest of the further free development of Yugoslav democratic socialism. Many philosophical associations, departments of philosophy, academies, and international institutions devoted to human rights and civil liberties passed resolutions of concern and sent them to Yugoslavia.

This discreet expression of solidarity of the international intellectual community made a considerable impact on Yugoslav authorities who were proud of their past international reputation and who, in the existing economic and foreign-political situation of the country, could not afford to disregard world public opinion. They decided to take their time and to give repression a more democratic appearance.

B. Recent Developments

Slowly crushing the resistance of the Faculty of Philosophy without provoking too much international publicity required a series of steps. Some of these were easy, some were met with unexpected difficulties or even failed completely.

It was relatively easy to introduce certain important changes into existing university law. The law as now amended requires a university professor not only to have scholarly and moral qualifications but also to be politically acceptable. Political organizations now have the right to initiate a procedure in order to establish whether any individual university teacher meets political criteria.

A third change was a general and vague limitation of the principle of self-management. While heretofore the vast majority of the members of the faculty councils had to be elected by the faculty and students themselves, now the law prescribed that the composition of the council had to be determined through a "self-managing agreement" between the faculty and its founder—the Republican Executive Council (i.e., the government of the given Federal Republic).

The next step was to translate those legal changes into more specific and practical demands. The plan was *first* to specify political criteria for being a university professor in such a way that they could be applied to ousting the eight Belgrade professors, who previously could not be removed; *second* to push the party organization and the students' organization into condemning their colleagues and teachers; *third* to compel the University of Belgrade to accept a sufficient number of outside voting members into the councils so as to enable political authorities to gain full control over the decision-making process in the Faculty of Philosophy.

These measures met with considerable resistance. When a text of Criteria for the Election of University Professors was first proposed to the University Assembly in June 1973, most speakers objected strongly to it. They found certain criteria too rigid, for example, the requirement that a university professor must accept Marxism and actively support the politics of the League of Communists in his lectures and in all his scholarly and public activity. But later the Rector of the University, most deans, and eventually the University Assembly succumbed to the pressure, and in November accepted the text of the criteria.

Only the Faculty of Philosophy rejected it, and gave the following grounds, among others: it was unconstitutional because the existing constitution guarantees freedom of scientific work and cultural creation and forbids any kind of pressure on individuals to declare what kind of beliefs they have; it was unacceptable because the vast majority of Belgrade University professors are not Marxists and are apolitical; it was discriminatory because it allows, by its vagueness, any conceivable kind of interpretation; and it was discriminatory also because these criteria were being imposed on the University of Belgrade only, and not on any other Yugoslav university.

In May 1973, the Belgrade University committee of the League of Communists sent an open letter to the party organization of the Faculty of Philosophy, demanding the ouster of eight professors: Mihailo Marković, Ljubomir Tadić, Svetozar Stojanović, Zaga Pešić (Golubović), Miladin Životić, Dragoljub Mićunović, Nebojša Popov, and Trivo Inđić. After a series of meetings, attended by a large number of higher-ranking party officials who exerted great pressure on students and professors to conform to the demand, the party organization of the Faculty of Philosophy nevertheless rejected the ouster demand. A few of the most active opponents were expelled from the party, but when the party organization of the faculty met again in November, it decided, again unanimously, that the eight professors should stay at the faculty. There was a complete conviction that a university professor cannot be fired for expressing critical views in his writings, especially taking into account that the party itself now was repeating many of the criticisms that were expressed by those same scholars several years ago.

In November 1973, a university committee of the student organization made an attempt to force students of the Faculty of Philosophy into action against their professors, threatening them with possible violence if the faculty continued to resist. But the philosophy students refused to undertake anything of the sort and, on the contrary, to everyone's surprise, organized a street demonstration (although strictly forbidden in recent years, and in the past forcefully dispersed by the police). This time, students protested against repression in Greece and against the massacre in the University of Athens. There was no violence.

The crucial issue during the last six months has been the composition of the faculty councils. Self-management in the university meant that even in the institutions of special social importance, such as educational ones, only a small number of outside members were nominated by political authorities. Now the executive council (the government) of the Serbian Republic demanded that half the members of the faculty councils must be nominated from outside the university. Taking into account that students and administration must also be represented in the councils, this would give only one sixth of the votes to both professors and assistants and would clearly replace self-management by compulsory management.

By October, after initial resistance, the rector of the university and all faculties except the Faculty of Philosophy succumbed to the pressure. They were told that this new structure had been prescribed by the university law and therefore could not be a matter of debate. As a matter of fact, the law only prescribed that the composition of the faculty councils had to be determined through a "self-managing agreement" between the faculty and its founder (the Republic's executive council). The Faculty of Philosophy refused to sign the agreement because it was unconstitutional and incompatible with the principle of self-management, and because the very concept of agreement involves negotiation. The faculty asked the Constitutional Court to decide about the legitimacy of the imposed "agreement." At the same time, the faculty also drew up a counterproposal. But there was no negotiation and communication was broken.

An extremely abusive campaign was launched against the Faculty of Philosophy through the party newspaper *Komunist*, as well as through the press, radio, and TV. The faculty was accused of opposing the introduction of "self-management" at the university, of opposing the policy of the League of Communists, of keeping a monopoly on education, and of opposing any influence from "society," of asking help from foreign scholars, etc. At the same time the faculty was threatened with expulsion from the University of Belgrade, with refusal to finance its further activity or to employ its graduated students, and with eventual closing down. Under growing pressure of this kind, the Faculty Council decided on December 14, 1973, to authorize its Dean to sign the "self-managing agreement."

C. The Present Situation

The Faculty Council will now have half of its members nominated by political authorities. They will certainly be carefully selected from among leading political officials and disciplined members of the League of Communists. They will surely pose the question of removing the eight professors from the Department of Philosophy and Sociology as they do not meet the recently accepted political criteria. The political leadership will obviously press to clear the situation up before the Congress of the League of Communists of Yugoslavia in the spring.

It may still not be an easy task. According to law, assistants are reelected every three years, associate professors and assistant professors every five years—which means that legally one would have to wait for the expiration of that period for each candidate. Full professors do not undergo the process of reelection at all (i.e., they have tenure), which means that two among the eight (Marković and Tadić) cannot at this time legally be removed at all.

Another important circumstance is also that the party organization of the Faculty of Philosophy—whose opinion counts when it comes to political evaluation—has never agreed to condemn, or endorse the elimination of, any one from the group.

A relevant fact is that the threatened scholars enjoy a considerable reputation in the university and among other intellectuals. The action against them is not popular and, despite great efforts, the apparatus of the League of Communists was not able to find any well-known Yugoslav philosopher, sociologist, or political scientist to attack them.

The crucial questions are now (1) whether the outside members of the council will be disciplined enough by the government to perform according to their orders when they face their victims in the council; and (2) whether some of the inner members of the council, professors from various other departments of the Faculty of Philosophy, will yield to pressure and eventually vote for the firing of their colleagues.

Neither development is inevitable, but both are possible. Without strong political pressure many outside members would—as in the past— not even attend the meetings, or would be passive or vote with the rest. Thus everything will now depend on how brutal the effort will be and how far the political authorities will go in pressing the members of the council. Meanwhile, during the past six months several of the eight philosophers under attack have again been deprived of their passports.

D. Call for Action

The degree of pressure will depend on whether the whole thing will pass in silence as a little episode in one of the world's many universities, or whether it will be understood for what it is: one of the last battles for survival of free, critical, progressive thought in the present-day socialist world, in a country which is still open to democratic development and where until recently it seemed to have every chance to flourish.

That is where the reaction of the international intellectual community may again play a decisive role. The whole political and economic position of Yugoslavia makes it sensitive to world public opinion. By showing an interest in what is going on now in Yugoslav cultural life, by spreading the information, by raising the issue in international organizations, by expressing concern and protest in the press or in letters to Tito (which, after the recent escalation, should have more resolute and sharp form than previous ones), scholars and intellectuals everywhere could help to relax the present grip of the Yugoslav leadership and induce it to live up somewhat better to its own ideology of self-management and socialist democracy.

All the repressive measures so far have not sufficed fully to isolate and suffocate Yugoslav philosophy. But this might well happen in the weeks to come if the scholarly world will tolerate the further escalation of brutality and fear in a country that until not long ago has been an island of hope for many.

★ Originally published as: Noam Chomsky and Robert S. Cohen, "The Repression at Belgrade University," *New York Review of Books*, February 7, 1974. The article relied on information from several key sources from the region and was published with a note indicating that "the following statement was prepared by experts on the situation in Yugoslavia whom we believe to be reliable."

Letter to Tito

Dear Marshal Tito,

The international community of scholars and scientists feels increasingly concerned about the news of repressive measures against intellectuals and attempts to curtail academic freedom in Yugoslavia. Particularly shocking is the recently introduced law for the Republic of Serbia, abridging the self-management of the universities and authorizing the Parliament to suspend, on political grounds, university teachers from their positions. It is understood that the introduction of the law is part of a concerted attack on a number of internationally known and respected Marxist philosophers and their students. If the law is applied, it threatens with ruin the entire inner organization of Yugoslav universities, the autonomy and self-management of which has been a pride of the nation and a model for the world at large.

In view of these developments, we in whose names the present letter is written have decided to form a standing International Committee of Concern for Academic Freedom in Yugoslavia. We are friends of the country, who admire Marshal Tito's achievements for the liberation of the Yugoslav peoples and for the building of a new, democratic, and humanist socialism. We should hate to see these achievements ruined by a return to authoritarian and reactionary forms of political management.

The aim of our Committee is to raise the issue of academic freedom in Yugoslavia in all national and international academic institutions and organizations and to keep the news media informed of the developments. The Committee will be in existence as long as repression in Yugoslavia continues.

We regard it as our right and duty to protest any further infringements on academic freedom and violations of the United Nations Charter on human rights in Yugoslavia. In particular, we protest the new amendments to the university law in Serbia and urge Marshal Tito to use his influence and statesmanship to repudiate this law and see that it is not applied. It is our conviction that only by restoring autonomy to the universities and abstaining from repressive measures against the country's intellectuals can Yugoslavia survive as a respected member of the family of progressive and peace-loving nations.

We who form the Committee are the following scholars and scientists:

Sir Alfred J. Ayer
Professor of Philosophy, University of Oxford, Past President, Institut International de Philosophie (Paris)

Professor Noam Chomsky
Professor of Linguistics, Massachusetts Institute of Technology, USA

Professor Robert S. Cohen
Professor of Physics and Philosophy, Boston University, USA

Professor Dagfinn Follesdal
Professor of Philosophy, University of Oslo, Norway, and Stanford University, USA

Dr. Jürgen Habermas
Max-Planck-Institut, Starnberg, BRD

Professor Jaakko Hintikka
Professor of Philosophy, Academy of Finland and Stanford University, USA, Vice President, International Union of History and Philosophy of Science

Professor Harald Ofstad
Professor of Philosophy, University of Stockholm, Sweden

Professor Chaim Perelman
Professor of Philosophy, Université Libre de Bruxelles, Belgium, President, Institut International de Philosophie, Paris

Professor Paul Ricoeur

Professor of Philosophy, Université de Paris

Professor Georg Henrik von Wright

Professor of Philosophy, Academy of Finland and Professor-at-Large, Cornell University, USA, Past President, International Union of History and Philosophy of Science

★ Originally published as: Noam Chomsky et al., "Letter to Tito," *New York Review of Books*, February 6, 1975. The letter, dated December 23, 1974, was sent on behalf of the International Committee of Concern for Academic Freedom in Yugoslavia.

PART II
YUGOSLAV WARS

Solutions and Dissolutions

Davor Džalto

The breakup of Yugoslavia and the civil wars of the 1990s attracted considerable attention from the international community and received broad media coverage. The Yugoslav wars also inspired a number of academic publications, both in Europe and in the U.S., that aspired to explain and contextualize the crisis.

A couple of factors made the Yugoslav conflicts at the end of the twentieth century one of the central issues in U.S. and EU foreign policy, as well as in the mass media and academic discourse.

The breakup of Yugoslavia followed the fall of the Berlin Wall in 1989 and the collapse of the Soviet Union in 1991. It was also the first major conflict in Europe after World War II and corresponded with a new phase of European integrations. The European Union was formed in 1993, effectively replacing the European Economic Community, with the prospect of the inclusion of the European ex-Soviet countries into its membership. This process was paralleled with the process of NATO integrations (for which the concept of "Euro-Atlantic" integrations was coined to simultaneously describe both of these processes).

There was also the dominant feeling of optimism that came as a result of the so-called fall of communism. Some strategists and political theorists (e.g., Francis Fukuyama) even prophesied the "end of history" that signified the universal triumph of the "liberal democracy" over all other forms of sociopolitical and economic organization.

In such a situation, the Yugoslav wars were a shock in the eyes of many and created the impression of a phantom coming from the darkest of (European) nightmares. The narrative about brutal conflicts on European soil at the end of the twentieth century did not really fit the optimistic and idealized image of the post–Cold War world and its hoped-for (bright) future.

The conflicts could not be reconciled, not easily at least, with the post–World War II European "success story" that should have simply been expanded and reinforced in the post-1989 world. With "liberal democracy" (i.e., the "West") seen as some kind of eschatological paradise which the entire world (especially the ex-communist world) was striving toward, it became difficult to reconcile the conflicts that immediately followed the "fall of communism" with such an idealized image of the post-Soviet world. This image of an outburst of barbarianism, irrationality, mass killings, and the destruction of entire cities and regions countered the image of the post-Soviet prosperity.

Given its unique position within the Cold War context and the fact that it was to a significant extent shaped by that context, Yugoslavia could not but be affected by the changed situation of the post-1989 world. But what led to its disintegration and war was a synergy of multiple internal and external factors.

There are at least three main internal factors that were behind the dissolution of Yugoslavia that I want to briefly address: the crisis of the central federal authority, the rise of nationalism, and economic instability.

The decentralization of Yugoslavia, which took place during the 1960s and 1970s, gave more prominent positions to the local governments in each of the republics and autonomous provinces, weakening the central Yugoslav government. This was not so significant as long as Tito was in power as the chief authority, and as long as the League of Communists of Yugoslavia was more or less united under his leadership. But the integrative factor of Tito disappeared in 1980, and the weakened central state authorities, faced with growing problems, were left with a significantly narrowed space for action.

The country was governed by a collective presidency, composed of members from each of the Yugoslav republics and autonomous provinces, the federal government ("Savezno izvršno v[ij]eće"), which coordinated its activities with the presidency and with the federal parliament. This complex structure of the federal authorities, combined with the decentralization through which the republics gained more autonomy, turned out to be a very inefficient way of dealing with the growing problems of the Yugoslav state. The result was that toward the mid- and late 1980s, the centers of power would effectively shift to political and party leaderships in each of the Yugoslav republics.

As already pointed out, national tensions were notable even during Tito's era. They only grew after Tito's death, which coincided with the deteriorating federal authority. Political elites in each of the Yugoslav republics were turning to national(istic) narratives as an effective way of obtaining popular support and as a means of staying in power, or seizing it.[1] It has already been observed that "as pressures for democratization grew in the course of the 1980s, canny political figures came to recognize that public support would be necessary to retain power. The obvious basis of support for all such politicians was nationalism, and in each of the republics the most powerful political parties to emerge were formed on the basis of ethnic affiliation."[2]

In each of the Yugoslav republics and among all the Yugoslav nations, narratives about oppression, exploitation, and the domination of other national groups (or other republics) against "us" or "our national being" would grow during the 1980s and 1990s. The Slovenian narrative, for instance, was one about the financial exploitation of the underdeveloped southern republics (combined with derogatory national and cultural stereotypes about the "Southerners"). The Croatian narrative was mostly about Serbian domination and exploitation, combined with the "centuries-long" Croatian quest for independence, which both the (Serb-dominated) kingdom and "Serbo-communist" Yugoslavia prevented. The Serbian narrative was not only about the World War II genocide against the Serbs but a more general ahistorical self-victimization tale, in which the suffering in both wars was just an episode in a long line of foreign invasions and battles against the "innocent Serbs," which all goes back to the 1389 Battle of Kosovo.

As is often the case, the national and radically nationalistic narratives were combined with the (real or declaratory) democratic aspirations of the Yugoslav nations and their republics, as well as with the quest for freedom and de-bureaucratization, often against "communist oppression."[3]

During the late 1980s and at the beginning of the 1990s, these internal tensions would be expressed through more articulated claims by Slovenia and Croatia for a less and less centralized government and a confederal model, as a step toward independence. The demands for democratization—that became dominant political platforms in other Yugoslav republics as well—would become a useful narrative in order to legitimize the secession claims. The leaderships in both republics looked toward the West for support.

It seems that the dominant position in Serbia and among the Serbian population in other Yugoslav republics was for the preservation of Yugoslavia. This was a logical impulse, given the fact that a significant number of Serbs lived outside of Serbia. But when it became clear that the SFRJ would not survive and that the prospects for Slovenian and Croatian independence were becoming real, the Serbian leadership redefined its position from one that was for the preservation of Yugoslavia (in which the position of Serbia and the Serbs would de facto be dominant) to one that was for the preservation of the territories in which Serbs lived within what would be left of Yugoslavia. Some Bosnian Muslim leaders also seem to have initially adopted a position that favored staying in Yugoslavia, even the "smaller" one.[4]

The difficulty of the situation was correctly captured by CIA analysts who, already in 1990, reported that

> the key question for Serbia is the "fate" of the Serbs who dwell outside the borders of Serbia. This is the issue of greatest psychological importance for Serbs, and no Belgrade leadership can lightly accept responsibility for splintering the unity of the Serbian people, the goal for which Serbs perceive they have fought—and won—four bloody wars in this century.[5]

The absence of a significant Serbian population in Slovenia and Macedonia is one explanation of why Slovenia's secession (in June 1991) involved only a minor conflict (the "Ten Days War") and Macedonia's secession went peacefully (while Montenegro would choose to stay in the "small" Yugoslavia).

The real problem, however, was the position of the Serbs in an independent Croatia and Bosnia and Herzegovina. The reasoning that prevailed among Serbian political elites, as well as among many intellectuals, was that if individual republics (dominated by one of the constitutive nations— meaning Croats or Muslims) were breaking away from Yugoslavia, the Serbs should have the same right to choose their future, including the right to *stay* in (smaller) Yugoslavia. This effectively meant breaking away from those republics that were breaking away from Yugoslavia.

The situation was further complicated by territorial aspirations, coming both from Serbia and Croatia, toward Bosnia and Herzegovina. In 1990, Croatian President Franjo Tuđman publicly advocated for the partition of Bosnia and Herzegovina as a solution to the Yugoslav crisis.[6] This gave birth to the "agreed war" theory ("dogovoreni rat"), which claims that the war in Yugoslavia, especially the war in Bosnia, was, initially at least, the product of coordinated activities between Franjo Tuđman and Slobodan Milošević.[7]

The other main factor of the Yugoslav drama was that the "international community" (meaning Western European countries and the U.S.) was not helping the situation. As Chomsky points out in his texts, the premature recognition of the independence of Croatia (in December 1991) was a "recipe for war."

In addition to the already highly charged political space, there was also a flow of arms into Yugoslavia from abroad. This topic (never fully and properly explored) was already being discussed in 1991. From a now declassified CIA document, we learn that:

> Foreign arms have been entering the Yugoslav republics for months, the product of smuggling, gray arms market transactions, and at least one confirmed government-to-republic sale. The acquisition of foreign weapons is extremely sensitive in Yugoslavia's supercharged political atmosphere, and Belgrade reacted sharply to Hungary's government authorized sale of assault rifles to the Croatian government. . . . It is quite likely that arms dealers from Israel, Europe and the Middle East have approached republic officials in Yugoslavia and concluded agreements with some of them. . . . The flow of foreign arms stepped up late last year as Slovenia and Croatia began to see a more immediate threat of Army intervention. Private Slovene groups covertly acquired weapons last fall [redacted] and we believe that the republic government has been buying arms commercially on the gray arms market. Croatian representatives directly solicited US and European military support late last year, and senior republic officials have publicly acknowledged their efforts to acquire weapons in international arms markets. The Croats were rebuffed by Western governments, but the Hungarian Government responded by authorizing a controversial sale of several thousand assault rifles. Hungarian officials and Yugoslav press reports claim they may also have received Czech weapons. At least one report indicates some Croatian paramilitary forces have been seen with weapons from Singapore and Germany. . . . Moreover, if conflict erupts, emigre groups elsewhere in Europe will almost certainly step up efforts to provide military support to their compatriots in Yugoslavia.[8]

Together with acquiring foreign arms, the formation of independent armed forces within the Yugoslav republics was possible because of the structure of the internal defense system of the SFRJ. The Yugoslav Territorial Defense Forces (TDF), organized and trained for guerrilla war in case of a foreign invasion, were under the command of the Yugoslav republics, and as such not directly subordinated to the Yugoslav People's Army ("Jugoslovenska Narodna Armija"—JNA) command. The JNA had realized that this was a potential threat, which led to the attempts to disarm the TDF (which probably only stimulated the acquisition of foreign arms).[9]

Last but not least, there were also the economic issues that troubled the SFRJ throughout the post-Tito period. The Yugoslav economic problems did not start with Tito's death, but they certainly worsened over the first decade following his departure. There were multiple factors that contributed to the economic difficulties.

First of all, there were debt issues caused by foreign borrowing that started during Tito's time. The effect of the oil price shock of 1973 increased this borrowing. Another issue was the already mentioned decentralization of Yugoslavia, which gave the republics' considerable autonomy in the economic sphere as well. This led to many uncoordinated, redundant, and inefficient major investments that could have been avoided if there had been more substantial federal coordination. In addition, Yugoslav industry started to lose pace with the latest technological advancements. This was combined with the ineffectiveness of the highly bureaucratized administration and redistributive political interference in the economy, by which the profits of successful companies were used to maintain unnecessary and inefficient businesses and institutions only because there was a political interest in their preservation.

The economic difficulties led to arrangements being made with the IMF. Already by 1981, the SFRJ had become the test subject for the implementation of new neoliberal policies that still continue to be implemented and advocated for in the region. The reforms started with the standard austerity measures. As British scholar and activist Kate Hudson pointed out, "The terms that were required by the IMF were designed to secure the privatization and dismantling of the public sector in Yugoslavia."[10] The response to the economic crisis was "to continue to implement the IMF's austerity programme,"[11] which ceased to lead to the desired effects.

The economic crisis had two important (and unfortunate) political consequences. It became an argument for nationalists (especially in the most developed Yugoslav republics) against the preservation of the unified state, and for abandoning even the positive achievements of Yugoslav society and its economic models from the past, under the pretext of its "communist" outdatedness. On the other hand, Western countries strongly supported (especially toward the end of the 1980s) the "democratic processes" that should have been combined with a "market economy" as a way of transforming Yugoslavia (or the ex-Yugoslav countries) into a Western-type postcommunist society. Predictably, the expectations of many who supported some of the new economic policies have not yet been met—except in neoliberal theory.

In spite of all the nationalistic upheaval and the media propaganda that accompanied it, there was also a significant pro-Yugoslav popular support, primarily in Bosnia and Herzegovina and Serbia during the relevant period. The last federal prime minister, Ante Marković (1989–1991), for instance, whose orientation was explicitly pro-Yugoslav, enjoyed strong popular support in 1990.[12] Yet this personal popularity never translated into an organized political force that could defeat the nationalistic parties.

There were also antiwar and pro-Yugoslav demonstrations, such as the Sarajevo protests of 1992.[13] But these demonstrations were attacked by both the Serbian and Muslim nationalistic parties in Bosnia and would finally be crushed. This is only one example, among many that would follow, of the political, economic, and military cooperation between the Croatian, Serbian, and Muslim nationalists and their armed forces.[14]

In Serbia there was also a significant anti-war, anti-Milošević, and pro-Yugoslav support that would soon be sidelined. On the wave of nationalism, presenting himself as the defender of Yugoslavia and the Serbs, Milošević would continue to consolidate his power, turning the country into a soft dictatorship and blocking democratic developments up until October 5, 2000, when popular upheaval and protests brought an end to his regime.[15]

In spite of this complexity and the long history behind the wars surrounding the Yugoslav dissolution, the dominant explanations that both the international media and the scholarship offered during and immediately after the Yugoslav conflicts of the 1990s followed two main patterns.

According to the first one, the conflicts were read through the prism of the (revitalized) *otherness* of the Balkans. This was a way to contextualize conflict in a "postcommunist" country without sacrificing the dominant discourse of post-Soviet optimism. The motif of the "otherness" of the Balkans offered, in this context, a useful conceptual tool to explain that the wars and ethnic cleansings happened because the territories in which the conflicts took place *were not really (civilized) Europe*. This pattern presented the war as an ethnic and religious conflict of the Balkan peoples who had killed each other throughout their history. The complex history that was behind this late-twentieth century appropriation of the image of the Balkans as the European (eternal) *other* was analyzed in detail by Maria Todorova, in her classic study *Imagining the Balkans*.

The second dominant approach to the conflicts (which sometimes coincides with the first one) followed the "good guys" vs. "bad guys" model. To save the image of an eschatological paradise that should have almost automatically come once the authoritarian ("communist") regimes were dismantled, and to make it easier for the average Western media consumer to make sense of this conflict on European soil, the "good guys/bad guys" model was quickly created and would remain the dominant way of describing and interpreting the conflicts. In this model one side in the conflict is predominantly, if not exclusively, responsible for the wars and their outcomes, whereas other sides are predominantly, if not exclusively, the victims. This theoretical framework would soon become the mainstream both in the media representations of the events and in the political agendas of the time, as well as in the scholarship. The result of this synergy can also be seen in the way in which even the International Criminal Tribunal for the Former Yugoslavia (ICTY) in The Hague formulated the charges and handled the processes against those accused of war crimes and crimes against humanity.

In both of these models the causes of the conflicts are to be found within the Yugoslav/Balkan context itself, either in its otherness and sui generis character or in the specific conjuncture of (more tangible) internal factors. The advantage of both of these models was that they could offer an explanation of what was happening without raising the issue of external factors and their role in, and responsibility for, the conflict.

In contrast to these dominant views, created and promoted in the media and the scholarship, Noam Chomsky offered, already during the Yugoslav drama, a different reading of the causes that led to the breakup of Yugoslavia and the subsequent wars. This made his interpretation of the conflicts and the atrocities that came as a result of them different from the already adopted conceptual frameworks in some important aspects.

Without negating the significance of the internal difficulties that the Yugoslav federation was facing, Chomsky focuses on the international context and the role of the "international community" (the U.S. and major European countries) in the breakup of the federation and the wars that followed. In his articles, lectures, and interviews published in this chapter, Chomsky explains the broader economic and political interests that influenced the way particular countries formulated their policies toward the region. Chomsky specifically points to the role of the German leadership at the early stages of the dissolution and to the traditional perception of the Balkans as a German sphere of interest. In his interview with Matic Primc, for instance, answering the question about the U.S. and the EU's roles in the breakup of Yugoslavia and, specifically, the question of whether the dissolution was "engineered" or merely "helped along," Chomsky points to some important aspects of the story of the Yugoslav dissolution that are largely neglected or completely ignored:

> Putting aside Slovenia, which is a special case, public opinion in Yugoslavia seemed to be in favor of maintaining the federation. The U.S. at first took the same position. Under German initiative, the EU quickly recognized Croatia without taking into account the rights of the substantial Serb minority. That was a recipe for civil conflict, which soon ensued. As Yugoslavia fractured, the U.S. entered in support of the Bosnian Muslims, mostly for great power reasons. Clinton convinced Izetbegović to reject the Vance-Owen plan, thereby undermining the best hope for a peaceful settlement and laying the basis for vicious conflict, which ended with a settlement not very different from that plan, except that hopes for peaceful reconstruction are far more remote. A great deal of self-serving mythology has been concocted by Western intellectuals about all of this, impossible to unravel here.[16]

Chomsky was also vocal about the way particular events have been reported or, sometimes more importantly, have not been reported in the mainstream media. One example is the 1995 ethnic cleansing in Croatia. Although this was the largest ethnic cleansing in the Yugoslav wars, it has been mostly ignored and often qualified as a legitimate military operation.

One of the most controversial, however, is the case of Srebrenica. The Srebrenica massacre has been qualified as "genocide," up to the point that the ICTY uses this qualification in a couple of its rulings, thus offering a new interpretation of the definition of genocide advanced by the Convention on the Prevention and Punishment of the Crime of Genocide (1948). In the articles and interviews presented in this chapter, Chomsky also warns of the important historical implications if qualifications such as "genocide" in respect to the atrocities committed on the ex-Yugoslav territory during the 1990s conflicts remain.

In both of these cases, as well as in the case of the NATO bombing of the Bosnian Serb territories, Chomsky attempted to understand and interpret these events both in the context of the whole chain of events of the Yugoslav wars as well as in the context of the broader European and U.S. policies of that time. This method enabled Chomsky to draw conclusions that significantly differ from mainstream discourse. Chomsky explains that:

> The massacre, whatever its scale, can hardly be used as justification for NATO intervention, though one could, I suppose, offer it as a condemnation of NATO non-intervention, and in particular U.S. refusal to send ground troops along with other NATO powers. Srebrenica was lightly defended by a small Dutch government contingent, and was regarded as unviable by the NATO command. The Dutch government did a careful inquiry. They concluded that Milošević knew nothing about the massacre and was appalled at the discovery of the facts, which undermines the charge of "genocide" at the Tribunal; and also reported that the Clinton administration had been involved, along with Iran, in bringing in radical Islamist mujahedeen to support its side in the civil war, in violation of the official embargo. Shortly after the Srebrenica massacre and the mass expulsion of Serbs from Krajina, shortly after by U.S.-backed Croat forces, the Clinton administration supervised the Dayton peace agreement, welcoming Milošević and Tuđman (his quite comparable Croatian counterpart) as participants. Serious questions were raised at once concerning the refusal of the U.S. to support the (rather similar) Vance-Owen proposals under consideration in [1991 and] 1992, and its encouragement of Bosnians to reject them in anticipation of direct U.S. military support which never came; and about whether not only Srebrenica, Krajina, and other atrocities but the slaughter of the intervening years could have been avoided.[17]

The Yugoslav wars of the early 1990s were the introduction into the decades of instability, political and economic crises that continue to trouble the region. The trauma of the 1990s would bear an everlasting impact in each of the ex-Yugoslav republics on the way in which the entire Yugoslav legacy is interpreted.

Notes

1 This multifaceted process can be illustrated by the example of the rise to power of Slobodan Milošević (1941–2006), Franjo Tuđman (1922–99) and Alija Izetbegović (1925–2003), three crucial political figures in the Balkans in the 1990s. As the head of the League of Communists of Serbia (1986–90), and then president of Serbia (1989–91 and 1991–97), Milošević would become an undisputed Serbian political leader by 1989. Effectively abolishing the autonomous status of the provinces of Vojvodina and Kosovo and Metohija within the Yugoslav federation (through the Constitutional Amendments of 1989 and the new Constitution of the Republic of Serbia of 1990) and having the support of the Montenegrin leadership, Milošević would consolidate and expend his power. His rise to power was perceived in other Yugoslav republics as an attempt to control the majority voices in the Yugoslav presidency and, that way, to take the control of the federation. On the other hand, unlike Milošević, who kept up the pretense of defending socialism and Yugoslavia, Franjo Tuđman (President of Croatia, 1990–99) openly advanced a nationalistic program. In post–World War II Yugoslavia, Tuđman held the rank of a general in the Jugoslav People's Army; the transition from communist ideology to nationalism was, in his case, a gradual process. By the time the Yugoslav breakup began, Tuđman would speak of the NDH as an expression of "historical aspirations of the Croatian people," minimizing at the same time the victims of the Ustaša regime. Unlike Tuđman, who had been loyal to the Yugoslav-communist ideas before turning to nationalism, Alija Izetbegović (leader of Bosnian Muslims 1990–2000) appeared on the Yugoslav political scene as an opponent of the official ideology, in the name of his vision of Islamic society. He was arrested in 1946 for his opposition to the new regime and his activities during the World War II. Many recognized elements of Islamic fundamentalism in Izetbegović's 1970 book *Islamic Declaration*. In 1983, he was arrested again and sentenced to fourteen years in prison for what was perceived as "Muslim nationalism" and anti-state activities. This would become the platform from which Izetbegović entered the political life of Yugoslavia and Bosnia and Herzegovina in the 1990s.

2 Andrew Wachtel and Christopher Bennett, "The Dissolution of Yugoslavia," in *Confronting the Yugoslav Controversies*, eds. Charles Ingrao and Thomas A. Emmert (West Lafayette, IN: Purdue University Press, 2009), 28.

3 This would result, as Xavier Bougarel pointed out, in the formation of dominant national-oriented political parties in all of the Yugoslav republics, which were either "neocommunist" (meaning reformed [ex]communists, as in Slovenia, Serbia, Montenegro and Macedonia) or "anticommunist" (in Croatia and Bosnia and Herzegovina). Smaller parties and political movements ranged from even more nationalistic to pro-Yugoslav and pro–civil society oriented. See Ksavije Bugarel, *Bosna: anatomija rata* (Belgrade: Fabrika knjiga, 2004), 80.

4 Muhamed Filipović, a prominent Bosnian Muslim intellectual and politician, initially opposed Bosnian secession. He was also a member of the Bosnian Muslim delegation (together with Adil Zulfikarpašić) that in 1991 negotiated with Bosnian

Serb leaders, and then also with Milošević, and made an initial agreement. As a sign of good will, Milošević even proposed that Alija Izetbegović be the first president of the future state. See Muhamed Filipović, "Historijski sporazum," *Nezavisne novine*, October 15, 2008, available at http://www.nezavisne.com/index/kolumne/ Historijski-sporazum/30644; see also Noel Malcolm, *Bosnia: A Short History* (London: Macmillan, 1996), 227. However, Alija Izetbegović withdrew from further negotiations and the agreement failed. According to Filipović, the agreement was rejected by the Bosnian Muslim leadership under the pressure of the radical elements among the Muslim SDA party. In Filipović's view, the Croatian president, Franjo Tuđman, was also against this agreement, since that would weaken his own position. In some media interviews, Filipović indicates that foreign elements (primarily the U.S.) might also have been involved in putting pressure on Izetbegović to reject the agreement. This corresponds with Izetbegović's 1991 claims that he would "sacrifice peace for sovereign [i.e., independent] Bosnia" but "would never sacrifice sovereign Bosnia for peace." See Bugarel, *Bosna*, 85.

5   Declassified document *Yugoslavia Transformed*, October 18, 1990, 5. The same document made an accurate prediction that "Serbia can 'save' the unity of the Serbian folk only at risk of civil war. Even if Serbia emerged 'victor,' it would be internationally discredited, bankrupt, left to impose its will on more numerous hostile peoples, and isolated in face of the problems of Kosovo and Metohija."

6   See Bugarel, *Bosna*, 89. This corresponds to some other testimonies, such as that of Hrvoje Šarinić—former advisor and emissary of President Tuđman (later also Croatian prime minister)—given to the International Criminal Tribunal for the Former Yugoslavia (ICTY). Šarinić claimed that Tuđman considered Bosnia "a historical absurdity resulting from Turkish conquests in the fifteenth century." Šarinić's testimony, January 22, 2004, available at http://www.icty.org/en/content/ hrvoje-%C5%A1arini%C4%87.

7   This theory was already advanced by many journalists and analysts in Yugoslavia during the war. The documentary "Tuđman, Milošević: Dogovoreni rat?" (Tuđman, Milošević: Agreed War?"), produced in 2011 by the Serbian Television (RTS) addresses this issue. In the film, many actors of the events of the 1990s (including Stipe Mesić, Croatian member of the Yugoslav presidency, and later president of Croatia) elaborate upon the issue.

8   *Yugoslavia: Military Dynamics of a Potential Civil War: An Intelligence Assessment*, from March 1991, iii and 3.

9   See Yugoslavia: Assessment, 1–2; Mile Bjelajac and Ozren Žunec, "The War in Croatia, 1991–1995," in *Confronting*, eds. Ingrao and Emmert, 239–41.

10 Kate Hudson, *Breaking the South Slav Dream: The Rise and Fall of Yugoslavia* (London: Pluto, 2003), 57.

11 Ibid.

12 "As the annual inflation rate dropped from 3,000 per cent to around zero in mid-1990, Marković became the most popular politician in Yugoslavia." Pavković, *The Fragmentation*, 102.

13 Demonstrations occurred on April 5, 1992, in Sarajevo, with some 60,000 to 100,000 people gathered in front of the Parliament Building. See Bugarel, *Bosna*, 87.

14 Very telling examples in this respect are those related to the cooperation between all of the ethnic military formations when it came to weapon supplies that sometimes went simultaneously to all three sides in the Bosnian conflict. See Bugarel, *Bosna*, 95.

15 Milošević was actually perceived by many as a *moderate* option, given the extreme nationalists on one end of the political spectrum and pro-Western oriented democratic political options on the other. He positioned himself as the chief political figure in Serbia for the next decade, based on populist policies that combined his image as defender of the Yugoslav legacy with a flirtation with both the nationalists and Western-oriented political options, if and when necessary to sustain his personal power.

16 "US-EU Relations: Noam Chomsky interviewed by Matic Primc," *Spekter*, September 10, 2008, available at https://chomsky.info/20080910/.

17 Noam Chomsky, "Serb Massacres and NATO Intervention," *Zblogs*, Feb 16, 2005, available at https://zcomm.org/zblogs/serb-massacres-and-nato-intervention-by-noam-chomsky/.

USA, Germany, and the Faith of Yugoslavia

Davor Džalto: *There is still much debate and much controversy over the real causes of the dissolution of Yugoslavia. Certainly, one can point to the internal and external factors. Some claim that it was primarily the responsibility of the political elites in the Yugoslav republics who, together with many intellectuals, turned to nationalism as a new ideological fuel toward the end of the Cold War, to sustain their positions and expand their power. Others point to the role of the international community. What is your view?*

Noam Chomsky: The way it looked to me was different, rather along the lines of what Susan Woodward described.[1] First of all, there was the effect of Tito's death, and then there were the effects of the neoliberal policies instituted all over the world, including the Western countries, by the usual triumvirate: the IMF, the World Bank, and the U.S. Treasury Department. They had pretty much the same effects in different countries, so if you go down to the Occupy Wall Street protests today they are protesting the impact of these programs on the U.S. If you go to Tahrir Square in Egypt, they are protesting the impact on Egypt. It was similar in other parts of the world. The countries that observed the rules most stringently, in South America or sub-Saharan Africa for instance, are the ones that suffered most due to the lost decades of expected growth and development. South America has finally pulled out of it. They have rejected the neoliberal policies and they are now progressing. Similar austerity programs (that the IMF, incidentally, is no longer approving of) are now imposed in Europe, by the World Bank, the European Central Bank, and German banks. They are a form of class warfare undermining welfare states. Their purpose is making sure that banks are rich enough, undermining the role of labor—pretty standard effects.

With Yugoslavia it was the same. You can either say that the neoliberal policies were accepted or that Yugoslavia was subjected to them, it depends on the way you look at it. There were structural adjustment type programs in the 1980s, which undermined a lot of the achievements of the society. They had the usual effects of centralizing wealth and power, harming the general population, eliminating state structures, many of which were beneficial, many not. The poster child for this, the person whom the West loved more than anyone else, was Slobodan Milošević. Right up until 1990, he was probably a real favorite of the West because of the policies he was pursuing. Of course, there was the issue of nationalism, but that is also an interesting phenomenon. If you look at polls throughout Yugoslavia, around 1990, there was still, I think, considerable majority support for keeping the Federation together.

DDž: *Slovenia and Croatia were the first to proclaim independence from Yugoslavia. How do you see this sequence of events in the broader European and international context of that time?*
NC: Yes, Slovenia declared independence and that wasn't much of an issue. They were pretty much a part of Central Europe anyway. There were a couple of days of conflict and it sort of went over smoothly. But the big move was Croatia.

First of all, there were a lot of memories in Yugoslavia from World War II, particularly among the Serbian population. The proclaimed independence of Croatia was immediately backed by Germany, which also raised war memories—the Nazis and the Croatian fascists were very closely linked. And Germany was plainly just trying to expand its influence over the areas where it had traditionally dominated. The German support for Croatian independence paid no attention to the rights of the Serbian minority in Croatia, which was pretty significant. So, quite naturally, the Yugoslav Army intervened and that led to the first conflicts. Actually, some of the first atrocities were committed by Croatians and, as I said, there was a plenty of baggage there in terms of historical memories.

A big question was how Europe would respond. Of course, Europe went along with Germany, which it usually does—it is, after all, the motor of Europe—which meant that they were supporting the breakup and certain conflict. Then the internal conflicts broke out.

First, the U.S. was standing aside and in fact even supporting some steps toward unification. There were proposals in 1993, the Vance-Owen plan, which could probably have resolved the conflict more or less peacefully, without the atrocities that followed. The U.S. at that point entered into the conflict and undermined the efforts. Apparently Washington wanted to have a piece of the action, not to leave it to Europe, so it entered in and had to have somebody to support, and so it supported the Bosniaks. Clinton pretty much urged Alija Izetbegović not to accept the settlements that were being proposed, which are incidentally not very different from the way the settlement ended up. After all the crimes and barbs it very likely could have been put together right at that point, but then followed what we all know—more and more violence. Current estimates are about, I think, one hundred thousand killed, maybe sixty thousand Bosniaks, a lot of atrocities, a lot of crimes.

Everybody for example knows about Srebrenica, but nobody knows about the Krajina expulsions,[2] which happened around the same time, the biggest ethnic cleansing in the fall of Yugoslavia. But the U.S. was behind it. It was Croatians, so therefore it was okay to forget about it. Finally, militarily, the lines were more or less drawn after Srebrenica and Krajina and so the U.S. stepped in and monitored the agreements, which essentially ratified what was there. As I said, it probably could have been done in 1992.

DDž: *Let us focus for a moment on this role of Germany in the breakup of Yugoslavia that you mentioned. Your position has been that Germany was the chief promoter of Croatian independence, and then the rest of Western Europe just followed that path. This is not something one often hears in the media or in the scholarship on the former Yugoslavia. I want to ask you, what was the main interest of Germany in supporting the independence of Croatia, thus laying the groundwork for the breakup of Yugoslavia and the conflicts that followed?*

NC: Germany has a historic interest in the Balkans. When Hitler moved in, that was not an innovation. Germany had been influential there. I think it was just trying to restore its influence over that part of Europe, just as Germany is the driving force right now in the austerity programs that are destroying Southern Europe.

DDž: *How do you see current developments? How do you see the political and economic situation in Europe? A British member of the European parliament just recently accused Germany of aspiring to dominate and control the entirety of Europe.*

NC: That is not a secret, and it is also not new—it goes back centuries. The Europeans do not go to war with each other anymore. In political science literature, it is called "democratic peace." It is the concept that democracies don't fight each other. Well, it's true that democracies don't fight each other if they understand that the next time they play their favorite game of slaughtering each other, they're going to destroy the world. So in 1945 a light dawned in Europe. They realized "We've been the most savage and brutal place for centuries, but we can't do it anymore," because the capacity for destruction has reached such a level that the next time there is a war between France, Germany, and Italy, it will follow Einstein's answer when he was asked "What will be the weapons used in the next war?" His point was, paraphrasing him, "Well, I don't know what they'll be, but I know what they'll be in the war after that—stone axes." When that realization dawned, they stopped fighting each other. They now carry out atrocities elsewhere.

★ Noam Chomsky interviewed by Davor Džalto, January 6, 2012, Cambridge, MA.

Notes

1 Susan L. Woodward, American political scientist, expert on the Balkans and Yugoslavia, and author of *Balkan Tragedy: Chaos and Dissolution after the Cold War* (Washington, DC: Brookings Institution, 1995).

2 Chomsky refers here to the "Bljesak" (Flash) and "Oluja" (Storm) actions of the Croatian Army (1995) that ended the existence of the Republic of Serb Krajina ("Republika Srpska Krajina"), with the expulsion of around 200,000 and the killing of a couple of thousand Croatian Serbs. The Republic of Serb Krajina (1991–1995) occupied mostly the territories of the former "Military Frontier" or "Military (Vojna) Krajina" in the Austro-Hungarian Empire, where Serbs represented the majority.

Most Guns, Most Atrocities

I do not think the current conflict in Bosnia and Herzegovina has been primarily a U.S. responsibility. The situation has probably reached a point where it not easy to think of a constructive solution anymore. A few years ago there were options. However, the way in which the Yugoslav breakup was handled was almost guaranteed to lead to extreme conflict.

I think it is primarily a European responsibility in this case. Germany insisted on a very rapid breakup of Yugoslavia without any preparation. In fact, Germany insisted that it was going to go through it alone if necessary, which means Europe had to go along. The insistence on Croatian independence, without recognition of the fact that there was a substantial Serbian minority, was a guarantee of war. Bosnia also was recognized without any preparation, again with a big Serbian and Croatian minority. It was done in such a fashion so as to maximize the possibility of everything going wrong, and everything did go wrong. And now at this point, when people ask for a constructive proposal, it is pretty hard to suggest one. To deal with the problem in a really constructive fashion is not easy.

I also do not agree with this dominant view that one often hears from the mass media that Serbs are exclusively "the killers, the rapists," and so on. In conflicts like this, the ones who commit most of the atrocities are the ones who have most of the guns. And in fact Serbs in this conflict have most of the guns, so they commit most of the atrocities.

There were a couple of military options proposed to stop the violence, including the arms supply and potential Western military intervention. To add to the violence by, say, sending planes to bomb could have quite unpredictable consequences. Take the possible reaction inside Russia. It's no big secret that there's an old tradition in Russia about saving the Serbs, from the Turks for instance, and a lot of similar stories. There's a lot of concern, especially in nationalist and military circles in Russia, about the breakup of the Soviet Union, the humiliation of Russia, and so on. It's entirely possible that there already are Russian so-called volunteers fighting with the Serbs. Suppose they go down there with tactical nuclear weapons on their backs, you can think of a lot of ugly possibilities. Or suppose that some sort of international intervention would stimulate the Serbs to carry out the kind of desperate and violent acts that are not uncommon. They might decide to move on to Kosovo, which might involve the Turks, and you could have a Balkan war. All of these are possible consequences of direct intervention and not to be treated lightly.

★ Based on Noam Chomsky's responses to Phil Donahue and Vladimir Pozner's questions about the war in Bosnia and Herzegovina, on *Pozner & Donahue*, CNBC, April 1993.

Open Letter to the *Guardian*

This is an open letter to a few of the people with whom I had discussed the *Guardian* interview of 31 October, on the basis of the electronic version, which is all that I had seen. Someone has just sent me a copy of the printed version, and I now understand why friends in England who wrote me were so outraged.

It is a nuisance, and a bit of a bore, to dwell on the topic, and I always keep away from personal attacks on me, unless asked, but in this case the matter has some more general interest, so perhaps it's worth reviewing what most readers could not know. The general interest is that the print version reveals a very impressive effort, which obviously took careful planning and work, to construct an exercise in defamation that is a model of the genre. It's of general interest for that reason alone.

A secondary matter is that it may serve as a word of warning to anyone who is asked by the *Guardian* for an interview and happens to fall slightly to the critical end of the approved range of opinion of the editors. The warning is: if you accept the invitation, be cautious and make sure to have a tape recorder that is very visibly placed in front of you. That may inhibit the dedication to deceit, and if not, at least you will have a record. I should add that in probably thousands of interviews from every corner of the world and every part of the spectrum for decades, that thought has never occurred to me before. It does now.

It was evident from the electronic version that it was a scurrilous piece of journalism. That's clear even from internal evidence. The reporter obviously had a definite agenda: to focus the defamation exercise on my denial of the Srebrenica massacre. From the character of what appeared, it is not easy to doubt that she was assigned this task. When I wouldn't go along, she simply invented the denial, repeatedly, along with others. The centerpiece of the interview was this, describing my alleged views, in particular, that: "during the Bosnian war the 'massacre' at Srebrenica was probably overstated. (Chomsky uses quotations marks to undermine things he disagrees with and, in print at least, it can come across less as academic than as witheringly teenage; like, Srebrenica was so not a massacre.)"

Transparently, neither I nor anyone speaks with quotation marks, so the reference to my claim that "Srebrenica was so not a massacre," shown by my using the term "massacre" in quotes, must be in print—hence "witheringly teenage," as well as disgraceful. That raises the obvious question: Where is it in print, or anywhere? I know from letters that were sent to me that a great many journalists and others asked the author of the interview and the relevant editors to provide the source and were met by stony silence—for a simple reason: it does not exist, and they know it. Furthermore, as Media Lens pointed out, with five minutes research on the internet, any journalist could find many places where I described the massacre as a massacre, never with quotes. That alone ends the story. I will skip the rest, which also collapses quickly.

More interesting, however, is the editorial contribution. One illustration actually is in the e-edition. I did write a very brief letter in response, which for some reason went to the ombudsman, who informed me that the word "fabrication" had to be removed. My truncated letter stating that I take no responsibility for anything attributed to me in the article that did appear, paired with a moving letter from a victim, expressing justified outrage that I or anyone could take the positions invented in the *Guardian* article. Pairing aside, the heading given by the editors was: "Fall out over Srebrenica." The editors are well aware that there was no debate or disagreement about Srebrenica, once the fabrications in their article are removed.

The printed version reveals how careful and well-planned the exercise was, and why it might serve as a model for the genre. The front-page announcement of the interview reads: "Noam Chomsky The Greatest Intellectual?" The question is answered by the following highlighted Q&A, above the interview:

Q: Do you regret supporting those who say the Srebrenica massacre was exaggerated?
A: My only regret is that I didn't do it strongly enough.

It is set apart in large print so that it can't be missed, and will be quoted separately (as it already has been). It also captures the essence of the agenda.

The only defect is that it didn't happen. The truthful part is that I said, and explained at length, that I regret not having strongly enough opposed the Swedish publisher's decision to withdraw a book by Diana (not "Diane," as the *Guardian* would have it) Johnstone after it was bitterly attacked in the Swedish press. As Brockes presumably knew, though I carefully explained anyway, there is one source for my involvement in this affair: an open letter that I wrote to the publisher, after editors there who objected to the decision and journalist friends sent me the Swedish press charges that were the basis for the rejection. In the open letter, readily available on the internet (and the only source), I went through the charges one by one, checked them against the book, and found that they all ranged from serious misrepresentation to outright fabrication. I then took—and take—the position that it is completely wrong to withdraw a book because the press charges (falsely) that it does not conform to approved doctrine. And I do regret that "I didn't do it strongly enough," the words Brockes managed to quote correctly. In the interview, whatever Johnstone may have said about Srebrenica never came up and is entirely irrelevant in any event, at least to anyone with a minimal appreciation of freedom of speech.

The article is then framed by a series of photographs. Let's put aside childhood photos and an honorary degree—included for no apparent reason other than, perhaps, to reinforce the image the reporter sought to convey of a rich elitist hypocrite who tells people how to live (citing a comment of her own, presumably supposed to be clever, which will not be found on the tape, I am reasonably confident). Those apart, there are three photos depicting my actual life. It's an interesting choice, and the captions are even more interesting.

One is a picture of me "talking to journalist John Pilger" (who isn't shown, but let's give the journal the benefit of the doubt of assuming he is actually in the original). The second is of me "meeting Fidel Castro." The third, and most interesting, is a picture of me "in Laos en route to Hanoi to give a speech to the North Vietnamese."

That's my life: honoring commie-rats and the renegade who is the source of the word "pilgerize," invented by journalists furious about his incisive and courageous reporting, and knowing that the only response they are capable of is ridicule.

Since I'll avoid speculation, you can judge for yourselves the role Pilger plays in the fantasy life of the editorial offices of the *Guardian*. And the choice is interesting in other ways. It's true that I have met John a few times, much fewer than I would like because we both have busy lives. And possibly a picture was taken. It must have taken some effort to locate this particular picture, assuming it to be genuine, among the innumerable pictures of me talking to endless other people. And the intended message is very clear.

Turn to the Castro picture. In this case the picture, though clipped, is real. As the editors surely know, at least if those who located the picture did two minutes of research, the others in the picture (apart from my wife) were, like me, participants in the annual meeting of an international society of Latin American scholars, with a few others from abroad. This annual meeting happened to be in Havana. Like all others, I was in a group that met with Castro. End of second story.

Turn now to the third picture, from 1970. The element of truth is that I was indeed in Laos and on my way to Hanoi. The facts about these trips are very easy to discover. I wrote about both in some detail right away, in two articles in the *New York Review of Books*, reprinted in my book *At War with Asia* in 1970. It is easily available to *Guardian* editors, because it was recently reprinted. If they want to be the first to question the account (unlike reviewers in such radical rags as the journal of the Royal Institute, *International Affairs*), it would be very easy for a journalist to verify it: contact the two people who accompanied me on the entire trip, one then a professor of economics at Cornell, the other a minister of the United Church of Christ. Both are readily accessible. From the sole account that exists, the editor would know that in Laos I was engaged in such subversive activities as spending many hours in refugee camps interviewing miserable people who had just been driven by the CIA "clandestine army" from the Plain of Jars, having endured probably the most intense bombing in history for over two years, almost entirely unrelated to the Vietnam War. And in North Vietnam, I did spend most of my time doing what I had been invited to do: many hours of lectures and discussion on any topic I knew anything about in the bombed ruins of the Hanoi Polytechnic, to faculty who were able to return to Hanoi from the countryside during a lull in the bombing and were very eager to learn about recent work in their own fields, to which they had had no access for years.

The rest of the trip "to Hanoi to give a speech to the North Vietnamese" is a *Guardian* invention. Those who frequent ultra-right defamation sites can locate the probable source of this ingenious invention, but even that ridiculous tale goes nowhere near as far as what the *Guardian* editors concocted, which is a new addition to the vast literature of vilification of those who stray beyond the approved bounds.

So that's my life: worshipping commie-rats and such terrible figures as John Pilger. Quite apart from the deceit in the captions, simply note how much effort and care it must have taken to contrive these images to frame the answer to the question on the front page.

It is an impressive piece of work and, as I said, provides a useful model for studies of defamation exercises or for those who practice the craft. And also, perhaps, provides a useful lesson for those who may be approached for interviews by this journal.

This is incidentally only a fragment. The rest is mostly what one might expect to find in the scandal sheets about movie stars, familiar from such sources, and of no further interest.

★ Originally published as: Noam Chomsky, "Chomsky Answers *Guardian*," *ZNet*, November 13, 2005.

On the Srebrenica Massacre

Srebrenica was theoretically a protected base, so nobody could get in. The Muslim forces were using it as a base to attack Serbian villages outside, and they were very frank and open about it. An officer that headed the militias bragged to the press that he was sending his troops out into the Serb villages, beheading people, torturing them, and then they would go back into the safe zone.[1] It was reported in the U.S.[2] Well, you know, it was pretty clear that sooner or later there was going to be a response to this. Now, what the commander then did was pull out his militias, and when the Serbs came in, which they did in reaction, they were kind of surprised that there was no military defense, and then they carried out a lot of atrocities.

Now, that is often called genocide. I don't use the word "genocide" much, and I don't think it's used properly. The way it's used strikes me as a kind of Holocaust denial. I mean, to use the term "genocide" when you kill a bunch of people you don't like, that demeans the victims of the Holocaust. If you kill, say, a couple of thousand men in a village, after you have allowed the women and children to escape—you have in fact trucked them out— that does not count as genocide. It's a horror story but it is not genocide.

In the case of Srebrenica, the figures are debated. The highest figures that are given are around eight thousand. However, when enemies carry out an atrocity there is a huge effort that goes into finding every piece of bone, into the DNA analysis, into trying to get the biggest number you can. When we carry out a comparable atrocity nobody even investigates it. I think we ought to tell the truth about it, and the truth is that it was an atrocity, but nothing like what was claimed in, say, the British press.

This is also true of the camps.[3] That's another interesting story. There were a couple of detention camps. The first one was investigated by a *Guardian* reporter, [Ed] Vulliamy, and some ITN TV people,[4] and they reported on this camp, which they described as a detention camp.[5] If you read the early report, they pointed out that people were not forced to stay there, they could get out if they wanted. This was an eyewitness report. Later, the story changed. It became Auschwitz. Incidentally, the same journalist reported that it was a kind of Auschwitz in Europe. The story was changed, not on the basis of new evidence, but just because the mood had changed.

There was a small newspaper called *LM*.[6] They sent a photographer to the camps who took photographs and essentially confirmed the original story.[7] What happened then is interesting. ITN and, incidentally, the *Guardian* as well, went after *LM*. They relied on the utterly scandalous British libel laws that make it possible for a big corporation to put a tiny newspaper out of business, since they can't pay the legal costs. Then there was a euphoria about it, saying it was great we managed to put out of business a tiny newspaper which published something we didn't like.

Then something else happened. Phillip Knightley, the most respected photojournalist, maybe anywhere in the world and certainly here, looked into it.[8] He has very respected work, which goes back to the Spanish Civil War. He did an analysis and he concluded that the *LM* analysis was probably correct. He didn't accuse anyone of distortion, he just said that if you looked at it, it was probably correct. He also wrote a very interesting article addressed to the British journalists, saying that they ought to learn something about the freedom of the press. I don't think any of those were published.

★ Based on Noam Chomsky's responses during a discussion on U.S. foreign policy with Jonathan Freedland. British Library, London, March 19, 2013.

Notes

1   Chomsky refers here to Naser Orić (b. 1967), a Bosniak war commander in charge of the Srebrenica region between 1992–1995.
2   Chomsky refers here to an article by John Pomfret, "Weapons, Cash and Chaos Lend Clout to Srebrenica's Tough Guy," *Washington Post*, February 16, 1994, available at https://www.washingtonpost.com/archive/politics/1994/02/16/weapons-cash-and-chaos-lend-clout-to-srebrenicas-tough-guy/f15d65af-356b-423b-a6cd-9ef36cb5b557/?utm_term=.c66add3b906d.
3   Chomsky refers here to the detention camps in Bosnia and Herzegovina, where people of other ethnic / national backgrounds were detained and often tortured.
4   Independent Television News is a British-based news service.
5   Chomsky refers here to the Trnopolje detention camp.

6   *Living Marxism* was a British magazine established in 1988. The magazine (later rebranded as *LM*) was closed in 2000 after the legal process that ITN launched against it, to which Chomsky refers later on.

7   In 1997 *LM* published an article by Thomas Deichmann ("The Picture That Fooled the World") attacking ITN reporting and questioning its authenticity.

8   The analysis of the photograph that Chomsky refers here was conducted in 1998.

PART III
KOSOVO CRISIS

Kosovo: A Drama in Multiple Acts

Davor Džalto

The Kosovo crisis and the NATO bombing of FRY in 1999 were the final acts in the decade-long Yugoslav disintegration process. The war that NATO launched against FRY was a unilateral action, not authorized by the UN Security Council. This divided the international community over the legitimacy of such intervention and its real objectives.

In the context of Noam Chomsky's interest in the region, the Kosovo issue and the events surrounding the NATO war against FRY represent the most thoroughly analyzed segment of the Yugoslav puzzle. Chomsky closely followed the events from the beginning of the bombing and continued to discuss the bombing and its consequences for more than a decade. In the texts in this chapter, Chomsky addresses a variety of issues, such as the causes of the intervention, the actual course of events, the media coverage, the impact of the bombing on the future of the region, as well as the parallels between the Kosovo crisis and broader international issues, such as the "right to defend" doctrine, the issues of justice and morality in international relations, international law, etc.

The significance of Chomsky's engagement with these issues consists of the fact that he was able to formulate, already during the 1999 intervention, alternative interpretations of the causes of the crisis, and to expose inconsistencies in the way the military campaign was presented and justified in the mainstream media and academic discourse. He also pointed to factual errors (such as the inverted chronology of events) that, through the media, entered the mainstream, becoming the basis for the legitimization of the bombing.

As outlined in the previous chapters, Kosovo and Metohija was not exactly a model of peaceful coexistence even before the crisis of the 1990s. Ethnic tensions existed even before World War II and they continued during Tito's rule, with various frequencies and levels of intensity. The situation became especially complex in the 1980s and 1990s, when the issues that were unique to Kosovo and Metohija were additionally complicated by the problems that the Yugoslav federation was facing as a whole. The complex situation in the province was a result of multiple factors, such as poor economic conditions, changed demographics, separatist tendencies among segments of the Albanian population, and police oppression that fueled ethnic tensions.

In spite of the significant amount of money poured into the province during Tito's rule (as a part of the broader Yugoslav policy to help poor regions), Kosovo and Metohija remained the most underdeveloped region of the Yugoslav federation.[1] An extremely high unemployment rate (at least two and half times the federal average),[2] high personal debt, and poor economic outcomes were among the factors that contributed to the rise of ethnic tensions. The situation was further complicated with the austerity measures applied in SFRJ in the 1980s, which especially affected the poorest regions.

Another important factor was the changing demographic picture of Kosovo and Metohija. With the highest birthrate in both Yugoslavia and Europe, ethnic Albanians constituted 77.4 percent of the population of Kosovo and Metohija in 1981 (as opposed to 68.5 percent in 1948), and this percentage would only grow further.[3] Another factor that contributed to the changing demographic picture of Kosovo and Metohija was the migration of Kosovo Serbs, for both economic and security reasons. The Serbian minority in Kosovo felt threatened in the predominantly Albanian surroundings, and cases of resentment against Kosovo Serbs and occasional violence against them were also reported.[4]

The first large-scale manifestation of nationalism in post-Tito Yugoslavia was the Albanian riots of 1981. The protests started over what were essentially socioeconomic issues, but they soon acquired the character of a political upheaval that advanced the claims for a changed status of Kosovo and Metohija within the Yugoslav federation. These claims ranged from demanding the province be given the status of a republic within Yugoslavia to demands for full independence and even the prospect of a union with Albania.[5] As the protests spread, the federal government responded by proclaiming a state of emergency and by sending tanks and the police to suppress the protests by force. The result was that many ethnic Albanian members of the League of Communists of Yugoslavia in Kosovo and Metohija were expelled from the party, and measures were also taken against all who were labeled as separatists. This only escalated the tensions.

Over the following years, representatives of Kosovo Serbs required the state authorities to take action in order to protect Serbs, stop the discrimination, improve the rights of Serbs in the province, and reverse the trend of migration. The expectations of Kosovo Serbs coincided with Slobodan Milošević's rise in the political life of Serbia in the mid- and late 1980s.

An important episode was Milošević's visit to Kosovo in 1987, as the head of the Serbian communists. Although he called for brotherhood and unity among all "citizens" and was nominally against divisions along ethnic/national lines, he won the sympathies of Kosovo Serbs by expressing his support for their claims and by publicly criticizing the police violence against Serb protestors.[6]

Milošević returned to Kosovo in 1989, as president of Serbia. On June 28, he addressed the crowd (estimates are that around one million people gathered at Gazimestan) as part of the celebration of the six-hundredth anniversary of the Battle of Kosovo (1389), which has a special symbolic meaning in Serbian history. Milošević used the opportunity to mobilize the masses, appealing to their patriotic feelings. Even though he stressed the importance of overcoming national tensions, peaceful coexistence, and the further development and modernization of Serbia and Yugoslavia, the masses most enthusiastically greeted his references to Serbian national pride, national unity, and national history. Not only the political leadership but also the intellectual and church elites exploited the symbolism of Kosovo and of the 1989 jubilee to mobilize and homogenize Serbian society.

As a response to the secessionist aspirations, and as a way to further solidify Milošević's popularity, Serbian authorities took steps in the 1989–1990 period aimed at limiting and revoking the autonomy of the province. The deteriorating status of the region's autonomy and various types of pressure against those who were perceived as "disloyal" citizens (which included dismissals from work, politically motivated arrests and trials, etc.) escalated nationalistic sentiments among Kosovo Albanians. This would change the initial demands for independence *within* Yugoslavia into demands for independence *from* Yugoslavia.

Over the course of the early 1990s, Kosovo Albanians would develop parallel institutions (both in Kosovo and abroad) meant to reduce reliance on Serbian state institutions in the province as much as possible. Yet it was not primarily Kosovo Albanians who were living in the province, but "the

Kosovar Albanians in the Diaspora who became the most radicalized part of the Kosovar Albanian community,"[7] and who, eventually, created the Kosovo Liberation Army (Ushtria Çlirimtare e Kosovës—UÇK, hereafter KLA).

The KLA started planning and executing terrorist activities, at first primarily targeting the Serbian police force, before expanding its activities against both Serbian and ("disloyal") Albanian civilians at a later stage.[8] The armed conflicts with the Serbian police escalated during 1997 and 1998, as the KLA started using northern Albania as its base.[9] It seems that the finances came mostly from the drug market, as well as from a special fund, based in Switzerland, called "Homeland Calling" established by the KLA and supported by the Albanian diaspora.[10] The armed conflict provoked another wave of Serb migration from Kosovo and Metohija into central Serbia, in the 1996–1999 period.

The escalation of KLA attacks led to the escalation of Serbian police violence. Serbian authorities launched not only a broader police campaign against KLA members and supporters but also various types of repressive measures against Albanian civilians, such as "arbitrary arrest, detention, physical abuse, illegal searches, and extra-judicial killing."[11] This, in turn, deepened the interethnic tensions and mistrust.

The escalation of the conflict in 1998 and the Serbian and Yugoslav government representatives' rejection of the ultimatum presented in Rambouillet (in February 1999) and in Paris (in March 1999) by the Contact Group were used as a rationale for launching the bombing on Mach 24, 1999. The reasons for the NATO attack were often portrayed as "humanitarian," being grounded in the "responsibility to protect." These pretexts are discussed at length in the texts published in this chapter.

Complementary to Chomsky's analyses, some scholars made attempts to understand the NATO attack within the broader context of U.S. policy in regards to the region, going beyond the immediate propaganda narrative that was employed by the majority of the mainstream media in the West to justify the attack. Kate Hudson, for instance, sees the NATO war against FRY as a step in a process that had started long before: "In fact, the US had decided to defeat Milosevic, who was obstructing the full integration of Yugoslavia into the western institutional framework. The legitimate grievances of the Kosovan Albanians were manipulated by the west and used to justify the attempts to destroy the remaining parts of the socialist economy of Yugoslavia in order to fully open up the region to capitalist expansion."[12]

The immediate consequence of the NATO bombing was that Milošević's internal position was strengthened. This led to even more oppressive and authoritarian measures being undertaken by the government, both against Kosovo Albanians and against the democratic opposition movement that was challenging the regime in the rest of Serbia.[13] With a state of war proclaimed on the whole territory of FRY, Milošević was strengthened, the opposition silenced, and his fall probably delayed.

The bombing ended with the so-called Kumanovo agreement (signed in Kumanovo, on June 9, 1999), which determined that the armed forces of FRY and Serbia would withdraw from Kosovo, and that the international security forces ("Kosovo Force" or KFOR) would take control of the province. UN resolution 1244 (June 10, 1999) further specified the steps and principles of establishing a UN-monitored administration in Kosovo, guaranteeing the "substantial autonomy" of Kosovo "within the Federal Republic of Yugoslavia."

But the end of the NATO bombing did not mean the end of the violence in Kosovo. Upon the withdrawal of the Yugoslav army and the Serbian police force and the takeover of the NATO-led KFOR, many Serbs would permanently leave Kosovo. Most of the remaining Serbs in the province were exposed to perpetual violence, which included forced migration, beatings, massacres, the desecration of graves, and the destruction of churches and of private property.[14] Unable or unwilling to protect the minorities in Kosovo, KFOR and the new Kosovo political leadership did not take any serious steps to stop the violence or punish the perpetrators. As a result, the violence continued, escalating in March 2004, when many Serbs across Kosovo and Metohija were forced to leave their homes, with dozens of them beaten and killed.[15] The pogrom of 2004 also brought the destruction of many Serbian cultural heritage sites, including many medieval churches.

Some of the atrocities committed in the post-NATO bombing period became known publicly only later. Such is the case of the trafficking of human organs taken from kidnapped people (most of them ethnic Serbs but also Albanians) by the KLA members and later sold on the black market. The report titled "Inhuman Treatment of People and Illicit Trafficking in Human Organs in Kosovo" by the Committee on Legal Affairs and Human Rights of the Parliamentary Assembly of the Council of Europe, concluded that:

> According to the information gathered by the Assembly and to the criminal investigations now under way, numerous concrete

and convergent indications confirm that some Serbians and some Albanian Kosovars were held prisoner in secret places of detention under KLA control in northern Albania and were subjected to inhuman and degrading treatment, before ultimately disappearing.

Numerous indications seem to confirm that, during the period immediately after the end of the armed conflict, before international forces had really been able to take control of the region and re-establish a semblance of law and order, organs were removed from some prisoners at a clinic on Albanian territory, near Fushë-Krujë, to be taken abroad for transplantation. . . . Although some concrete evidence of such trafficking already existed at the beginning of the decade, the international authorities in charge of the region did not consider it necessary to conduct a detailed examination of these circumstances, or did so incompletely and superficially.[16]

In violation of UN Resolution 1244, and with major diplomatic support from the U.S., Kosovo declared independence on February 17, 2008. As of February 2017, according to the Ministry of Foreign Affairs of Kosovo, 113 countries recognized its independence.[17] Yet given that many countries still do not recognize its independence, including two of the permanent members of the Security Council (Russia and China), five EU countries (Cyprus, Greece, Romania, Slovakia, and Spain), and many of the non-aligned countries, the independence of Kosovo remains an open and greatly divisive issue in international affairs.

To solve the still highly inflammatory situation in the Balkans, another "borders adjustment" resolution was proposed in a recent issue of *Foreign Affairs*. Recognizing the "miserable reality" in the region (although without acknowledging that this reality is significantly, if not crucially, the result of the Western-imposed policies in the region over the past decades, combined with the rule of corrupt local elites), the article suggests adjustments of borders between Albania, Bosnia and Herzegovina, Croatia, Kosovo, Montenegro, Macedonia, and Serbia as a way to secure long-term stability in the region.[18]

Notes

1   See Kate Hudson, *Breaking the South Slav Dream: The Rise and Fall of Yugoslavia* (London: Pluto, 2003), 66–68; Žil Trud (Gilles Troude), *Etnički sukobi u Titovoj Jugoslaviji (1960–1980)* (Sremski Karlovci: Izdavačka knjižarnica Zorana Stojanovića, 2010), 228–37.

2   Momčilo Pavlović, *Kosovo under Autonomy 1974–1990* (report), 13, available at https://www.cla.purdue.edu/si/Team1Reporte.pdf. See Hudson, *Breaking*, 66.

3   Pavlović, *Kosovo*, 10; and Hudson, *Breaking*, 68.

4   In 1981, Ali Shukriu, the Kosovo Albanian communist leader, famously said: "What nation and what honorable person can be proud of the fact that the girls of Serbian nationality dare not go to school, that graves are desecrated or that church windows are broken? How would Albanian families feel if their graves were desecrated and their religious objects damaged?" Quoted in Benedikt Harzl, "Kosovo in Abkhazia or the Universality of De Facto States," *Minorities in South Asia and in Europe: A New Agenda*, ed. Samir Kumar Das (Kolkata: Samya, 2010), 206.

5   See Hudson, *Breaking*, 66.

6   "Speech of Slobodan Milosevic at Kosovo Polje," April 24–25, 1987, available at http://www.slobodan-milosevic.org/news/milosevic-1987-3-eng.htm.

7   Independent International Commission on Kosovo, *The Kosovo Report* (Oxford: Oxford University Press, 2000), 45.

8   See *Report*, 52.

9   *Report*, 52.

10 *Report*, 52.

11 *Report*, 53.

12 Hudson, *Breaking*, 123.

13 At this time, the Serbian government was composed of the Milošević-controlled Socialist Party of Serbia, Yugoslav Left (led by Milošević's wife Mira Marković), and members of the ultra-nationalist Serbian Radical Party.

14 See Human Rights Watch Report, "Federal Republic of Yugoslavia: Abuses Against Serbs and Roma in the New Kosovo," August 1999, available at https://www.hrw.org/reports/1999/kosov2/.

15 Human Rights Watch Report, "The Violence: Ethnic Albanian Attacks on Serbs and Roma," available at https://www.hrw.org/reports/2004/kosovo0704/7.htm.

16 Dick Marty, "Inhuman Treatment of People and Illicit Trafficking in Human Organs in Kosovo" (Doc. 12462 from January 7, 2011), available at https://sitf.eu/images/110107CoEReport.pdf.

17 "International recognitions of the Republic of Kosovo," available at http://www.mfa-ks.net/?page=2,224.

18 Timothy Less, "Dysfunction in the Balkans: Can the Post-Yugoslav Settlement Survive?," *Foreign Affairs*, December 20, 2016, available at https://www.foreignaffairs.com/articles/bosnia-herzegovina/2016-12-20/dysfunction-balkans.

Crisis in the Balkans

On March 24, U.S.-led NATO forces launched cruise missiles and bombs at targets in Yugoslavia, "plunging America into a military conflict that President Clinton said was necessary to stop ethnic cleansing and bring stability to Eastern Europe," lead stories in the press reported. In a televised address, Clinton explained that by bombing Yugoslavia, "we are upholding our values, protecting our interests, and advancing the cause of peace."[1]

In the preceding year, according to Western sources, about two thousand people had been killed in the Yugoslav province of Kosovo and there were several hundred thousand internal refugees. The humanitarian catastrophe was overwhelmingly attributable to Yugoslav military and police forces, the main victims being ethnic Albanian Kosovars, commonly said to constitute about 90 percent of the population. After three days of bombing, according to the UN High Commissioner for Refugees, several thousand refugees had been expelled to Albania and Macedonia, the two neighboring countries. Refugees reported that the terror had reached the capital city of Priština, largely spared before, and provided credible accounts of large-scale destruction of villages, assassinations, and a radical increase in generation of refugees, perhaps an effort to expel a good part of the Albanian population. Within two weeks the flood of refugees had reached some 350,000, mostly from the southern sections of Kosovo adjoining Macedonia and Albania, while unknown numbers of Serbs fled north to Serbia to escape the increased violence from the air and on the ground.

On March 27, U.S.-NATO Commanding General Wesley Clark declared that it was "entirely predictable" that Serbian terror and violence would intensify after the NATO bombing. On the same day, State Department spokesperson James Rubin said that "The United States is extremely alarmed by reports of an escalating pattern of Serbian attacks on Kosovar

Albanian civilians," now attributed in large part to paramilitary forces mobilized after the bombing. General Clark's phrase "entirely predictable" is an overstatement. Nothing is "entirely predictable," surely not the effects of extreme violence. But he is surely correct in implying that what happened at once was highly likely. As observed by Carnes Lord of the Fletcher School of Law and Diplomacy, formerly a Bush Administration national security adviser, "enemies often react when shot at," and "though Western officials continue to deny it, there can be little doubt that the bombing campaign has provided both motive and opportunity for a wider and more savage Serbian operation than what was first envisioned."

In the preceding months, the threat of NATO bombing—again, predictably—was followed by an increase in atrocities. The withdrawal of international observers, sharply condemned by the Serb Parliament, predictably had the same consequence. The bombing was then undertaken under the rational expectation that killing and refugee generation would escalate as a result, as indeed happened, even if the scale may have come as a surprise to some, though apparently not the commanding general.

Under Tito, Kosovars had had a considerable measure of self-rule. So matters remained until 1989, when Kosovo's autonomy was rescinded by Slobodan Milošević, who established direct Serbian rule and imposed "a Serbian version of Apartheid," in the words of former U.S. government specialist on the Balkans James Hooper, no dove: he advocates direct NATO invasion of Kosovo. The Kosovars "confounded the international community," Hooper continues, "by eschewing a war of national liberation, embracing instead the nonviolent approach espoused by leading Kosovo intellectual Ibrahim Rugova and constructing a parallel civil society," an impressive achievement, for which they were rewarded by "polite audiences and rhetorical encouragement from Western governments." The nonviolent strategy "lost its credibility" at the Dayton Accords in November 1995, Hooper observes. At Dayton, the U.S. effectively partitioned Bosnia-Herzegovina between an eventual greater Croatia and greater Serbia, after having roughly equalized the balance of terror by providing arms and training for the forces of Croatian dictator Tuđman and supporting his violent expulsion of Serbians from Krajina and elsewhere. With the sides more or less balanced, and exhausted, the U.S. took over, displacing the Europeans who had been assigned the dirty work, much to their annoyance. "In deference to Milošević," Hooper writes, the U.S. "excluded Kosovo Albanian delegates" from the Dayton negotiations and "avoided discussion of the

Kosovo problem." "The reward for nonviolence was international neglect"—more accurately, U.S. neglect.

Recognition that the U.S. understands only force led to "the rise of the guerrilla Kosovo Liberation Army (KLA) and expansion of popular support for an armed independence struggle." By February 1998, KLA attacks against Serbian police stations led to a "Serbian crackdown" and retaliation against civilians, another standard pattern: Israeli atrocities in Lebanon, particularly under Nobel Peace laureate Shimon Peres, are or should be a familiar example, though one that is not entirely appropriate. These Israeli atrocities are typically in response to attacks on its military forces occupying foreign territory in violation of longstanding Security Council orders to withdraw. Many Israeli attacks are not retaliatory at all, including the 1982 invasion that devastated much of Lebanon and left twenty thousand civilians dead (a different story is preferred in U.S. commentary, though the truth is familiar in Israel). We need scarcely imagine how the U.S. would respond to attacks on police stations by a guerrilla force with foreign bases and supplies.

Fighting in Kosovo escalated, the scale of atrocities corresponding roughly to the resources of violence. An October 1998 cease-fire made possible the deployment of two thousand European monitors. Breakdown of U.S.-Milošević negotiations led to renewed fighting, which increased with the threat of NATO bombing and the withdrawal of the monitors, again as predicted. Officials of the UN refugee agency and Catholic Relief Services had warned that the threat of bombing "would imperil the lives of tens of thousands of refugees believed to be hiding in the woods," predicting "tragic" consequences if "NATO made it impossible for us to be here."

Atrocities then sharply escalated as the late March bombing provided "motive and opportunity," as was surely "predictable," if not "entirely" so.

The bombing was undertaken, under U.S. initiative, after Milošević had refused to accept a U.S. ultimatum, the Rambouillet Agreement of the NATO powers in February. There were disagreements within NATO, captured in a *New York Times* headline that reads: "Trickiest Divides Are Among Big Powers at Kosovo Talks." One problem had to do with deployment of NATO peacekeepers. The European powers wanted to ask the Security Council to authorize the deployment, in accord with treaty obligations and international law. Washington, however, refused to allow the "neuralgic word 'authorize,'" the *New York Times* reported, though it did finally permit "endorse." The Clinton administration "was sticking to its stand that NATO should be able to act independently of the United Nations."

The discord within NATO continued. Apart from Britain (by now, about as much of an independent actor as Ukraine was in pre-Gorbachev years), NATO countries were skeptical of Washington's preference for force and annoyed by Secretary of State Albright's "saber-rattling," which they regarded as "unhelpful when negotiations were at such a sensitive stage," though "US officials were unapologetic about the hard line."

Turning from generally uncontested fact to speculation, we may ask why events proceeded as they did, focusing on the decisions of U.S. planners—the factor that must be our primary concern on elementary moral grounds, and that is a leading if not decisive factor on grounds of equally elementary considerations of power.

We may note at first that the dismissal of Kosovar democrats "in deference to Milošević" is hardly surprising. To mention another example, after Saddam Hussein's repeated gassing of Kurds in 1988, in deference to its friend and ally the U.S. barred official contacts with Kurdish leaders and Iraqi democratic dissidents, who were largely excluded from the media as well. The official ban was renewed immediately after the Gulf War, in March 1991, when Saddam was tacitly authorized to conduct a massacre of rebelling Shi'ites in the south, and then Kurds in the north. The massacre proceeded under the steely gaze of "Stormin'" Norman Schwarzkopf, who explained that he was "suckered" by Saddam, not anticipating that Saddam might carry out military actions with the military helicopters he was authorized by Washington to use. The Bush administration explained that support for Saddam was necessary to preserve "stability," and its preference for a military dictatorship that would rule Iraq with an "iron fist" just as Saddam had done was sagely endorsed by respected U.S. commentators.

Tacitly acknowledging past policy, Secretary of State Albright announced in December 1998 that "we have come to the determination that the Iraqi people would benefit if they had a government that really represented them." A few months earlier, on May 20, Albright had informed Indonesian President Suharto that he was no longer "our kind of guy," having lost control and disobeyed IMF orders, so that he must resign and provide for "a democratic transition." A few hours later, Suharto transferred formal authority to his handpicked vice president. We now celebrate the May 1999 elections in Indonesia, hailed by Washington and the press as the first democratic elections in forty years—but without a reminder of the major U.S. clandestine military operation forty years ago that brought Indonesian democracy to an end, undertaken in large measure because the democratic system was unacceptably open, even allowing participation of the left.

We need not tarry on the plausibility of Washington's discovery of the merits of democracy in the past few months; the fact that the words can be articulated, eliciting no comment, is informative enough. In any event, there is no reason to be surprised at the disdain for nonviolent democratic forces in Kosovo; or at the fact that the bombing was undertaken with the likely prospect that it would undermine a courageous and growing democratic movement in Belgrade, now probably demolished as Serbs are "unified from heaven—but by the bombs, not by God," in the words of Aleksa Đilas, the historian son of Yugoslav dissident Milovan Đilas. "The bombing has jeopardized the lives of more than 10 million people and set back the fledgling forces of democracy in Kosovo and Serbia," having "blasted . . . [its] germinating seeds and insured that they will not sprout again for a very long time," according to Serbian dissident Veran Matić, editor in chief of the independent station Radio B-92 (now banned). Former *Boston Globe* editor Randolph Ryan, who has been working for years in the Balkans and living in Belgrade, writes that "Now, thanks to NATO, Serbia has overnight become a totalitarian state in a frenzy of wartime mobilization," as NATO must have expected, just as it "had to know that Milošević would take immediate revenge by redoubling his attacks in Kosovo," which NATO would have no way to stop.

As to what planners "envisioned," Carnes Lord's confidence is hard to share. If the documentary record of past actions is any guide, planners probably were doing what comes naturally to those with a strong card—in this case violence. Namely, play it, and then see what happens.

With the basic facts in mind, one may speculate about how Washington's decisions were made. Turbulence in the Balkans qualifies as a "humanitarian crisis" in the technical sense: it might harm the interests of rich and privileged people, unlike slaughters in Sierra Leone or Angola, or crimes we support or conduct ourselves. The question, then, is how to control the authentic crisis. The U.S. will not tolerate the institutions of world order, so the problems have to be handled by NATO, which the U.S. pretty much dominates. The divisions within NATO are understandable: violence is Washington's strong card. It is necessary to guarantee the "credibility of NATO"—meaning, of U.S. violence: others must have proper fear of the global hegemon. "One unappealing aspect of nearly any alternative" to bombing, Barton Gellman observed in a *Washington Post* review

of "the events that led to the confrontation in Kosovo," "was the humiliation of NATO and the United States." National Security Adviser Samuel
Berger "listed among the principal purposes of bombing 'to demonstrate
that NATO is serious.'" A European diplomat concurred: "Inaction would
have involved 'a major cost in credibility, particularly at this time as we
approach the NATO summit in celebration of its fiftieth anniversary.'" "To
walk away now would destroy NATO's credibility," Prime Minister Tony
Blair informed Parliament. Blair is not concerned with the credibility of
Italy or Belgium, and understands "credibility" in the manner of any Mafia
Don.

Violence may fail, but planners can be confident that there is always
more in reserve. Side benefits include an escalation of arms production
and sales—the cover for the massive state role in the high tech economy for
years. Just as bombing unites Serbs behind Milošević, it unites Americans
behind Our Leaders. These are standard effects of violence; they may not
last for long, but planning is for the short term.

There are two fundamental issues: (1) What are the accepted and applicable "rules of world order"? (2) How do these or other considerations apply
in the case of Kosovo?

(1) There is a regime of international law and international order
binding on all states, based on the UN Charter and subsequent resolutions
and World Court decisions. In brief, the threat or use of force is banned
unless explicitly authorized by the Security Council after it has determined
that peaceful means have failed or in self-defense against "armed attack" (a
narrow concept) until the Security Council acts.

There is, of course, more to say. Thus there is at least a tension, if not
an outright contradiction, between the rules of world order laid down in
the UN Charter and the rights articulated in the Universal Declaration of
Human Rights (UD), a second pillar of the world order established under
U.S. initiative after World War II. The Charter bans force violating state
sovereignty; the UD guarantees the rights of individuals against oppressive
states. The issue of "humanitarian intervention" arises from this tension.
It is the right of "humanitarian intervention" that is claimed by the U.S./
NATO in Kosovo, with the general support of editorial opinion and news
reports.

The question was addressed at once in a *New York Times* report headed
"Legal Scholars Support Case for Using Force." One example is offered: Allen
Gerson, former counsel to the U.S. mission to the UN. Two other legal

scholars are cited. One, Ted Galen Carpenter, "scoffed at the Administration argument" and dismissed the alleged right of intervention. The third is Jack Goldsmith, a specialist on international law at Chicago Law School. He says that critics of the NATO bombing "have a pretty good legal argument," but "many people think [an exception for humanitarian intervention] does exist as a matter of custom and practice." That summarizes the evidence offered to justify the favored conclusion stated in the headline.

Goldsmith's observation is reasonable, at least if we agree that facts are relevant to the determination of "custom and practice." We may also bear in mind a truism: the right of humanitarian intervention, if it exists, is premised on the "good faith" of those intervening, and that assumption is based not on their rhetoric but on their record, in particular their record of adherence to the principles of international law, World Court decisions, and so on. That is indeed a truism, at least with regard to others. Consider, for example, Iranian offers to intervene in Bosnia to prevent massacres at a time when the West would not do so. These were dismissed with ridicule (in fact, generally ignored); if there was a reason beyond subordination to power, it was because Iranian good faith could not be assumed. A rational person then asks obvious questions: Is the Iranian record of intervention and terror worse than that of the U.S.? And other questions, for example: How should we assess the "good faith" of the only country to have vetoed a Security Council resolution calling on all states to obey international law? What about its historical record? Unless such questions are prominent on the agenda of discourse, an honest person will dismiss it as mere allegiance to doctrine. A useful exercise is to determine how much of the literature—media or other—survives such elementary conditions as these.

(2) When the decision was made to bomb, there had been a serious humanitarian crisis in Kosovo for a year. In such cases, outsiders have three choices:

(I)   act to escalate the catastrophe
(II) do nothing
(III) try to mitigate the catastrophe

The choices are illustrated by other contemporary cases. Let's keep to a few of approximately the same scale, and ask where Kosovo fits into the pattern.

(A) *Colombia.* In Colombia, according to State Department estimates, the annual level of political killing by the government and its paramilitary associates is about at the level of Kosovo, and refugee flight primarily from their atrocities is well over a million, another three hundred thousand last year. Colombia has been the leading Western hemisphere recipient of U.S. arms and training as violence increased through the 1990s, and that assistance is now increasing under a "drug war" pretext dismissed by almost all serious observers. The Clinton administration was particularly enthusiastic in its praise for President Gaviria, whose tenure in office was responsible for "appalling levels of violence," according to human rights organizations, even surpassing his predecessors. Details are readily available.

In this case, the U.S. reaction is (I): escalate the atrocities.

(B) *Turkey*. For years, Turkish repression of Kurds has been a major scandal. It peaked in the 1990s; one index is the flight of over a million Kurds from the countryside to the unofficial Kurdish capital Diyarbakir from 1990 to 1994, as the Turkish army was devastating the countryside. Two million were left homeless according to the Turkish State Minister for Human Rights, a result of "state terrorism" in part, he acknowledged. "Mystery killings" of Kurds (assumed to be death squad killings) alone amounted to 3,200 in 1993 and 1994, along with torture, destruction of thousands of villages, bombing with napalm, and an unknown number of casualties, generally estimated in the tens of thousands; no one was counting. The killings are attributed to Kurdish terror in Turkish propaganda, generally adopted in the U.S. as well. Presumably Serbian propaganda follows the same practice. The year 1994 marked two records in Turkey: it was "the year of the worst repression in the Kurdish provinces," Jonathan Randal reported from the scene, and the year when Turkey became "the biggest single importer of American military hardware and thus the world's largest arms purchaser. Its arsenal, 80 percent American, included M-60 tanks, F-16 fighter-bombers, Cobra gunships, and Blackhawk 'slick' helicopters, all of which were eventually used against the Kurds." When human rights groups exposed Turkey's use of U.S. jets to bomb villages, the Clinton administration found ways to evade laws requiring suspension of arms deliveries, much as it was doing in Indonesia and elsewhere. Turkish aircraft have now shifted to bombing Serbia, while Turkey is lauded for its humanitarianism.

Colombia and Turkey explain their (U.S.-supported) atrocities on grounds that they are defending their countries from the threat of terrorist guerrillas. As does the government of Yugoslavia.

Again, the example illustrates (I): act to escalate the atrocities.

(C) *Laos*. Every year thousands of people, mostly children and poor farmers, are killed in the Plain of Jars in Northern Laos, the scene of the heaviest bombing of civilian targets in history it appears and arguably the most cruel: Washington's furious assault on a poor peasant society had little to do with its wars in the region. The worst period was from 1968, when Washington was compelled to undertake negotiations (under popular and business pressure), ending the regular bombardment of North Vietnam. Kissinger-Nixon then shifted the planes to bombardment of Laos and Cambodia.

The deaths are from "bombies," tiny antipersonnel weapons, far worse than land mines: they are designed specifically to kill and maim, and have no effect on trucks, buildings, etc. The Plain was saturated with hundreds of millions of these criminal devices, which have a failure-to-explode rate of 20 to 30 percent according to the manufacturer, Honeywell. The numbers suggest either remarkably poor quality control or a rational policy of murdering civilians by delayed action. These were only a fraction of the technology deployed, including advanced missiles to penetrate caves where families sought shelter. Current annual casualties from "bombies" are estimated from hundreds a year to "an annual nationwide casualty rate of 20,000," more than half of them deaths, according to the veteran Asia reporter Barry Wain of the *Wall Street Journal* in its Asia edition. A conservative estimate, then, is that the crisis last year was approximately comparable to Kosovo, though deaths are far more highly concentrated among children, over half according to studies reported by the Mennonite Central Committee, which has been working there since 1977 to alleviate the continuing atrocities.

There have been efforts to publicize and deal with the humanitarian catastrophe. A British-based Mine Advisory Group (MAG) is trying to remove the lethal objects, but the U.S. is "conspicuously missing from the handful of Western organisations that have followed MAG," the British press reports, though it has finally agreed to train some Laotian civilians. The British press also reports, with some annoyance, the allegation of MAG specialists that the U.S. refuses to provide them with "render harmless procedures" that would make their work "a lot quicker and a lot safer." These remain a state secret, as does the whole affair in the U.S. The Bangkok press reports a very similar situation in Cambodia, particularly the Eastern region where U.S. bombardment from early 1969 was most intense.

In this case, the U.S. reaction is (II): do nothing. The reaction of the media and commentators is to keep silent, following the norms under which the war against Laos was designated a "secret war," meaning well-known but suppressed, as also in the case of Cambodia from March 1969. The level of self-censorship was extraordinary then, as is the current phase. The relevance of this shocking example should be obvious without further comment.

President Clinton explained to the nation that "there are times when looking away simply is not an option"; "we can't respond to every tragedy in every corner of the world," but that doesn't mean that "we should do nothing for no one."[2] But the president and commentators, failed to add that the "times" are well defined. The principle applies to "humanitarian crises," in the technical sense discussed earlier: when the interests of rich and privileged people are endangered. Accordingly, the examples just mentioned do not qualify as "humanitarian crises," so looking away and not responding are definitely options, if not obligatory. On similar grounds, Clinton's policies on Africa are understood by Western diplomats to be "leaving Africa to solve its own crises." For example, in the Republic of Congo, scene of a major war and huge atrocities; here Clinton refused a UN request for a trivial sum for a battalion of peacekeepers, according to the UN's senior Africa envoy, the highly respected diplomat Mohamed Sahnoun, a refusal that "torpedoed" the UN proposal. In the case of Sierra Leone, "Washington dragged out discussions on a British proposal to deploy peacekeepers" in 1997, paving the way for another major disaster, but also of the kind for which "looking away" is the preferred option. In other cases too, "the United States has actively thwarted efforts by the United Nations to take on peacekeeping operations that might have prevented some of Africa's wars, according to European and UN diplomats," correspondent Colum Lynch reported as the plans to bomb Serbia were reaching their final stages.

I will skip other examples of (I) and (II), which abound, and also contemporary atrocities of a different kind, such as the slaughter of Iraqi civilians by means of a vicious form of what amounts to biological warfare "a very hard choice," Madeleine Albright commented on national TV in 1996 when asked for her reaction to the killing of half a million Iraqi children in five years, but "we think the price is worth it." Current estimates remain about five thousand children killed a month, and the price is still "worth it." These and other examples might be kept in mind when we read admiring accounts of how the "moral compass" of the Clinton administration is at last functioning properly, in Kosovo (Columbia University professor of preventive diplomacy David Phillips).

Kosovo is another illustration of (I): act in such a way as to escalate the violence, with exactly that expectation.

To find examples illustrating (III) is all too easy, at least if we keep to official rhetoric. The most extensive recent academic study of "humanitarian intervention" is by George Washington University law professor Sean Murphy. He reviews the record after the Kellogg-Briand Pact of 1928, which outlawed war, and then after the UN Charter, which strengthened and articulated these provisions. In the first phase, he writes, the most prominent examples of "humanitarian intervention" were Japan's attack on Manchuria, Mussolini's invasion of Ethiopia, and Hitler's occupation of parts of Czechoslovakia, all accompanied by uplifting humanitarian rhetoric and factual justifications as well. Japan was going to establish an "earthly paradise" as it defended Manchurians from "Chinese bandits," with the support of a leading Chinese nationalist, a far more credible figure than anyone the U.S. was able to conjure up during its attack on South Vietnam. Mussolini was liberating thousands of slaves as he carried forth the Western "civilizing mission." Hitler announced Germany's intention to end ethnic tensions and violence and "safeguard the national individuality of the German and Czech peoples," in an operation "filled with earnest desire to serve the true interests of the peoples dwelling in the area," in accordance with their will; the Slovakian president asked Hitler to declare Slovakia a protectorate.

Another useful intellectual exercise is to compare those obscene justifications with those offered for interventions, including "humanitarian interventions," in the post–UN Charter period. In that period, perhaps the most compelling example of (III) is the Vietnamese invasion of Cambodia in December 1978, terminating Pol Pot's atrocities, which were then peaking.

Vietnam pleaded the right of self-defense against armed attack, one of the few post-Charter examples when the plea is plausible: the Khmer Rouge regime (Democratic Kampuchea, DK) was carrying out murderous attacks against Vietnam in border areas. The U.S. reaction is instructive. The press condemned the "Prussians" of Asia for their outrageous violation of international law. They were harshly punished for the crime of having ended Pol Pot's slaughters, first by a (U.S.-backed) Chinese invasion, then by U.S. imposition of extremely harsh sanctions. The U.S. recognized the expelled DK as the official government of Cambodia, because of its "continuity" with the Pol Pot regime, the State Department explained. Not too subtly, the U.S. supported the Khmer Rouge in its continuing attacks in Cambodia. The example tells us more about the "custom and practice" that underlies "the emerging legal norms of humanitarian intervention."

Another illustration of (III) is India's invasion of East Pakistan in 1971, which terminated an enormous massacre and refugee flight (over ten million, according to estimates at the time). The U.S. condemned India for aggression; Kissinger was particularly infuriated by India's action, in part it seems because it was interfering with a carefully staged secret trip to China. Perhaps this is one of the examples that historian John Lewis Gaddis had in mind in his fawning review of the latest volume of Kissinger's memoirs, when he reports admiringly that Kissinger "acknowledges here, more clearly than in the past, the influence of his upbringing in Nazi Germany, the examples set by his parents and the consequent impossibility, for him, of operating outside a moral framework."[3] The logic is overpowering, as are the illustrations, too well-known to record.

Again, the same lessons.

Despite the desperate efforts of ideologues to prove that circles are square, there is no serious doubt that the NATO bombings further undermine what remains of the fragile structure of international law. The U.S. made that clear in the debates that led to the NATO decision, as already discussed. Today, the more closely one approaches the conflicted region, the greater the opposition to Washington's insistence on force, even within NATO (Greece and Italy). Again, that is not an unusual phenomenon: another current example is the U.S.-UK bombing of Iraq, undertaken in December with unusually brazen gestures of contempt for the Security Council, even the timing coinciding with an emergency session to deal with the crisis. Still another illustration, minor in context, is the destruction of half the pharmaceutical production of a small African country a few months earlier, another event that does not indicate that the "moral compass" is straying from righteousness, though comparable destruction of U.S. facilities by Islamic terrorists might evoke a slightly different reaction. It is unnecessary to emphasize that there is a far more extensive record that would be prominently reviewed right now if facts were considered relevant to determining "custom and practice."

It could be argued, rather plausibly, that further demolition of the rules of world order is by now of no significance, as in the late 1930s. The contempt of the world's leading power for the framework of world order has become so extreme that there is little left to discuss. A review of the internal documentary record demonstrates that the stance traces back to the earliest days, even to the first memorandum of the newly formed National Security Council in 1947. During the Kennedy years, the stance began to gain overt expression, as, for example, when the highly respected statesperson and Kennedy adviser Dean Acheson justified the blockade of Cuba in 1962 by informing the American Society for International Law that a situation in which our country's "power, position, and prestige" are involved cannot be treated as a "legal issue."

The main innovation of the Reagan–Clinton years is that defiance of international law and solemn obligations has become entirely open. It has also been backed with interesting explanations, which would be on the front pages and prominent in the school and university curriculum, if honesty and human consequences were considered significant values. The highest authorities explained that international law and agencies had become irrelevant because they no longer follow U.S. orders, as they did in the early postwar years, when U.S. power was overwhelming. When the World Court was considering what it later condemned as Washington's "unlawful use of force" against Nicaragua, Secretary of State George Shultz derided those who advocate "utopian, legalistic means like outside media-tion, the United Nations, and the World Court, while ignoring the power element of the equation." Clear and forthright, and by no means original. State Department Legal Adviser Abraham Sofaer explained that members of the UN can no longer "be counted on to share our view," and the "majority often opposes the United States on important international questions," so we must "reserve to ourselves the power to determine" how we will act.

One can follow standard practice and ignore "custom and practice" or dismiss it on some absurd grounds ("change of course," "Cold War," and other familiar pretexts). Or we can take custom, practice, and explicit doc-trine seriously, departing from respectable norms but at least opening the possibility of understanding what is happening in the world.

While the Reaganites broke new ground, under Clinton the defiance of world order has become so extreme as to be of concern even to hawkish policy analysts. In the current issue of the leading establishment journal, *Foreign Affairs*, Samuel Huntington warns that Washington is treading a dangerous course. In the eyes of much of the world, probably most of the world, he suggests the U.S. is "becoming the rogue superpower," considered "the single greatest external threat to their societies." Realist "international relations theory," he argues, predicts that coalitions may arise to counter-balance the rogue superpower. On pragmatic grounds, then, the stance should be reconsidered. Americans who prefer a different image of their society might have other grounds for concern over these tendencies, but they are probably of little concern to planners, with their narrower focus and immersion in ideology.

Where does that leave the question of what to do in Kosovo? It leaves it unanswered. The U.S. has chosen a course of action which, as it explicitly recognizes, escalates atrocities and violence; a course that strikes yet another blow against the regime of international order, which does offer the weak at least some limited protection from predatory states; a course that undermines, perhaps destroys, promising democratic developments within Yugoslavia, probably Macedonia as well. As for the longer term, consequences are unpredictable.

One plausible observation is that "every bomb that falls on Serbia and every ethnic killing in Kosovo suggests that it will scarcely be possible for Serbs and Albanians to live beside each other in some sort of peace" (*Financial Times*). Other possible long-term outcomes are not pleasant to contemplate. The resort to violence has, again predictably, narrowed the options. Perhaps the least ugly that remains is an eventual partition of Kosovo, with Serbia taking the northern areas that are rich in resources and have the main historical monuments, and the southern sector becoming a NATO protectorate where some Albanians can live in misery. Another possibility is that with much of the population gone, the U.S. might turn to the Carthaginian solution. If that happens, it would again be nothing new, as large areas of Indochina can testify.

A standard argument is that we had to do something: we could not simply stand by as atrocities continue. The argument is so absurd that it is rather surprising to hear it voiced. Suppose you see a crime in the streets and feel that you can't just stand by silently, so you pick up an assault rifle and kill everyone involved: criminal, victim, bystanders. Are we to understand that to be the rational and moral response?

One choice always available is to follow the Hippocratic principle: "First, do no harm." If you can think of no way to adhere to that elementary principle, then do nothing; at least that is preferable to causing harm. But there are always other ways that can be considered. Diplomacy and negotiations are never at an end. That was true right before the bombing, when the Serb Parliament, responding to Clinton's ultimatum, called for negotiations over an "international presence in Kosovo immediately after the signing of an accord for self-administration in Kosovo which will be accepted by all national communities" living in the province, reported on wire services worldwide but scarcely noted here. Just what that meant we cannot know, since the two warrior states preferred to reject the diplomatic path in favor of violence.

Another argument, if one can call it that, has been advanced most prominently by Henry Kissinger. He believes that intervention was a mistake ("open-ended," quagmire, etc.). That aside, it is futile. "Through the centuries, these conflicts [in the Balkans] have been fought with unparalleled ferocity because none of the populations has any experience with and essentially no belief in Western concepts of toleration." At last we understand why Europeans have treated each other with such gentle solicitude "through the centuries," and have tried so hard over many centuries to bring to others their message of nonviolence, toleration, and loving kindness. One can always count on Kissinger for some comic relief, though in reality, he is not alone. He is joined by those who ponder "Balkan logic" as contrasted with the Western record of humane rationality. And those who remind us of the "distaste for war or for intervention in the affairs of others" that is "our inherent weakness," of our dismay over the "repeated violations of norms and rules established by international treaty, human rights conventions" (historian Tony Judt). We are to consider Kosovo as "A New Collision of East and West," a *Times* think piece is headlined, a clear illustration of Samuel Huntington's "Clash of Civilizations": "a democratic West, its humanitarian instincts repelled by the barbarous inhumanity of Orthodox Serbs," all of this "clear to Americans" but not to others, a fact that Americans fail to comprehend (Huntington, interview).

Or we may listen to the inspiring words of Secretary of Defense William Cohen, introducing the president at Norfolk Naval Air Station. He opened by quoting Theodore Roosevelt, speaking "at the dawn of this century, as America was awakening into its new place in the world." President Roosevelt said, "Unless you're willing to fight for great ideals, those ideals will vanish," and "today, at the dawn of the next century, we're joined by President Bill Clinton" who understands as well as Teddy Roosevelt that "standing on the sidelines . . . as a witness to the unspeakable to take place, that would in fact affect the peace and stability of NATO countries, was simply unacceptable."[4] One has to wonder what must pass through the mind of someone invoking this famous racist fanatic and raving jingoist as a model of American values, along with the events that illustrated his cherished "great ideals" as he spoke: the slaughter of hundreds of thousands of

Filipinos who had sought liberation from Spain, shortly after Roosevelt's contribution to preventing Cubans from achieving the same goal.

Wiser commentators will wait until Washington settles on an official story. After two weeks of bombing, the story is that they both knew and didn't know that a catastrophe would follow. On March 28, "when a reporter asked if the bombing was accelerating the atrocities, [President Clinton] replied, 'absolutely not'" (Adam Clymer). He reiterated that stand in his April 1 speech at Norfolk: "Had we not acted, the Serbian offensive would have been carried out with impunity." The following day, Pentagon spokesperson Kenneth Bacon announced that the opposite was true: "I don't think anyone could have foreseen the breadth of this brutality," the first acknowledgment by the Administration that "it was not fully prepared for the crisis," the press reported, a crisis that was "entirely predictable," the commanding general had informed the press a week earlier. From the start, reports from the scene were that "the Administration had been caught off guard" by the Serbian military reaction (Jane Perlez and many others).

The right of "humanitarian intervention" is likely to be more frequently invoked in coming years maybe with justification, maybe not now that Cold War pretexts have lost their efficacy. In such an era, it may be worthwhile to pay attention to the views of highly respected commentators—not to speak of the World Court, which ruled on the matter of intervention and "humanitarian aid" in a decision rejected by the U.S., its essentials not even reported.

In the scholarly disciplines of international affairs and international law it would be hard to find more respected voices than Hedley Bull or Louis Henkin. Bull warned fifteen years ago that "Particular states or groups of states that set themselves up as the authoritative judges of the world common good, in disregard of the views of others, are in fact a menace to international order, and thus to effective action in this field." Henkin, in a standard work on world order, writes:

> [The] pressures eroding the prohibition on the use of force are deplorable, and the arguments to legitimize the use of force in those circumstances are unpersuasive and dangerous. . . . Even "humanitarian intervention" can too readily be used as the occasion or pretext for aggression. Violations of human rights are indeed all too common, and if it were permissible to remedy them by external use of force, there would be no law to forbid the use of force by almost any state

against almost any other. Human rights, I believe, will have to be vindicated, and other injustices remedied, by other, peaceful means, not by opening the door to aggression and destroying the principal advance in international law, the outlawing of war and the prohibition of force.[5]

Recognized principles of international law and world order, treaty obligations, decisions by the World Court, considered pronouncements by the most respected commentators, these do not automatically yield solutions to particular problems. Each has to be considered on its merits. For those who do not adopt the standards of Saddam Hussein, there is a heavy burden of proof to meet in undertaking the threat or use of force in violation of the principles of international order. Perhaps the burden can be met, but that has to be shown, not merely proclaimed with passionate rhetoric. The consequences of such violations have to be assessed carefully—in particular, what we take to be "predictable." For those who are minimally serious, the reasons for the actions also have to be assessed on rational grounds, with attention to historical fact and the documentary record, not simply by adulation of our leaders and their "moral compass."

★ Originally published as: Noam Chomsky, "Crisis in the Balkans," *Z Magazine*, May 1999

Notes

1   The issues surrounding the Kosovo crisis prior, during, and after the bombing of 1999 are documented and discussed in detail in Noam Chomsky, *A New Generation Draws the Line: Kosovo, East Timor and the Standards of the West* (London: Verso, 2000).

2   Kevin Cullen and Anne Kornblut, "Crisis Swells at Closed Border Macedonia Blocks Refugees; NATO Plans Albania Relief Force," *Boston Globe*, April 4, 1999, available at https://www.highbeam.com/doc/1P2-8542025.html; "Clinton's Speech on Kosovo: 'We Also Act to Prevent a Wider War,'" *New York Times*, April 2, 1999, available at http://www.nytimes.com/1999/04/02/world/crisis-balkans-clinton-s-speech-kosovo-we-also-act-prevent-wider-war.html.

3   John Lewis Gaddis, "The Old World Order," *New York Times Book Review*, March 21, 1999, available at http://www.nytimes.com/books/99/03/21/reviews/990321.21gaddist.html.

4   1999 Federal Information Systems Corporation, *Federal News Service*, April 1, 1999.

5   Hedley Bull, *Justice in International Relations (1983–84 Hagey Lectures)* (Waterloo, ON: University of Waterloo, 1984), 1–35.

Wiping Out the Democratic Movement

Terms like "massacre" and "genocide" are often used very freely. This also applies to the current conflict in the Balkans.

Let's take a look at what the U.S. and NATO claimed to be the case in Kosovo, and let's assume that everything they say is true. What they say is that up to February or March this year [1999], until the bombing started, there were about two thousand people killed on all sides in Kosovo, most of them Albanian, probably the large majority of the two thousand. There were probably a couple hundred thousand refugees. This was largely according to the U.S.

The violence began with attacks on Serbian police in Kosovo (a province of FRY) by the KLA. These attacks were supported from abroad. The Serbian army and police reacted very brutally to that, pretty much in a way we're familiar with in, let's say, Lebanon. There Israel reacts to attacks on its soldiers with retaliation against civilians that leads to further retaliation.

We have a similar situation in Kosovo, with KLA attacks. It's a humanitarian crisis, but, unfortunately, it's one that's duplicated in many, many parts of the world.

For example, its almost identical to the one that the State Department describes as occurring in Colombia, where approximately the same number of people have been killed, along with three hundred thousand refugees last year (according to the State Department). It added to the well over a million atrocities attributed to the army and its paramilitary associates who are funded by the U.S., increasing the flow of arms around the world.

Now, what happened on March 23 and 24 this year? The U.S. presented the Yugoslav government with an ultimatum—the Rambouillet Agreement. Although it wasn't reported here, the Serbian national assembly rejected it but made a counterproposal. The State Department Representative James

Rubin was asked during a press conference on March 24 about this Serbian assembly counteroffer and he said, "We saw no silver lining in it so we decided to bomb." That's the end of the diplomacy.

First of all, the Serbian government very strongly condemned the withdrawal of the international monitors. The monitors withdrew because the U.S. told them to leave. The Serbian government was strongly opposed to that. They wanted the monitors back and suggested a resolution saying something like this: after autonomy is negotiated among the various ethnic communities we will consider the question of an international presence to guarantee safety. Maybe it was a good offer, maybe it was not a good offer, but there was certainly room for diplomacy. The U.S. simply refused.

In this, just as in other similar cases, the concept of the "international community" has often been evoked to justify certain positions as the position of the international community. The term international community is a term of propaganda—U.S. propaganda. There is no involvement of the international community here as in Europe; the U.S. would not allow it. The real international community is the United Nations. The international community is not NATO. The NATO powers, with varying degrees of commitment, follow the U.S. lead. They do not constitute the international community. That term is used here to refer to the U.S. and its allies. In reality, India is part of the international community, China is part of it, South Africa is part of it, Latin America is part of it—and they mostly opposed the U.S. actions.

The Intellectual Class

It is also interesting to look at how the intellectual class reacted to the war. The majority of educated people, the overwhelming majority, in fact, tend to support state atrocities. They supported the U.S. war in Vietnam, for example. Vietnam was a liberals' war. It started with the aggressive attack against South Vietnam, which was launched by John F. Kennedy. He's the one who sent U.S. Air Force planes to bomb South Vietnamese civilians, authorized the use of napalm, initiated crop destructions, started driving millions of people into the concentration camps. The liberal, educated community supported it right through, until the time when business turned against it. Corporate America turned against it on pragmatic grounds—it was becoming too costly. If you want to see what the attitude of the liberals was, look at yesterday's lead editorial of the *New York Times*, which happens to capture it quite accurately. They say that we shouldn't be hobbled by the Vietnam analogy in the bombing of Kosovo, and maybe invading it. Their reasons are that in the case of Vietnam the sacrifices of the U.S. were too high and the gains were uncertain. There were people on the German general staff who said the same thing about Hitler after Stalingrad. That's not opposition to the war.

If the issue here is humanitarian there are very simple ways to stop much worse humanitarian crises, in fact right in that region. Notice that the U.S. and NATO bombing radically escalated the atrocities exactly as was expected. There were certainly atrocities but they were at the level that you find all over the world. Once the bombing started, it was beginning to become comparable to other cases. There was an article in one of the leading Israeli journals pointing out that Kosovo was becoming like Palestine in 1947 and 1948, except with TV cameras. That's accurate since the numbers of people expelled are similar, and in fact the numbers killed are about the same as well.

U.S. propaganda has succeeded in presenting the bombing as a humanitarian endeavor, and a lot of people who are in favor of humanitarian endeavors are just caught up in the propaganda. But if you think it through, it's plain that it can't be the case. For one thing, the bombing sharply increased the humanitarian catastrophe exactly as expected. In fact, let me just quote the U.S. NATO commander Wesley Clark. Two days after the bombing started, he said it was entirely predictable that Serbia would respond by expelling people, joined by more entirely predictable atrocities. In fact, that's what happened. In Kosovo, the bombing increased the humanitarian disaster enormously. Furthermore, we know that the U.S. government does not care about humanitarian catastrophes, and most of the people who are getting excited about this in the U.S. do not care either. You can see that very easily by looking right next door in Turkey, where they have been massively supporting even worse atrocities, and it takes nothing to stop that support. Stop sending the jet planes, napalm, and antipersonnel weapons. That's all it takes.

The Media

The media coverage of the events is also telling and follows the pattern of the intellectual class. CNN, for instance, is being driven by U.S. foreign policy and they know that perfectly well. It wasn't the choice of CNN to focus attention solely on Kosovo and not look at Turkey. That was the choice of the U.S. government. How many pictures have you seen of the thousands of Kurdish villages that were destroyed in Southeast Turkey? The tens of thousands of people who were killed, 2.5 million refugees, and so on—how many pictures have we seen about that? Well, the answer is zero.

Of course, there are some very fine journalists—not many, though. For example, Jonathan Randal, a long-time Middle East correspondent for the *Washington Post*. He recently came out with a very good book on the atrocities in Turkey and the U.S. support for them. Now there's the occasional journalist who tries to be independent, but it's very difficult. If you want to keep your job, you'd better follow the line.

The Question of "Moral Outrage"

We have to make a distinction between the majority of the American population and the elite educated sectors that are involved in planning and management. They are completely different. Let's take a look back at the Vietnam War again. I mentioned the way it's analyzed by the *New York Times*, which is quite typical of the educated sectors. The war was wrong because it became too costly for us. That's the general view. Take a look at the view of the American population. It's a question that's been asked on polls regularly since the late 1960s: What do you think about the war in Vietnam? Since that's an open question, you don't expect high numbers, but roughly 70 percent since around 1970 have said: the war was "fundamentally wrong and immoral," not "a mistake." Among educated people, the percentage of those who hold this view is statistically insignificant, maybe 1 percent. Well that's a dramatic difference between the general population and the educated sectors, which is found in a lot of other issues. As far as the population is concerned, one can speak of moral outrage. But remember that people have no way to feel a moral outrage about Turkey because they have never heard of it. This is significant because here we're directly and massively contributing to the atrocities committed there.

For example, in yesterday's *New York Times* they had a major article on sovereignty and human rights by one of their intellectuals, Judith Miller, who simply attests to the fact that the U.S. has been an aggressive leader in the struggle for human rights. Anyone who even pays attention to the most elementary data knows that that's not true. Look at international reports. But that's the kind of thing you say if you are a well-educated person. Well-educated people understand what the position is that they must assume.

You are supposed to accept the framework and not question it. There's nothing new about this.

That is clear already in George Orwell's work. Virtually everyone has read *Animal Farm*, but ask how many people read the introduction to *Animal Farm*. The answer will be very few, if any. The reason for that is that initially it wasn't published. Why wasn't it published? Well, it was generally held that *Animal Farm* was a satire about the West's totalitarian enemies, like the Soviet Union. That, of course, was wonderful, so everybody praised it. But in the introduction Orwell said he was writing about England. He warned that people in Britain shouldn't feel so self-righteous because England was not all that different. His introduction was called "Freedom of the Press." He described how in free England unpopular ideas were suppressed, marginalized, and never heard—not by the same means they use in Russia, but the end result is not very different. He even gave some reasons for this. He said that well-educated people come to understand that there were certain things that it simply wouldn't do to say (or even to think). And that's part of the process of education.

So, yes, you end up with the result that we've been talking about. For a properly educated person the idea that the U.S. might not have honorable motivations is just unthinkable. You can have that idea about every other country in history or in the present world, and in fact you do have it. But not about our state and the states that we support with a dedication of the kind that Soviet commissars would be impressed with. That is part of education.

Why Are We There?
One could ask a simple question: Why is the U.S. involved in the Kosovo crisis? We can exclude the possibility of humanitarian concerns because that is simply impossible. Then we can speculate. Turbulence in the Balkans, no matter what kind it is, is a threat to the interests of rich and powerful people. It poses a kind of a danger to Europe and hence to the U.S., which is heavily involved in European economic investment. That means that any kind of turbulence in the Balkans becomes what is called a "humanitarian crisis." It's a technical term, and it means anything that might threaten the interests of rich and powerful people. In contrast, when people slaughter each other in Sierra Leone or southeastern Turkey, Colombia, or anywhere else, it is not a humanitarian crisis because it doesn't threaten the interests of rich and powerful people. In fact, the U.S. is very often involved in escalating those conflicts.

One could also ask: What do you do if you have a crisis and you want to resolve it? The first and obvious thing to do is to try to reduce the turbulence. Now there is a way to do that through the UN, which would be in accord with world order, international law, and our treaty obligations. However, the U.S. completely refuses that. The U.S. has been strongly opposed to the international community, to international law, to the UN, and to the World Court for at least thirty years. You can tell that just by looking at the vetoes of Security Council resolutions. The U.S. has been way in the lead since the 1960s, Britain is second, France a distant third, and Russia's fourth, along with China. The same is true of the World Court. The U.S. doesn't want to allow the UN to take the leading role.

Well then, what do you do in such a situation? If you can't allow the international community to get involved you shift over to NATO. There at least the U.S. dominates. Within NATO there's also a disagreement. The U.S. and Britain are essentially warrior states. They have an overwhelming monopoly regarding force so they quite naturally turn to the use of force as the obvious way to deal with anything.

Comparisons with the Holocaust

The violence in Kosovo has been compared with the Holocaust. That is simply an insult, a horrendous insult to the victims of Hitler. If the Kosovo crisis is a holocaust, then there have been thousands of holocausts since 1945, beginning, for example, with what happened in Palestine in 1947 and 1948, and other much worse events that occurred at the same time. What was happening up until the bombing was a humanitarian crisis of a kind that unfortunately exists all over the world. What is going on right now is beginning to approach other cases like Palestine in 1947 and 1948. It's not even close yet to what was happening in Turkey right in the 1990s. It's nothing like what's going on in Africa. Why is the term "holocaust" being used by people who we ought to call Holocaust revisionists? These are people who are denying the reality of the Holocaust. Why are those people now using it to refer to what's going on in Kosovo? Well, it is used as a justification for the U.S. violence—that's all.

Conflict between Islam and Christianity

The Kosovo crisis has also been described as a conflict between Islam and Christianity. This is what we can find in Emil Harding, the dean of Harvard, who's been peddling that idea for some years. To me, it seems to be complete nonsense. If you look at the interactions of Christianity and Islam, they go in every possible direction. The most fundamentalist Islamic state in the world—Saudi Arabia—happens to be a U.S. ally. In the 1980s, the U.S. was fighting a virtual war with the Catholic Church in Central America. That's why the decade began with an archbishop and six leading Jesuit intellectuals being murdered by military forces that we were supporting.[1] In fact, there are lots and lots of complications around the world, but Islam versus Christianity is a very minor element.

Questions about World War II

Many of the issues in the Balkans today have their roots in the war against Hitler, in the 1940s. That war was overwhelmingly fought by the Russians. The overwhelming majority of Hitler's forces were on the Eastern Front. The U.S. and Britain were mostly fighting elsewhere. At the end of the war the region was essentially partitioned pretty much where the armies were, and the U.S. then returned to what had been its position in the 1930s, when the U.S. and Britain mainly supported the traditional structures, which were mostly profascist, suppressing the antifascist resistance. That's why people like Klaus Barbie, to pick a famous case, shifted directly from working for the Nazis to working for the U.S. occupying forces.

Perhaps the most dramatic example is Reinhard Gehlen, a leading Nazi war criminal who was the head of military intelligence operations in the Eastern Front. Anybody who knows the history knows what that means. He was immediately picked up by the U.S. and the CIA and was made the head of the U.S. operations in the East. The same thing happened in Japan. For example, Japan had a horrifying biological warfare program run by doctors who were the perfect equivalent of Mengele, testing on human subjects. They were taken over by the U.S. and immunized so they were protected from any war-crimes trials. They were taken to the U.S. and they formed the basis of the U.S. biological warfare program. When the Russians put some of them on trial for war crimes it was ridiculed here as a communist show trial.

There's an interesting question some people pose nowadays: Who won World War II then? Let me quote a leading Central American democrat, Juan José Arévalo, who was the first democratic leader in Guatemala. He wrote a book around the mid-1950s in which he claimed that judging by what was going on in Central America, Roosevelt, unfortunately, lost the war and Hitler won.

How to Stop the Massacres?

In Turkey it's easy to just stop contributing to the massacres. In Kosovo it is harder. In my view the bombing has been a catastrophe. Predictively, it has made things far worse. It almost wiped out the very promising and courageous democratic movement in Belgrade and the rest of Yugoslavia, which was the best hope for getting rid of Milošević. If you want a dramatic example of that, look at this morning's *New York Times*, with the front-page story that describes the new NATO strategy. One of the things they talk about is attacking the economy in order to harm Milošević. One of the main examples they give us is to do with attacking the automobile manufactory, which is going to really hurt Milošević. What they don't point out is that the workers in that plant had formed a very decent union, which carried out major strikes against Milošević. That's what NATO was destroying. From every point of view I think that's a disaster. So the first thing to do is to stop it. When you are carrying out something that is a disaster, the first thing to do is to stop it. Then the next thing to do is to pursue whatever remains of the diplomatic negotiating options that were there on March 23, 1999. However, I don't think that the U.S. and NATO want to be involved in this and discredit themselves, but there are other people in the world who could perform that role. They could get Nelson Mandela, for instance, to come in.

We support murderers and dictators that are far worse than Milošević. But Milošević is going to be a warning to them—since they look at the way we act. They will discover that the U.S. has continued to support dictators as long as they follow orders. In 1995, the Dayton Peace Agreement was an agreement with Milošević. We sold out the Kosovar Albanians. That's one of the reasons that their nonviolent movement in Kosovo turned to violence. They recognized that the U.S. understands nothing but violence.

The goal is always to ensure that the U.S. dominates the region. A specific proposal was made to that end, which involved the ground forces inside Yugoslavia. They know they're not going to achieve the goals by bombing, so therefore they are turning to the question of ground forces. They obviously think, "Okay, let's arm this group that we called a terrorist army just recently." After all, the U.S. has often done that. They did it in Nicaragua. They armed murderers, a brutal terrorist army, and sent them in to attack civilian targets in Nicaragua. That's why the U.S. was condemned by the World Court.

It seems that NATO is not harming the Yugoslav army. American correspondents on the ground said they did not see much effect on the Yugoslav army, which is not surprising if it's true. After all, remember that for forty, almost fifty, years, the Yugoslav military has been preparing for a ground attack. They expected the ground attack from the Soviet Union and that's what they are set up for. This kind of attack is probably not going to have much effect on them, just as the U.S. journalists are reporting right now. On the other hand, if the bombing continues, and it really becomes something like Indochina, then maybe an army, the Albanian-based army, supported by NATO forces, might be able to do something on the ground. That would be a complete disaster.

★ Based on a Noam Chomsky interview with Erik Siljak and The A-Infos Radio Project, April 19, 1999.

Notes

1   Chomsky refers here to the assassination of Óscar Romero, archbishop of San Salvador, in 1980, and the assassinations of Jesuit priests, Ignacio Ellacuría, Ignacio Martín Baró, Segundo Montes, Joaquín López y López, Amando López, and Juan Ramón Moreno, as well as their housekeeper Julia Elba Ramos and her daughter, Celina Maricet Ramos, in 1989.

The Truth about Kosovo

Patrick Cain: *Let's define some of the language we are hearing around this war. Can you comment on the use of the terms "humanitarian crisis," "genocide," and "ethnic cleansing" as they are being applied to Kosovo?*

Noam Chomsky: Well, for starters, the concept called "humanitarian crisis" has a technical meaning, which does not have much to do with what might reasonably be assumed to be the defining criteria of the term. The technical meaning of humanitarian crisis is a problem somewhere that threatens the interests of rich and powerful people. That is the essence of what makes it a crisis. Now, any disturbance in the Balkans does threaten the interests of rich and powerful people, namely, the elites of Europe and the U.S. So when there are humanitarian issues in the Balkans, they become a "humanitarian crisis." On the other hand, if people slaughter each other in Sierra Leone or the Congo, it's not a humanitarian crisis. As a matter of fact, Clinton just refused to provide the relatively puny sum of $100,000 for a peace-making force in the Republic of the Congo, which might well have averted a huge massacre. But those deaths do not constitute a humanitarian crisis. Neither do the many other deaths and tragedies to which the U.S. directly contributes: the massacres in Colombia, for example, or the slaughters and expulsions of people in southeastern Turkey, which are being carried out with crucial support from Clinton. Those aren't humanitarian crises. But Kosovo is a crisis because it is in the Balkans.

Now the term "genocide," as applied to Kosovo, is an insult to the victims of Hitler. In fact, it's revisionist to an extreme. If this is genocide, then there is genocide going on all over the world—and Bill Clinton is decisively implementing a lot of it. If this is genocide, then what do you call what is happening in the southeast of Turkey? The number of refugees there is huge; it's already reached about half the level of Palestinians expelled from Palestine.

If it increases further, it may reach the number of refugees in Colombia, where the number of people killed every year by the army and paramilitary groups armed and trained by the U.S. is approximately the same as the number of people killed in Kosovo last year.

"Ethnic cleansing," on the other hand, is real. Unfortunately, it's something that goes on and has been going on for a long time. It's no big innovation. How come I'm living where I am, instead of the original people who lived here? Did they happily walk away?

PC: *So human rights abuses in Kosovo are termed a "humanitarian crisis" by the world's most powerful state. But how did we get from that to all-out war?*
NC: Well, let's look at the situation from the U.S. point of view: there's a crisis, what do we do about it? One possibility is to work through the United Nations, which is the agency responsible under treaty obligations and international law for dealing with such matters. But the U.S. made it clear a long time ago that it has total contempt for the institutions of world order, the UN, the World Court, and so on. In fact the U.S. has been very explicit about that. This was not always the case. In the early days of the UN, the majority of countries backed the U.S. because of its overwhelming political power. But that began to change when decolonization was extended and the organization and distribution of world power shifted. Now the U.S. can no longer count on the majority of countries to go along with its demands. The UN is no longer a pliant, and therefore no longer a relevant, institution. This proposition became very explicit during the Reagan years and even more brazen during the Clinton years. So brazen that even right-wing analysts are worried about it. There is an interesting article in the current issue of *Foreign Affairs*, an establishment journal in the U.S., warning Washington that much of the world regards the U.S. as a "rogue superpower" and the single greatest threat to their existence. In fact, the U.S. has placed itself totally above the rule of international law and international institutions.

NATO at least has the advantage of being pretty much under U.S. domination. Within NATO there are differences of opinion, so when there was a question last September of sending unarmed NATO monitors into Kosovo, every NATO country (with the possible exception of Britain) wanted the operation authorized by the UN Security Council as is required by treaty obligation.

But the U.S. flatly refused. It would not allow the use of the word "authorize." It insisted that the UN has no right to authorize any U.S. action. When the issue moved on to negotiations and the use of force, the U.S. and Britain, typically the two warrior states, were eager to use force and abandon negotiations. In fact, continental European diplomats were telling the press that they were annoyed by the saber-rattling mentality of Washington. So NATO as a whole was driven to the use of force, in part, reluctantly. In fact, the reluctance increases as you get closer to the region. So England and the U.S. are quite enthusiastic, others quite reluctant, and some in between.

PC: *Why was the U.S. so eager to use force?*
NC: The reason is obvious. When involved in a confrontation, you use your strong card and try to shift the confrontation to the area in which you are most powerful. The strong card of the U.S. is the use of force. That's perhaps the only realm of international relations where the U.S. has a near monopoly. The consequences of using force in Yugoslavia were more or less anticipated. NATO Commanding General Wesley Clark stated that it was entirely predictable that the bombing would sharply increase the level of atrocities and expulsion. As indeed it did. The NATO leadership could not have failed to know that the bombing would destroy the quite courageous and promising democracy movement in Serbia, as indeed it did; and cause all sorts of turmoil in surrounding countries, as indeed it has, though still not at the same level of crisis as Turkey or other places.

Nevertheless, it was necessary, as the Clinton foreign policy team kept stressing, to preserve the credibility of NATO. Now, when they talk about credibility, they are not talking about the credibility of Denmark or France. The Clinton administration doesn't care about those countries' credibility. What they care about is U.S. credibility. Credibility means fear: what they are concerned with is maintaining fear of the global enforcer, namely, the U.S. And that's much more important than the fate of hundreds of thousands of Kosovars or whatever other consequences are incurred. So the U.S. and NATO have helped to create a humanitarian catastrophe by knowingly escalating an already serious crisis to catastrophic proportions.

PC: *Some people say that unless American soldiers start being shipped home in body bags, there will not be a serious antiwar effort in the U.S. What is your assessment of that?*

NC: I don't agree with that at all. I mean, look at the history. During the 1980s, there was overwhelming opposition to U.S. atrocities in Central America. As a matter of fact, opposition was so strong that the Reagan administration had to back off and resort to using international terrorist networks like the Contras to carry out its policies. And there were no Americans in body bags then. Today there's strong opposition to U.S. support for Indonesian slaughter in East Timor, and there are no American body bags. If you look at the opposition to the Vietnam War, Americans were of course being killed, but that was by no means the decisive factor. I think that the notion that only dead American soldiers will inspire a peace movement—in other words, that people are motivated only by self-interest—is U.S. propaganda. It's intolerable for the propaganda system to concede that people might act on moral instinct, which is in fact what they do.

PC: *How do you reconcile that view with the fact that, according to polls at least, the majority of Americans would support an escalation of the war, for example, through the deployment of NATO ground troops?*
NC: You have to keep in mind what these people are hearing. The public is getting its marching orders from Washington. And those orders are to disregard all other atrocities, even ones much worse than Kosovo, especially in places where the U.S. is involved. Focus your attention only on this disaster and pretend to yourself that the crisis is all about one evil man who is carrying out genocide. This is what we are being told by our media day and night. It's effective. Most people accept the marching orders. Then they say we've got to do something, like send ground troops.

The Pentagon and the European forces are strongly against it, mainly for technical reasons. I mean, it would be a catastrophe. Sounds easy to send ground troops, but think about it. First of all, it would not be easy to get them in and would most probably take months to get them ready. It would mean facing a major guerrilla war that would probably level the whole region. That's what happens when you send in ground troops and cause greater catastrophes. It would simply escalate the atrocities.

PC: *What steps do you think people who oppose this war should take now?*
NC: There is no question that people of conscience must take action against this. What can we do to end this war? Same thing as always, there's no

magical trick. It requires education, explanation, organizing, demonstrating, exerting pressure . . . all things that we know. And this is very hard to do; it's not like flipping on a light switch. It takes work.

★ "Kosovo: Noam Chomsky interviewed by Patrick Cain," *The Activist*, June 1999.

Kosovo Peace Accord

On March 24, 1999, U.S.-led NATO air forces began to pound the Federal Republic of Yugoslavia (FYR), including Kosovo, which NATO regards as a province of Serbia. On June 3, NATO and Serbia reached a Peace Accord. The U.S. declared victory, having successfully concluded its "10-week struggle to compel Mr. Milošević to say uncle," Blaine Harden reported in the *New York Times*. It would therefore be unnecessary to use ground forces to "cleanse Serbia," as Harden had recommended in a lead story headlined "How to Cleanse Serbia." The recommendation was natural in the light of American history, which is dominated by the theme of ethnic cleansing from its origins and to the present day, achievements celebrated in the names given to military attack helicopters and other weapons of destruction. A qualification is in order, however: the term "ethnic cleansing" is not really appropriate: U.S. cleansing operations have been ecumenical—Indochina and Central America are two recent illustrations.

While declaring victory, Washington did not yet declare peace: the bombing continues until the victors determine that their interpretation of the Kosovo Accord has been imposed. From the outset, the bombing had been cast as a matter of cosmic significance, a test of a New Humanism, in which the "enlightened states" (*Foreign Affairs*) open a new era of human history guided by "a new internationalism where the brutal repression of whole ethnic groups will no longer be tolerated" (Tony Blair). The enlightened states are the U.S. and its British associate, perhaps also others who enlist in their crusades for justice.

Apparently the rank of "enlightened states" is conferred by definition. One finds no attempt to provide evidence or argument, surely not from their history. The latter is in any event deemed irrelevant by the familiar doctrine of "change of course," invoked regularly in the ideological institutions to dispatch the past into the deepest recesses of the memory hole, thus deterring the threat that some might ask the most obvious questions: With institutional structures and distribution of power essentially unchanged, why should one expect a radical shift in policy—or any at all, apart from tactical adjustments?

But such questions are off the agenda. "From the start the Kosovo problem has been about how we should react when bad things happen in unimportant places," global analyst Thomas Friedman explained in the *New York Times* as the Accord was announced. He proceeds to laud the enlightened states for pursuing his moral principle that "once the refugee evictions began, ignoring Kosovo would be wrong . . . and therefore using a huge air war for a limited objective was the only thing that made sense."[1]

A minor difficulty is that concern over the "refugee evictions" could not have been the motive for the "huge air war." The UNHCR reported its first registered refugees outside of Kosovo on March 27 (4,000), three days after the bombings began. The toll increased until June 4, reaching a reported total of 670,000 in the neighboring countries (Albania, Macedonia), along with an estimated 70,000 in Montenegro (within the FYR), and 75,000 who had left for other countries. The figures, which are unfortunately all too familiar, do not include the unknown numbers who have been displaced within Kosovo, some 200,000–300,000 in the year before the bombing according to NATO, a great many more afterwards.

Uncontroversially, the "huge air war" precipitated a sharp escalation of ethnic cleansing and other atrocities. That much has been reported consistently by correspondents on the scene and in retrospective analyses in the press. The same picture is presented in the two major documents that seek to portray the bombing as a reaction to the humanitarian crisis in Kosovo. The most extensive one, provided by the State Department in May, is suitably entitled "Erasing History: Ethnic Cleansing in Kosovo"; the second is the Indictment of Milošević and associates by the International Tribunal on War Crimes in Yugoslavia after the U.S. and Britain "opened the way for what amounted to a remarkably fast indictment by giving [prosecutor Louise] Arbour access to intelligence and other information long denied to her by Western governments," the *New York Times* reported, with two full pages devoted to the Indictment. Both documents hold that the atrocities began "on or about January 1"; in both, however, the detailed chronology reveals that atrocities continued about as before until the bombing led to a very sharp escalation. That surely came as no surprise. Commanding

General Wesley Clark at once described these consequences as "entirely predictable"—an exaggeration of course, as nothing in human affairs is that predictable, though ample evidence is now available revealing that the consequences were anticipated, for reasons readily understood without access to secret intelligence.

One small index of the effects of "the huge air war" was offered by Robert Hayden, director of the Center for Russian and East European Studies of the University of Pittsburgh: "the casualties among Serb civilians in the first three weeks of the war are higher than all of the casualties on both sides in Kosovo in the three months that led up to this war, and yet those three months were supposed to be a humanitarian catastrophe." True, these particular consequences are of no account in the context of the jingoist hysteria that was whipped up to demonize Serbs, reaching intriguing heights as bombing openly targeted the civilian society and hence required more fervent advocacy.

By chance, at least a hint of a more credible answer to Friedman's rhetorical question was given in the *Times* on the same day, in a report from Ankara by Stephen Kinzer. He writes that "Turkey's best-known human rights advocate entered prison" to serve his sentence for having "urged the state to reach a peaceful settlement with Kurdish rebels."[2] A few days earlier, Kinzer had indicated obliquely that there is more to the story: "Some [Kurds] say they have been oppressed under Turkish rule, but the Government insists that they are granted the same rights as other citizens." One may ask whether this really does justice to some of the most extreme ethnic cleansing operations of the mid-1990s, with tens of thousands killed, 3,500 villages destroyed, some 2.5 to 3 million refugees, and hideous atrocities that easily compare to those recorded daily in the front pages for selected enemies, reported in detail by the major human rights organizations but ignored. These achievements were carried out thanks to massive military support from the U.S., increasing under Clinton as the atrocities peaked, including jet planes, attack helicopters, counterinsurgency equipment, and other means of terror and destruction, along with training and intelligence information for some of the worst killers.

Recall that these crimes have been proceeding through the 1990s within NATO itself, and under the jurisdiction of the Council of Europe and the European Court of Human Rights, which continues to hand down judgments against Turkey for its U.S.-supported atrocities. It took real discipline for participants and commentators "not to notice" any of this at the celebration of NATO's fiftieth anniversary in April. The discipline was particularly impressive in light of the fact that the celebration was clouded by somber concerns over ethnic cleansing—by officially designated enemies, not by the enlightened states that are to rededicate themselves to their traditional mission of bringing justice and freedom to the suffering people of the world, and to defend human rights, by force if necessary, under the principles of the New Humanism.

These crimes, to be sure, are only one illustration of the answer given by the enlightened states to the profound question of "how we should react when bad things happen in unimportant places." We should intervene to escalate the atrocities, not "looking away" under a "double standard," the common evasion when such marginalia are impolitely adduced. That also happens to be the mission that was conducted in Kosovo, as revealed clearly by the course of events, though not the version refracted through the prism of ideology and doctrine, which do not gladly tolerate the observation that a consequence of the "the huge air war" was a change from a year of atrocities on the scale of the annual (U.S.-backed) toll in Colombia in the 1990s to a level that might have approached atrocities within NATO/Europe itself in the 1990s had the bombing continued.

The marching orders from Washington, however, are the usual ones: focus laser-like on the crimes of today's official enemy, and do not allow yourself to be distracted by comparable or worse crimes that could easily be mitigated or terminated thanks to the crucial role of the enlightened states in perpetuating them or escalating them when power interests so dictate. Let us obey the orders, then, and keep to Kosovo.

A minimally serious investigation of the Kosovo Accord must review the diplomatic options of March 23, the day before "huge air war" was launched, and compare them with the agreement reached by NATO and Serbia on June 3. Here we have to distinguish two versions: (1) the facts, and (2) the spin—that is, the U.S./NATO version that frames reporting and commentary in the enlightened states. Even the most cursory look reveals that the facts and the spin differ sharply. Thus the *New York Times* presented the text of the Accord with an insert headed: "Two Peace Plans: How they Differ." The two peace plans are the Rambouillet (Interim) Agreement presented to Serbia as a "take-it-or-be-bombed" ultimatum on March 23 and the Kosovo Peace Accord of June 3. But in the real world there are three "peace plans," two of which were on the table on March 23: the Rambouillet Agreement and the Serb National Assembly Resolutions responding to it.

Let us begin with the two peace plans of March 23, asking how they differed and how they compare with the Kosovo Peace Accord of June 3, then turning briefly to what we might reasonably expect if we break the rules and pay some attention to the (ample) precedents.

The Rambouillet Agreement called for complete military occupation and political control of Kosovo by NATO and effective NATO military occupation of the rest of Yugoslavia at NATO's will. NATO is to "constitute and lead a military force" (KFOR) that "NATO will establish and deploy" in and around Kosovo, "operating under the authority and subject to the direction and political control of the North Atlantic Council (NAC) through the NATO chain of command"; "the KFOR commander is the final authority within theater regarding interpretation of this chapter [Implementation of the Military Agreement] and his interpretations are binding on all Parties and persons" (with an irrelevant qualification). Within a brief time schedule, all Yugoslav army forces and Ministry of Interior police are to redeploy to "approved cantonment sites," then to withdraw to Serbia, apart from small units assigned to border guard duties with limited weapons (all specified in detail). These units would be restricted to defending the borders from attack and "controlling illicit border crossings" and not permitted to travel in Kosovo apart from these functions.

"Three years after the entry into force of this Agreement, an international meeting shall be convened to determine a mechanism for a final settlement for Kosovo." This paragraph has regularly been construed as calling for a referendum on independence, not mentioned.

With regard to the rest of Yugoslavia, the terms for the occupation are set forth in Appendix B: Status of Multi-National Military Implementation Force. The crucial paragraph reads: "8. NATO personnel shall enjoy, together with their vehicles, vessels, aircraft, and equipment, free and unrestricted passage and unimpeded access throughout the FRY including associated airspace and territorial waters. This shall include, but not be limited to, the right of bivouac, maneuver, billet, and utilization of any areas or facilities as required for support, training, and operations."[3]

The remainder spells out the conditions that permit NATO forces and those they employ to act as they choose throughout the territory of the FRY, without obligation or concern for the laws of the country or the jurisdiction of its authorities, who are, however, required to follow NATO orders "on a priority basis and with all appropriate means." One provision states that "all NATO personnel shall respect the laws applicable in the FRY," but with a qualification to render it vacuous: "Without prejudice to their privileges and immunities under this Appendix."

It has been speculated that the wording was designed so as to guarantee rejection. Perhaps so. It is hard to imagine that any country would consider such terms, except in the form of unconditional surrender.

In the massive coverage of the war one will find little reference to the Agreement that is even close to accurate, notably the crucial article of Appendix B just quoted. The latter was, however, reported as soon as it had become irrelevant to democratic choice. On June 5, after the peace agreement of June 3, the *New York Times* reported that under the annex to the Rambouillet Agreement "a purely NATO force was to be given full permission to go anywhere it wanted in Yugoslavia, immune from any legal process," citing also the wording. Evidently, in the absence of clear and repeated explanation of the basic terms of the Rambouillet Agreement— the official "peace process"—it has been impossible for the public to gain any serious understanding of what was taking place or to assess the accuracy of the preferred version of the Kosovo Accord.

The second peace plan was presented in resolutions of the Serbian National Assembly on March 23. The Assembly rejected the demand for NATO military occupation and called on the OSCE (Organization for Security and Cooperation in Europe) and the UN to facilitate a peaceful diplomatic settlement. It condemned the withdrawal of the OSCE Kosovo Verification Mission ordered by the U.S. on March 19 in preparation for the March 24 bombing. The resolutions called for negotiations leading "toward the reaching of a political agreement on a wide-ranging autonomy for Kosovo and Metohija [the official name for the province], with the securing of a full equality of all citizens and ethnic communities and with respect for the sovereignty and territorial integrity of the Republic of Serbia and the Federal Republic of Yugoslavia." Furthermore, though "The Serbian Parliament does not accept presence of foreign military troops in Kosovo and Metohija," "The Serbian Parliament is ready to review the size and character of the international presence in Kosmet [Kosovo/Metohija] for carrying out the reached accord, immediately upon signing the political accord on the self-rule agreed and accepted by the representatives of all national communities living in Kosovo and Metohija."[4]

The essentials of these decisions were reported on major wire services, and therefore certainly known to every newsroom. Several database searches have found scarce mention, none in the national press and major journals.

The two peace plans of March 23 thus remain unknown to the general public, even the fact that there were two, not one. The standard line is that "Milosevic's refusal to accept . . . or even discuss an international peace-keeping plan [namely, the Rambouillet Agreement] was what started NATO bombing on March 24" (Craig Whitney, *New York Times*), one of the many articles deploring Serbian propaganda—accurately no doubt but with a few oversights.

As to what the Serb National Assembly Resolutions meant, the answers are known with confidence by fanatics—different answers, depending on which variety of fanatics they are. For others, there would have been a way to find out the answers: to explore the possibilities. But the enlightened states preferred not to pursue this option; rather, to bomb, with the antici-pated consequences.

Further steps in the diplomatic process and their refraction in the doctrinal institutions, merit attention, but I will skip that here, turning to the Kosovo Accord of June 3. As might have been expected, it is a com-promise between the two peace plans of March 23. On paper at least, the U.S./NATO abandoned their major demands, cited above, which had led to Serbia's rejection of the ultimatum. Serbia in turn agreed to an "interna-tional security presence with substantial NATO participation [which] must be deployed under unified command and control . . . under U.N. auspices." An addendum to the text stated: "Russia's position [that] the Russian con-tingent will not be under NATO command and its relationship to the inter-national presence will be governed by relevant additional agreements."[5] There are no terms permitting access to the rest of the FYR for NATO or the "international security presence" generally. Political control of Kosovo is not to be in the hands of NATO but of the UN Security Council, which will establish "an interim administration of Kosovo." The withdrawal of Yugoslav forces is not specified in the detail of the Rambouillet Agreement, but is similar, though accelerated. The remainder is within the range of agreement of the two plans of March 23.

The outcome suggests that diplomatic initiatives could have been pursued on March 23, averting a terrible human tragedy with consequences that will reverberate in Yugoslavia and elsewhere and are in many respects quite ominous.

To be sure, the current situation is not that of March 23. A *Times* head-line the day of the Kosovo Accord captures it accurately: "Kosovo Problems Just Beginning." Among the "staggering problems" that lie ahead, Serge

Schmemann observed, are the repatriation of the refugees "to the land of ashes and graves that was their home" and the "enormously costly challenge of rebuilding the devastated economies of Kosovo, the rest of Serbia and their neighbors." He quotes Balkans historian Susan Woodward of the Brookings Institution, who adds "that all the people we want to help us make a stable Kosovo have been destroyed by the effects of the bombings," leaving control in the hands of the KLA. The U.S. had strongly condemned the KLA as "without any question a terrorist group" when it began to carry out organized attacks in February 1998, actions that Washington condemned "very strongly" as "terrorist activities," probably giving a "green light" thereby to Milošević for the severe repression that led to the Colombia-style violence before the bombings precipitated a sharp escalation.

These "staggering problems" are new. They are "the effects of the bombings" and the vicious Serb reaction to them, though the problems that preceded the resort to violence by the enlightened states were daunting enough.

Turning from facts to spin, headlines hailed the grand victory of the enlightened states and their leaders, who compelled Milošević to "capitulate," to "say uncle," to accept a "NATO-led force," and to surrender "as close to unconditionally as anyone might have imagined,"[6] submitting to "a worse deal than the Rambouillet plan he rejected." Not exactly the story but one that is far more useful than the facts. The only serious issue debated is whether this shows that air power alone can achieve highly moral purposes, or whether, as the critics allowed into the debate allege, the case still has not been proven. Turning to broader significance, Britain's "eminent military historian" John Keegan "sees the war as a victory not just for air power but for the 'New World Order' that President Bush declared after the Gulf War," military expert Fred Kaplan reports. Keegan wrote that "If Milosevic really is a beaten man, all other would-be Milosevics around the world will have to reconsider their plans, [recognizing] that there are now no places on Earth that cannot be subjected to the same relentless harrowing as the Serbs have suffered in the past six weeks."[7]

The assessment is realistic, though not in the terms Keegan may have had in mind: rather, in the light of the actual goals and significance of the New World Order, as revealed by an important documentary record of the 1990s that remains unreported and a plethora of factual evidence that helps us understand the true meaning of the phrase "Miloševićs around the world." Merely to keep to the Balkans region, the strictures do not hold of huge ethnic cleansing operations and terrible atrocities within NATO itself, under European jurisdiction and with decisive and mounting U.S. support, and not conducted in response to an attack by the world's most awesome military force and the imminent threat of invasion. These crimes are legitimate under the rules of the New World Order, perhaps even meritorious, as are atrocities elsewhere that conform to the perceived interests of the leaders of the enlightened states and are regularly implemented by them when necessary. These facts, not particularly obscure, reveal that in the "new internationalism . . . the brutal repression of whole ethnic groups" will not merely be "tolerated" but actively expedited—exactly as in the "old internationalism" of the Concert of Europe, the U.S. itself, and many other distinguished predecessors.

While the facts and the spin differ sharply, one might argue that the media and commentators are realistic when they present the U.S./NATO version as if it were the facts. It will become The Facts as a simple consequence of the distribution of power and the willingness of articulate opinion to serve its needs. That is a regular phenomenon. Recent examples include the Paris Peace Treaty of January 1973 and the Esquipulas Accords of August 1987. In the former case, the U.S. was compelled to sign after the failure of the Christmas bombings to induce Hanoi to abandon the U.S.-Vietnam agreement of the preceding October. Kissinger and the White House at once announced quite lucidly that they would violate every significant element of the Treaty they were signing, presenting a different version which was adopted in reporting and commentary, so that when North Vietnam finally responded to serious U.S. violations of the accords, it became the incorrigible aggressor which had to be punished once again, as it was. The same tragedy/farce took place when the Central American Presidents reached the Esquipulas Accord (often called "the Arias plan") over strong U.S. opposition. Washington at once sharply escalated its wars in violation of the one "indispensable element" of the Accord, then proceeded to dismantle its other provisions by force, succeeding within a few months, and continuing to undermine every further diplomatic effort until its final victory. Washington's version of the Accord, which sharply deviated from it in crucial respects, became the accepted version. The outcome could therefore be heralded in headlines as a "Victory for US Fair Play" with Americans "United in Joy" over the devastation and bloodshed, overcome with rapture "in a romantic age" (Anthony Lewis, headlines in the *New York Times*, all reflecting the general euphoria over a mission accomplished).

It is superfluous to review the aftermath in these and numerous similar cases. There is little reason to expect a different story to unfold in the present case—with the usual and crucial proviso: if we let it.

★ Originally published as Noam Chomsky, "Kosovo Peace Accord," *Z Magazine*, July 1999.

Notes

1   Thomas Friedman, "Foreign Affairs; Good News, Bad News," *New York Times*, June 4, 1999, available at http://www.nytimes.com/1999/06/04/opinion/foreign-affairs-good-news-bad-news.html.
2   Stephen Kinzer, "Top Activist for Rights In Turkey Is Imprisoned," *New York Times*, June 4, 1999, available at http://www.nytimes.com/1999/06/04/world/top-activist-for-rights-in-turkey-is-imprisoned.html.
3   Quoted in Noam Chomsky, *The New Military Humanism* (Monroe, ME: Common Courage Press, 1999), 107.
4   Quoted in Chomsky, *New Military Humanism*, 109.
5   Guy Dinmore, "Deal Met with Relief, Scepticism and Anger," *Financial Times*, June 4, 1999, 2.
6   David Nyhan, "NATO Wins the War," *Boston Globe*, June 4, 1999, available at https://www.highbeam.com/doc/1P2-8546588.html; Fred Kaplan, "Milosevic's yield may disprove doubts on air war," *Boston Globe*, June 6, 1999, available at https://www.highbeam.com/doc/1P2-8546800.html; Editorial, "Summing up Kosovo," *Boston Globe*, June 8, 1999, available at https://www.highbeam.com/doc/1P2-8547034.html.
7   Quoted in Chomsky, *New Military Humanism*, 120.

Lessons from Kosovo

The crisis in Kosovo has excited passion and visionary exaltation of a kind rarely witnessed. The events have been portrayed as "a landmark in international relations," opening the gates to a stage of world history with no precedent, a new epoch of moral rectitude under the guiding hand of an "idealistic New World bent on ending inhumanity." This New Humanism, timed fortuitously with a new millennium, will displace the crass and narrow interest politics of a mean-spirited past. Novel conceptions of world order are being forged, interlaced with inspirational lessons about human affairs and global society. If the picture is true, if it has even a particle of truth, then remarkable prospects lie before us. Material and intellectual resources surely are at hand to overcome terrible tragedies at little cost, with only a modicum of goodwill. It takes little imagination or knowledge to compile a wish list of tasks to be undertaken that should confer enormous benefits on suffering people. In particular, crimes of the nature and scale of Kosovo are all too easily found, and many could be overcome, at least significantly alleviated, with a fraction of the effort and zeal expended in the cause that has consumed the Western powers and their intellectual cultures in early 1999.

If the high-minded spirit of the liberation of Kosovo has even shreds of authenticity, if at last leaders are acting "in the name of principles and values" that are truly humane, as Vaclav Havel confidently proclaimed, then there will be exciting opportunities to place critically important issues on the agenda of practical and immediate action. And even if reality turns out to fall short of the flattering self-portrait, the effort still has the merit of directing attention to what should be undertaken by those who regard the fine words as something more than cynical opportunism.

On March 24, U.S.-led NATO forces launched cruise missiles and bombs at targets throughout the Federal Republic of Yugoslavia (FRY), "plunging

America into a military conflict that President Clinton said was necessary to stop ethnic cleansing and bring stability to Eastern Europe," lead stories in the press reported. By bombing the FRY, Clinton informed the nation, "we are upholding our values, protecting our interests and advancing the cause of peace." "We cannot respond to such tragedies everywhere," he said, "but when ethnic conflict turns into ethnic cleansing where we can make a difference, we must try, and that is clearly the case in Kosovo." "Had we faltered" in what the heading of his speech calls "A Just and Necessary War," "the result would have been a moral and strategic disaster. The Albanian Kosovars would have become a people without a homeland, living in difficult conditions in some of the poorest countries in Europe," a fate that the U.S. cannot tolerate for suffering people.

Clinton's European allies agreed. Under the heading "A New Generation Draws the Line," British Prime Minister Tony Blair declared that this was a new kind of war in which we were fighting "for values," for "a new internationalism where the brutal repression of whole ethnic groups will no longer be tolerated," "for a world where those responsible for such crimes have nowhere to hide."

"The New Interventionism" was hailed by intellectual opinion and legal scholars who proclaimed a new era in world affairs in which the "enlightened states" will at last be able to use force where they "believe it to be just," discarding the "restrictive old rules" and obeying "modern notions of justice" that they fashion. "The crisis in Kosovo illustrates . . . America's new willingness to do what it thinks is right—international law not withstanding," wrote University of California law professor Michael Glennon in *Foreign Affairs*. Now freed from the shackles of the Cold War and old-fashioned constraints of world order, the enlightened states can dedicate themselves with full vigor to the mission of upholding human rights and bringing justice and freedom to suffering people everywhere, by force if necessary.

The enlightened states are the U.S. and its British associate, perhaps also others who enlist in their crusades for justice and human rights. Their mission is resisted, Glennon notes, only by "the defiant, the indolent, and the miscreant," the "disorderly" elements of the world. The rank of enlightenment is apparently conferred by definition. One will search in vain for credible attempts to provide evidence or argument for the critical distinction between enlightened and disorderly, surely not from history. The history is in any event deemed irrelevant by the familiar doctrine of "change of course," which holds that, yes, in the past we have erred out of naiveté or faulty information, but now we are returning to the traditional path of righteousness. There is, accordingly, no purpose in asking what might be learned from old, musty stories about the past, even though the decision-making structure and its institutional base remain intact and unchanged.

On June 3, NATO and Serbia reached a peace accord. The U.S. triumphantly declared victory, though not yet peace: the iron fist remains poised until the victors determine that their interpretation of the peace accord has been imposed. A broad consensus was articulated by the *New York Times* global analyst Thomas Friedman: "From the start the Kosovo problem has been about how we should react when bad things happen in unimportant places." The enlightened states have opened a new millennium by providing an answer to this critical question of the modern era, pursuing the moral principle that, in Friedman's words, "once the refugee evictions began, ignoring Kosovo would be wrong . . . and therefore using a huge air war for a limited objective was the only thing that made sense."

While Friedman's own (and conventional) answer to his rhetorical question is untenable, a credible answer appears in the same journal on the same day, though only obliquely. Reporting from Ankara, correspondent Stephen Kinzer writes that "Turkey's best-known human rights advocate [Akin Birdal] entered prison" to serve his sentence for having "urged the state to reach a peaceful settlement with Kurdish rebels." Looking beyond the sporadic and generally uninformative or misleading news reports and commentary, we discover that the sentencing of the courageous president of the Human Rights Association of Turkey is only one episode of a campaign of intimidation and harassment of human rights advocates who are investigating and reporting horrendous atrocities and calling for peaceful resolution of a conflict that has been marked by one of the most savage campaigns of ethnic cleansing and state terror of the 1990s. The campaign has proceeded with mounting fury thanks to the active participation of the U.S., "upholding our values, protecting our interests, and advancing the cause of peace" (in the president's words), in a way that is all too familiar to those who do not prefer intentional ignorance. These events, continuing right now and taking place within NATO and under European jurisdiction, provide a rather striking illustration—far from the only one—of the answer given by the enlightened states to the question of "how we should react when bad things happen in unimportant places": we should react by helping to escalate the atrocities, a mission accomplished in Kosovo as well.

Such elements of the real world of today raise some rather serious questions about the New Humanism. In the Balkans war of 1999, these questions remain out of sight—within the "enlightened states," at least. Elsewhere, they are readily perceived over a broad spectrum. To select several remote points for illustration, Amos Gilboa, a prominent Israeli commentator on military and strategic affairs, sees the enlightened states as "a danger to the world." He describes their new rules of the game as a reversion to the colonial era, with the resort to force "cloaked in moralistic righteousness," as the rich and powerful do "what seems to them to be justified."

At a very different point on the spectrum, Alexander Solzhenitsyn (a Western idol when he is saying the right things) offers a succinct definition of the New Humanism: "The aggressors have kicked aside the UN, opening a new era where might is right."[1] They and many others like them throughout the world might agree with an observation by the prominent and influential—though little celebrated—radical pacifist A.J. Muste: "The problem after a war is with the victor. He thinks he has just proved that war and violence pay. Who will now teach him a lesson?"[2] The larger issues highlighted by the most recent of the wars of Yugoslav secession came into focus with the fading of the Cold War. Central among these is the claimed right of intervention on the part of states or alliances on humanitarian grounds, which extends the scope of legitimated use of force. There is general agreement on the timing, but the conclusions about "humanitarian intervention" are phrased in different ways, reflecting the evaluation of the intent and likely consequences of the "emerging norms of justified intervention."[3] The enlarged options are of two kinds: those carried out under UN auspices and in conformity with the UN charter, which is agreed to be the foundation of international law in the post–World War II period; and those carried out unilaterally, with no Security Council authorization, by states or alliances (the U.S. and NATO, for example, or the Warsaw Pact in earlier years). If sufficiently powerful, arrogant, and internally well disciplined, such alliances may designate themselves "the international community."

Questions arise about the first category, but that is not our topic here. Rather, we are concerned with the states or alliances that do not seek or are not granted authorization from the international community, but use force because "they believe it to be just." In practice, that reduces to "America's new willingness to do what it thinks is right," apart from operations in "unimportant countries" of no concern to the reigning global superpower (for example, peacekeeping interventions of the West African states, which received retroactive authorization from the United Nations). From one perspective, the extended scope of intervention has always been legitimate, indeed meritorious, but was obstructed during the Cold War because "the defiant, the indolent, and the miscreant" who resist the mission were then able to rely for support on the Communist powers, dedicated to subversion and insurrection as they sought to conquer the world. With the Cold War over, the "disorderly" can no longer impede the good works of the enlightened states, and the New Humanism can therefore flourish under their wise and just leadership.

From a contrasting perspective, "the new interventionism" is replaying an old record. It is an updated variant of traditional practices that were impeded in a bipolar world system that allowed some space for non-alignment—a concept that effectively vanishes when one of the two poles disappears. The Soviet Union, and to some extent China, set limits on the actions of the Western powers in their traditional domains—not only by virtue of the military deterrent but also because of their occasional willingness, however opportunistic, to lend support to targets of Western subversion and aggression. With the Soviet deterrent in decline, the Cold War victors are more free to exercise their will under the cloak of good intentions but in pursuit of interests that have a very familiar ring outside the realm of enlightenment. The self-described bearers of enlightenment happen to be the rich and powerful, the inheritors of the colonial and neocolonial systems of global dominion: they are the North, the First World. The disorderly miscreants who defy them have been at the other end of the stick: they are the South, the Third World.

The division is not sharp and clear; nothing is in the dominion of human affairs. But the tendencies are hard to miss, and they suggest some of the reasons for the difference of perspective in interpretation of the emerging norms of justified intervention. The conflict of interpretation is difficult to resolve if history is declared irrelevant and the present scene is glimpsed only through the filters established by the enlightened states, which transmit the evil deeds of official enemies while blocking unwanted images. To take the most obvious current illustration, images of atrocities pass through unhindered, even magnified, if they are attributable to Belgrade but not if they trace back to Ankara and Washington. If we hope to understand anything about the world, we should ask why decisions on forceful intervention are made one way or another by the states with the power to exercise their judgment and will.

At the 1993 American Academy Conference on Emerging Norms, one of the most distinguished figures in the academic discipline of international relations, Ernest Haas, raised a simple and cogent question, which has since received a clear and instructive answer. He observed that NATO was then intervening in Iraq and Bosnia to protect Kurds and Muslims and asked: "Will NATO take the same interventionist view if and when Turkey begins to lean more heavily on its Kurdish insurgents?" The question poses a clear test of the New Humanism: Is it guided by power interests or by humanitarian concern? Is the resort to force undertaken "in the name of principles and values," as professed? Or are we witnessing something more crass and familiar? The test was a good one, and the answer was not long in coming. As Haas raised the question, Turkey was leaning much more heavily on the Kurdish population of the Southeast while rejecting offers of peaceful settlement that would permit cultural and linguistic rights. Very shortly the operation escalated to extremes of ethnic cleansing and state terror. NATO took a very definite "interventionist view," in particular NATO's leader, which intervened decisively to escalate the atrocities.

The implications concerning the larger issues seem rather clear, particularly when we compare this "interventionist view" to the one adopted for the Kosovo crisis, a lesser one on moral grounds, not only for reasons of scale (crucially and dramatically, prior to the decision to bomb the FRY) but also because it is outside the bounds and jurisdiction of the NATO powers and their institutions, unlike Turkey, which is squarely within. The two cases differ sharply in a different dimension, however: Serbia is one of those disorderly miscreants that impede the institution of the U.S.-dominated global system, while Turkey is a loyal client state that contributes substantially to this project. Again, the factors that drive policy do not seem hard to discern, and the North-South divisions over the larger issues and their interpretation seem to fall into place as well. Even a cursory examination shows that the proclamations of the New Humanism are at best highly dubious. The narrowest focus, on the NATO intervention in Kosovo alone, suffices to undermine the lofty pronouncements.

A broader look at the contemporary world powerfully reinforces the conclusion and brings forth with stark clarity "the values" that are actually being upheld. If we deviate further from the marching orders that issue from Washington and London and allow the past to enter the discussion, we quickly discover that the new generation is the old generation, and that the "new internationalism" replays old and unpleasant records. The actions of distinguished forebears, as well as the justifications offered and their merits, should also give us pause. Let us begin by keeping to the rules and focusing attention on the designated case: Serb atrocities in Kosovo, which are quite real and often ghastly. We immediately discover that the bombing was not undertaken in "response" to ethnic cleansing and to "reverse" it, as leaders alleged. With full awareness of the likely consequences, Clinton and Blair decided in favor of a war that led to a radical escalation of ethnic cleansing along with other deleterious effects. In the year before the bombing, according to NATO sources, about 2,000 people had been killed in Kosovo and several hundred thousand had become internal refugees. The humanitarian catastrophe was overwhelmingly attributable to Yugoslavian police and military forces, the main victims being ethnic Albanians, commonly assumed to constitute about 90 percent of the population. Prior to the bombing, and for two days following its onset, the United Nations High Commissioner for Refugees (UNHCR) reported no data on refugees, though many Kosovars—Albanian and Serb—had been leaving the province for years, and entering as well, sometimes as a consequence of the Balkan wars, sometimes for economic and other reasons. After three days of bombing, UNHCR reported on March 27 that 4,000 had fled Kosovo to Albania and Macedonia, the two neighboring countries. By April 5, the *New York Times* reported that "more than 350,000 have left Kosovo since March 24," relying on UNHCR figures, while unknown numbers of Serbs fled north to Serbia to escape the increased violence from the air and on the ground. After the war, it was reported that half the Serb population had "moved out when the NATO bombing began." There have been varying estimates of the number of refugees within Kosovo before that NATO bombing. Cambridge University Law Professor Marc Weller, legal adviser to the Kosovar Albanian delegation at the Rambouillet Conference, reports that after the withdrawal of the international monitors on March 19, "within a few days the number of displaced had again risen to over 200,000." House Intelligence Committee Chairman Porter Goss gave the estimate of 250,000 internally displaced. By the time of the peace accord on June 3, the UNHCR reported 671,500 refugees beyond the borders of the FRY, in addition to 70,000 in Montenegro and 75,000 who went to other countries. To these we may add the unknown numbers displaced within Kosovo, perhaps as many as 300,000 in the year before the bombing, far more afterwards, with varying estimates; and according to the Yugoslavian Red Cross, more than a million displaced within Serbia after the bombing, along with many who left Serbia. The numbers reported from

Kosovo are, unfortunately, all too familiar. To mention only two cases that are prime illustrations of "our values" in the '90s, the refugee total prior to the NATO bombing is similar to the State Department estimate for Colombia in the same year; and the UNHCR totals at the war's end are about the same as the number of Palestinians who fled or were expelled in 1948, another policy issue that is very much alive today. In that case, refugees numbered about 750,000, or 85 percent of the population, with more than 400 villages leveled and ample violence. The comparison was not overlooked in the Israeli press, where Gideon Levy of *Ha'aretz* described Kosovo as Palestine 1948 with TV cameras. Israeli Foreign Minister Ariel Sharon warned that if "NATO's aggression" is "legitimized" the next step might be a call for autonomy and links to the Palestinian Authority for Galilee. Elsewhere, Ian Williams, a fervent supporter of the NATO bombing, commented, "The Serbs could almost have studied Israeli tactics in 1948 in their village destruction campaign, except of course the Palestinians had no NATO to back them up."

The distinction between worthy and unworthy victims is traditional, as is its basis, remote from any moral principle apart from the rights demanded by power and privilege. Washington simultaneously rejects the principles of the Universal Declaration of Human Rights (for unworthy victims, Palestinians and many others) and passionately upholds them (for worthy victims, now Kosovar Albanians). Though readily understood in terms of power interests, the distinctions, when noticed at all, are portrayed as "double standards" or "mistakes" in respectable commentary. Attention to the facts reveals that there is a single standard, the one that great powers typically observe, and that although plans may go awry (aggressors have been defeated, etc.), the "mistakes" are overwhelmingly tactical.

Continuing with Kosovo, refugees reported that immediately after the bombing began, the terror reached the capital city of Priština, mostly spared before, and provided credible accounts of large-scale destruction of villages, brutal atrocities, and a radical increase in the generation of refugees, perhaps an effort to expel the Albanian population. Similar reports, generally quite credible, were prominently featured throughout the media, in extensive and horrifying detail, the usual practice in the case of worthy victims under attack by official enemies.

One index of the effects of "the huge air war" was offered by Robert Hayden, director of the Center for Russian and East European Studies at the University of Pittsburgh: "The casualties among Serb civilians in the first three weeks of the war are higher than all of the casualties on both sides in Kosovo in the three months that led up to this war, and yet those three months were supposed to be a humanitarian catastrophe." Admittedly, casualties among Serb civilians amount to little in the context of the jingoist hysteria that was whipped up for a war against the Serbs. But the toll from the bombing among Albanians in the first three weeks, estimated at the time in the hundreds, though presumably much higher, was surely far beyond that of the preceding three months and probably the preceding years.

On March 27, U.S.-NATO Commanding General Wesley Clark announced that it was "entirely predictable" that Serb terror and violence would intensify after the bombing. On the same day, State Department spokesman James Rubin said, "The United States is extremely alarmed by reports of an escalating pattern of Serbian attacks on Kosovar Albanian civilians," now attributed in large part to paramilitary forces. Shortly after, Clark reported again that he was not surprised by the sharp escalation of Serb terror after the bombing: "The military authorities fully anticipated the vicious approach that Milosevic would adopt, as well as the terrible efficiency with which he would carry it out."[4] Clark's phrase "entirely predictable" is an overstatement. Nothing in human affairs is "entirely predictable," surely not the effects of extreme violence. But what happened at once was highly likely. "Enemies often react when shot at," observed Carnes Lord, a former Bush administration national security adviser. "Though Western officials continue to deny it, there can be little doubt that the bombing campaign has provided both motive and opportunity for a wider and more savage Serbian operation than what was first envisioned."

The outcome was not unanticipated in Washington. House Intelligence Committee Chairman Goss informed the media, "Our intelligence community warned us months and days before [the bombing] that we would have a virtual explosion of refugees over the 250,000 that was expected as of the last year [pre-bombing], that the Serb resolve would increase, that the conflict would spread, and that there would be ethnic cleansing." As far back as 1992, European monitors in Macedonia had "predicted a sudden, massive influx of ethnic Albanian refugees if hostilities spread into Kosovo."[5]

The reasons for these expectations are clear enough. People "react when shot at" not by garlanding the attacker with flowers, and not where the attacker is strong—but where they are strong: in this case, on the ground, not by sending jet planes to bomb Washington and London. It takes no particular genius to reach these conclusions, nor access to secret intelligence. The overt NATO threat of direct invasion made the brutal reaction even more likely, again for reasons that could hardly have escaped Clinton and Blair. The threat of bombing presumably had already led to an increase in atrocities, though evidence is slight. The withdrawal of international monitors on March 19 in preparation for the bombing presumably had the same consequence, again predictably. "The monitors were widely seen as the only remaining brake on Yugoslav troops," the *Washington Post* observed in a retrospective account; and releasing the brake, it must have been assumed, would lead to disaster. Other accounts agree. A subsequent detailed retrospective in the *New York Times* concluded, "The Serbs began attacking the Kosovo Liberation Army strongholds on March 19, but their attack kicked into high gear on March 24, the night NATO began bombing in Yugoslavia." It would take a heavy dose of intentional ignorance to interpret the facts as mere coincidence.

Serbia officially opposed the withdrawal of the monitors. That resolution in the National Assembly was not reported by the mainstream media, which also did not publish the terms of the Rambouillet Agreement, though the latter was identified throughout the war as right and just. It was "the peace process," emphasis on "the," a term used reflexively to refer to Washington's stand whatever it may be (often efforts to undermine diplomacy), a practice that has been particularly instructive with regard to the Middle East and Central America. The bombing was undertaken five days after the withdrawal of the monitors with the rational expectation that "the result" would be atrocities and ethnic cleansing, and a "sudden, massive" flight and expulsion of Albanians. That indeed happened, even if the scale may have come as a surprise to some, though the commanding general apparently expected nothing less.

★ Originally published in: Noam Chomsky, *The New Military Humanism* (Monroe, ME: Common Courage Press, 1999).

Notes

1   Quoted in Noam Chomsky, *A New Generation Draws the Line* (London: Verso, 2000), 6.
2   A.J. Muste, "Crisis in the World and in the Peace Movement," in *The Essays of A.J. Muste*, ed. Nat Hentoff (Indianapolis: Bobbs-Merrill, 1967).
3   The phrase is borrowed from the tile of one of the first and best of the general studies: Laura Reed and Carl Kaysen, eds., *Emerging Norms of Justified Intervention* (Cambridge, MA: American Academy of Arts and Sciences, 1993).
4   "Overview," *New York Times*, March 27, 1999; *Sunday Times*, March 28, 1999; "The Nightmare," *Newsweek*, April 11, 1999.
5   Elaine Sciolino and Ethan Bronner, "How a President, Distracted by Scandal, Entered Balkan War," *New York Times*, April 18, 1999.

A Review of NATO's War over Kosovo

The tumult having subsided, it should be possible to undertake a relatively dispassionate review and analysis of NATO's war over Kosovo. One might have expected the theme to have dominated the year-end millenarianism, considering the exuberance the war elicited in Western intellectual circles and the tidal wave of self-adulation by respected voices, lauding the first war in history fought "in the name of principles and values," the first bold step toward a "new era" in which the "enlightened states" will protect the human rights of all under the guiding hand of an "idealistic New World bent on ending inhumanity," now freed from the shackles of archaic concepts of world order. But it received scant mention.

A rare exception was the *Wall Street Journal*, which devoted its lead story on December 31 [1999] to an in-depth analysis of what had taken place. The headline reads: "War in Kosovo Was Cruel, Bitter, Savage; Genocide It Wasn't." The conclusion contrasts rather sharply with wartime propaganda. A database search of references to "genocide" in Kosovo for the first week of bombing alone was interrupted when it reached its limit of 1,000 documents.

As NATO forces entered Kosovo, tremendous efforts were undertaken to discover evidence of war crimes, a "model of speed and efficiency" to ensure that no evidence would be lost or overlooked. The efforts "build on lessons learned from past mistakes." They reflect "a growing international focus on holding war criminals accountable." Furthermore, analysts add, "proving the scale of the crimes is also important to NATO politically, to show why 78 days of airstrikes against Serbian forces and infrastructure were necessary."

The logic, widely accepted, is intriguing. Uncontroversially, the vast crimes took place after the bombing began: they were not a cause but a consequence. It requires considerable audacity, therefore, to take the crimes to provide retrospective justification for the actions that contributed to inciting them.

One "lesson learned," and quickly applied, was the need to avoid a serious inquiry into crimes in East Timor.[1] Here there was no "model of speed and efficiency." Few forensic experts were sent despite the pleas of the UN peacekeeping mission, and those were delayed for four months, well after the rainy season would remove essential evidence. The mission itself was delayed even after the country had been virtually destroyed and most of its population expelled. The distinction is not hard to comprehend. In East Timor, the crimes were attributable directly to state terrorists who were supported by the West right through the final days of their atrocities. Accordingly, issues of deterrence and accountability can hardly be on the agenda. In Kosovo, in contrast, evidence of terrible crimes can be adduced to provide retrospective justification for the NATO war, on the interesting principle that has been established by the doctrinal system.

Despite the intensive efforts, the results of "the mass-grave obsession," as the WSJ analysts call it, were disappointingly thin. Instead of "the huge killing fields some investigators were led to expect . . . the pattern is of scattered killings," a form of "ethnic cleansing light." "Most killings and burnings [were] in areas where the separatist Kosovo Liberation Army [KLA] had been active" or could infiltrate, some human-rights researchers reported, an attempt "to clear out areas of KLA support, using selective terror, robberies and sporadic killings." These conclusions gain some support from the detailed review the Organization for Security and Co-operation in Europe (OSCE) released in December, which "suggests a kind of military rationale for the expulsions, which were concentrated in areas controlled by the insurgents and along likely invasion routes."

The WSJ analysis concludes that "NATO stepped up its claims about Serb 'killing fields'" when it "saw a fatigued press corps drifting toward the contrarian story: civilians killed by NATO's bombs." NATO spokesperson Jamie Shea presented "information" that can be traced to KLA sources. Many of the most lurid and prominently published atrocity reports attributed to refugees and other sources were untrue, the WSJ concludes. Meanwhile NATO sought to deny its own atrocities, for example, by releasing a falsified videotape "shown at triple its real speed" to make it appear that "the killing of at least 14 civilians aboard a train on a bridge in Serbia last April" was unavoidable because "the train had been traveling too fast for the trajectory of the missiles to have been changed in time."

The WSJ analysts nevertheless conclude that the "heinous" crimes, including the huge campaign of expulsion, "may well be enough to justify" the NATO bombing campaign, on the principle of retrospective justification.

The OSCE study is the third major source concerning Serb crimes. The first is the State Department's case against Slobodan Milošević and his associates in May; the second, their formal indictment shortly after by the International Tribunal on War Crimes. The two documents are very similar, presumably because the "remarkably fast indictment" by the Tribunal was based on U.S.-UK "intelligence and other information long denied to [the Tribunal] by Western governments." Few expect that such information would be released for a War Crimes Tribunal on East Timor, in the unlikely event that there is one. The State Department updated its case in December 1999, with what is intended to be the definitive justification for the bombing, adding whatever information could be obtained from refugees and investigations after the war.

In the two State Department reports and the Tribunal indictment, the detailed chronologies are restricted, almost entirely, to the period that followed the bombing campaign initiated on March 24. Thus the final State Department report of December 1999 refers vaguely to "late March" or "after March," apart from a single reference to refugee reports of an execution on March 23, the day of NATO's official declaration that the air operations announced on March 22 would begin.

The one significant exception is the January 15 Račak massacre of forty-five people. But that cannot have been the motive for the bombing, for two sufficient reasons: first, the OSCE monitors and other international observers (including NATO) report this to be an isolated event, with nothing similar in the following months up to the bombing; we return to that record directly. And second, such atrocities are of little concern to the U.S. and its allies. Evidence for the latter conclusion is overwhelming, and it was confirmed once again shortly after the Račak massacre, when Indonesian forces and their paramilitary subordinates brutally murdered fifty or more people who had taken refuge from Indonesian terror in a church in the remote Timorese village of Liquiçá. Unlike Račak, this was only one of many massacres in East Timor at that time, with a toll well beyond anything attributed to Milošević in Kosovo: three to five thousand killed from January 1999, credible church sources reported on August 6, about twice the number killed on all sides in Kosovo in the year prior to the bombing, according to NATO. Historian John Taylor estimates the toll at five to six thousand from January to the August 30 referendum.

The U.S. and its allies reacted to the East Timor massacres in the familiar way: by continuing to provide military and other aid to the killers and maintaining other military arrangements, including joint training exercises as late as August, while insisting that security in East Timor "is the responsibility of the Government of Indonesia, and we don't want to take that responsibility away from them."

In summary, the State Department and the Tribunal make no serious effort to justify the bombing campaign or the withdrawal of the OSCE monitors on March 20 in preparation for it.

The OSCE inquiry conforms closely to the indictments produced by the State Department and the Tribunal. It records "the pattern of the expulsions and the vast increase in lootings, killings, rape, kidnappings and pillage once the NATO air war began on March 24." "The most visible change in the events was after NATO launched its first airstrikes" on March 24, the OSCE reports. "On one hand, the situation seemed to have slipped out of the control of any authorities, as lawlessness reigned in the form of killings and the looting of houses. On the other, the massive expulsion of thousands of residents from the city, which mostly took place in the last week of March and in early April, followed a certain pattern and was conceivably organized well in advance."

The word "conceivably" is surely an understatement. Even without documentary evidence, one can scarcely doubt that Serbia had contingency plans for expulsion of the population and would be likely to put them into effect under NATO bombardment, with the prospect of direct invasion. It is commonly argued that the bombing is justified by the contingency plans that were implemented in response to the bombing. Again, the logic is interesting. Adopting the same principle, terrorist attacks on U.S. targets would be justified if they elicited a nuclear attack, in accord with contingency plans—which exist—for first strike, even preemptive strike against nonnuclear states that have signed the nonproliferation treaty. An Iranian missile attack on Israel with a credible invasion threat would be justified if Israel responded by implementing its detailed contingency plans—which presumably exist—for expelling the Palestinian population.

The OSCE inquiry reports further that "once the OSCE-KVM [monitors] left on 20 March 1999 and in particular after the start of the NATO bombing of the FRY on 24 March, Serbian police and/or VJ (army), often accompanied by paramilitaries, went from village to village and, in the towns, from area to area threatening and expelling the Kosovo Albanian population."

The departure of the monitors also precipitated an increase in KLA ambushes of Serbian police officers, "provoking a strong reaction" by police, an escalation from "the prewar atmosphere, when Serbian forces were facing off against the rebels, who were kidnapping Serbian civilians and ambushing police officers and soldiers."

For understanding of NATO's resort to war, the most important period is the months leading up to the decision. Of course, what NATO knew about that period is a matter of critical significance for any serious attempt to evaluate the decision to bomb Yugoslavia without Security Council authorization. Fortunately, that is the period for which we have the most detailed direct evidence: namely, from the reports of the KVM monitors and other international observers. Unfortunately, the OSCE inquiry passes over these months quickly, presenting little evidence and concentrating rather on the period after monitors were withdrawn. A selection of KVM reports is, however, available, along with others by NATO and independent international observers. These merit close scrutiny.

The relevant period begins in December (1998), with the breakdown of the cease-fire that had permitted the return of many people displaced by the fighting. Throughout these months, the monitors report that "humanitarian agencies in general have unhindered access to all areas of Kosovo," with occasional harassment from Serb security forces and KLA paramilitaries, so the information may be presumed to be fairly comprehensive.

The "most serious incidents" reported by the International Committee of the Red Cross in December are clashes along the FRY-Albanian border and "what appear to be the first deliberate attacks on public places in urban areas." The UN Inter-Agency Update (December 24) identifies these as an attempt by armed Albanians to cross into Kosovo from Albania, leaving at least thirty-six armed men dead, and the killing of six Serbian teenagers by masked men spraying gunfire in a cafe in the largely Serbian city of Peć. The next incident is the abduction and murder of the deputy mayor of Kosovo Polje, attributed by NATO to the KLA. Then follows a report of "abductions attributed to the KLA." The UN secretary-general's report (December 24) reviews the same evidence, citing the figure of 282 civilians and police abducted by the KLA as of December 7 (FRY figures). The general picture is that after the October cease-fire, "Kosovo Albanian paramilitary units have taken advantage of the lull in the fighting to re-establish their control over many villages in Kosovo, as well as over some areas near urban centres and highways . . . leading to statements [by Serbian authorities] that if the [KVM] cannot control these units the Government would."

The UN Inter-Agency Update on January 11 is similar. It reports fighting between Serb security forces and the KLA. In addition, in "the most serious incident since the declaration of the ceasefire in October 1998, the period under review has witnessed an increase in the number of murders (allegedly perpetrated by the KLA), which have prompted vigorous retaliatory action by government security forces." "Random violence" killed twenty-one people in the preceding eleven days. Only one example is cited: a bomb outside "a cafe in Priština, injuring three Serbian youths and triggering retaliatory attacks by Serbian civilians on Albanians," the first such incident in the capital. The other major incidents cited are KLA capture of eight soldiers, the killing of a Serbian civilian, and the reported killing of three Serbian police. NATO's review of the period is similar, with further details: VJ shelling of civilian and KLA facilities with "at least 15 Kosovo Albanians" killed, KLA killing of a Serb judge, police and civilians, etc.

Then comes the Račak massacre of January 15, after which the reports return pretty much to what preceded. The OSCE monthly Report of February 20 describes the situation as "volatile." Serb-KLA "direct military engagement . . . dropped significantly," but KLA attacks on police and "sporadic exchange of gunfire" continued, "including at times the use of heavy weapons by the VJ." The "main feature of the last part of the reporting period has been an alarming increase in urban terrorism with a series of indiscriminate bombing or raking gunfire attacks against civilians in public places in towns throughout Kosovo"; these are "non-attributable," either "criminally or politically motivated." Then follows a review of police-KLA confrontations, KLA abduction of "five elderly Serb civilians," and the refusal of KLA and VJ to comply with Security Council resolutions. Five civilians were killed as "urban violence increased significantly," including three killed by a bomb outside an Albanian grocery store. "More reports were received of the KLA 'policing' the Albanian community and administering punishments to those charged as collaborators with the Serbs," also murder and abduction of alleged Albanian collaborators and Serb police. The "cycle of confrontation can be generally described" as KLA attacks on Serb police and civilians, "a disproportionate response by the FRY authorities," and "renewed KLA activity elsewhere."

In his monthly report, March 17, the UN secretary-general reports that clashes between Serb security forces and the KLA "continued at a relatively lower level," but civilians "are increasingly becoming the main target of violent acts," including killings, executions, mistreatment, and abductions. The UNHCR [UN Refugee Agency] "registered more than 65 violent deaths" of Albanian and Serb civilians (and several Roma) from January 20 to March 17. These are reported to be isolated killings by gunmen and grenade attacks on cafes and shops. Victims included alleged Albanian collaborators and "civilians known for open-mindedness and flexibility in community relations." Abductions continued, the victims almost all Serbs, mostly civilians. The OSCE report of March 20 gave a similar picture, reporting "unprovoked attacks by the KLA against the police" and an increase in casualties among Serb security forces, along with "Military operations affecting the civilian population," "Indiscriminate urban terrorist attacks targeting civilians," "non-attributable murders," mostly Albanians, and abduction of Albanian civilians, allegedly by a "centrally controlled" KLA "security force." Specific incidents are then reported.

The last NATO report (January 16–March 22) cites several dozen incidents, about half initiated by KLA, half by Serb security forces, in addition to half a dozen responses by Serb security forces and engagements with the KLA, including "Aggressive Serb attacks on villages suspected of harbouring UCK forces or command centres." Casualties reported are mostly military, at the levels of the preceding months.

As a standard of comparison, one might consider the regular murderous and destructive U.S.-backed Israeli military operations in Lebanon when Israeli forces occupying southern Lebanon in violation of Security Council orders or their local mercenaries are attacked by the Lebanese resistance. Through the 1990s, as before, these have far exceeded anything attributed to the FRY security forces within what NATO insists is their territory.

Within Kosovo, no significant changes are reported from the breakdown of the cease-fire in December until the March 22 decision to bomb. Even apart from the (apparently isolated) Račak massacre, there can be no doubt that the FRY authorities and security forces were responsible for serious crimes. But the reported record also lends no credibility to the claim that these were the reason for the bombing; in the case of comparable or much worse atrocities during the same period, the U.S. and its allies either did not react or—more significantly—maintained and even increased their support for the atrocities. Examples are all too easy to enumerate, East Timor in the same months, to mention only the most obvious one.

The vast expulsions from Kosovo began immediately after the March 24 bombing campaign. On March 27, the UNHCR reported that four thousand had fled Kosovo, and on April 1, the flow was high enough for UNHCR to begin to provide daily figures. Its Humanitarian Evacuation Programme began on April 5. From the last week of March to the end of the war in June, "forces of the FRY and Serbia forcibly expelled some 863,000 Kosovo Albanians from Kosovo," the OSCE reports, and hundreds of thousands of others were internally displaced, while unknown numbers of Serbs, Gypsies (Roma), and others fled as well.

The U.S. and the UK had been planning the bombing campaign for many months and could hardly have failed to anticipate these consequences. In early March, Italian Prime Minister Massimo D'Alema warned Clinton of the huge refugee flow that would follow the bombing; Clinton's National Security Adviser Sandy Berger responded that in that case "NATO will keep bombing," with still more horrific results. U.S. intelligence also warned that there would be "a virtual explosion of refugees" and a campaign of ethnic cleansing, reiterating earlier predictions of European monitors.

As the bombing campaign began, U.S.-NATO Commanding General Wesley Clark informed the press that it was "entirely predictable" that Serb terror would intensify as a result. Shortly after, Clark explained again that "The military authorities fully anticipated the vicious approach that Milosevic would adopt, as well as the terrible efficiency with which he would carry it out." Elaborating a few weeks later, he observed that the NATO operation planned by "the political leadership . . . was not designed as a means of blocking Serb ethnic cleansing. It was not designed as a means of waging war against the Serb and MUP [internal police] forces in Kosovo. Not in any way. There was never any intent to do that. That was not the idea."[2]

General Clark stated further that plans for Operation Horseshoe "have never been shared with me," referring to the alleged Serb plan to expel the population that was publicized by NATO after the shocking Serb reaction to the bombing had become evident.

The agency that bears primary responsibility for care of refugees is UNHCR. "At the war's end, British Prime Minister Tony Blair privately took the agency to task for what he considered its problematic performance."

Evidently, the performance of UNHCR would have been less problematic had the agency not been defunded by the great powers. For this reason, the UNHCR had to cut staff by over 15 percent in 1998. In October, while the bombing plans were being formulated, the UNHCR announced that it would have to eliminate a fifth of its remaining staff by January 1999 because of the budgetary crisis created by the "enlightened states."

In summary, the KVM monitors were removed and a bombing campaign initiated with the expectation, quickly fulfilled, that the consequence would be a sharp escalation of ethnic cleansing and other atrocities, after the organization responsible for care of refugees was defunded. Under the doctrine of retrospective justification, the heinous crimes that ensued are now held to be, perhaps, "enough to justify" the NATO bombing campaign.

The person who commits a crime bears the primary responsibility for it; those who incite him, anticipating the consequences, bear secondary responsibility, which only mounts if they act to increase the suffering of the victims. The only possible argument for action to incite the crimes is that they would have been even more severe had the action not been undertaken. That claim, one of the most remarkable in the history of support for state violence, requires substantial evidence. In the present case, one will seek evidence in vain—even recognition that it is required.

Suppose, nevertheless, that we take the argument seriously. It plainly loses force to the extent that the subsequent crimes are great. If no Kosovar Albanians had suffered as a result of the NATO bombing campaign, the decision to bomb might be justified on the grounds that crimes against them were deterred. The force of the argument diminishes as the scale of the crimes increases. It is, therefore, rather curious that supporters of the bombing seek to portray the worst possible picture of the crimes for which they share responsibility; the opposite should be the case. The odd stance presumably reflects the success in instilling the doctrine that the crimes incited by the NATO bombing provide retrospective justification for it.

This is by no means the only impressive feat of doctrinal management. Another is the debate over NATO's alleged "double standards," revealed by its "looking away" from other humanitarian crises, or "doing too little" to prevent them. Participants in the debate must agree that NATO was guided by humanitarian principles in Kosovo—precisely the question at issue. That aside, the Clinton administration did not "look away" or "do too little" in the face of atrocities in East Timor, or Colombia, or many other places. Rather, along with its allies, it chose to escalate the atrocities, often vigorously and decisively. Perhaps the case of Turkey—within NATO and under European jurisdiction—is the most relevant in the present connection. Its ethnic cleansing operations and other crimes, enormous in scale, were carried out with a huge flow of military aid from the Clinton administration, increasing as atrocities mounted. They have also virtually disappeared from history. There was no mention of them at the fiftieth anniversary meeting of NATO in April 1999, held under the shadow of ethnic cleansing—a crime that cannot be tolerated near the borders of NATO, participants and commentators declaimed; only within its borders, where the crimes are to be expedited. With rare exceptions, the press has kept to occasional apologetics, though the participation of Turkish forces in the Kosovo campaign was highly praised. More recent debate over the problems of "humanitarian intervention" evades the crucial U.S. role in the Turkish atrocities or ignores the topic altogether.

It is a rare achievement for a propaganda system to have its doctrines adopted as the very presuppositions of debate. These are among the "lessons learned," to be applied in future exercises cloaked in humanitarian intent.

The absurdity of the principle of retrospective justification is, surely, recognized at some level. Accordingly, many attempts to justify the NATO bombing take a different tack. One typical version is that "Serbia assaulted Kosovo to squash a separatist Albanian guerrilla movement, but killed 10,000 civilians and drove 700,000 people into refuge in Macedonia and Albania. NATO attacked Serbia from the air in the name of protecting the Albanians from ethnic cleansing [but] killed hundreds of Serb civilians and provoked an exodus of tens of thousands from cities into the countryside."[3] Assuming that order of events, a rationale for the bombing can be constructed. But uncontroversially, the actual order is the opposite.

The device is common in the media, and scholarship often adopts a similar stance. In a widely praised book on the war, historian David Fromkin asserts without argument that the U.S. and its allies acted out of "altruism" and "moral fervor" alone, forging "a new kind of approach to the use of power in world politics" as they "reacted to the deportation of more than a million Kosovars from their homeland" by bombing so as to save them "from horrors of suffering, or from death." He is referring to those expelled as the anticipated consequence of the bombing campaign. Opening her legal defense of the war, law professor Ruth Wedgwood assumes without argument that the objective of the NATO bombing was "to stem Belgrade's expulsion of ethnic Albanians from Kosovo"—namely, the expulsion precipitated by the bombing, and an objective unknown to the military commander and forcefully denied by him. International affairs and security specialist Alan Kuperman writes that in East Timor and Kosovo "the threat of economic sanctions or bombing has provoked a tragic backlash," and "Western intervention arrived too late to prevent the widespread atrocities." In Kosovo the bombing did not arrive "too late to prevent the widespread atrocities" but preceded them and, as anticipated, incited them. In East Timor, no Western action "provoked a tragic backlash." The use of force was not proposed, and even the threat of sanctions was delayed until after the consummation of the atrocities. The "intervention" was by a UN peacekeeping force that entered the Portuguese-administered territory, under UN jurisdiction in principle, after the Western powers finally withdrew their direct support for the Indonesian invasion and its massive atrocities, and its army quickly left.

Such revision of the factual record has been standard procedure throughout. In a typical earlier version, the *New York Times* foreign policy specialist Thomas Friedman wrote at the war's end that, "once the refugee evictions began, ignoring Kosovo would be wrong . . . and therefore using a huge air war for a limited objective was the only thing that made sense." The refugee evictions to which he refers followed the "huge air war," as anticipated. Again, the familiar inversion, which is understandable: without it, defense of state violence becomes difficult indeed.

One commonly voiced retrospective justification is that the resort to force made it possible for Kosovar Albanians to return to their homes; a significant achievement, if we overlook the fact that almost all were driven from their homes in reaction to the bombing. By this reasoning, a preferable alternative—grotesque, but less so than the policy pursued—would have been to wait to see whether the Serbs would carry out the alleged threat, and if they did, to bomb the FRY to ensure the return of the Kosovars, who would have suffered far less harm than they did when expelled under NATO's bombs.

An interesting variant appears in Cambridge University Law Professor Marc Weller's introduction to the volume of documents on Kosovo that he edited. He recognizes that the NATO bombing, which he strongly supported, is in clear violation of international law and might be justified only on the basis of an alleged "right of humanitarian intervention." That justification in turn rests on the assumption that the FRY refusal "to accept a very detailed settlement of the Kosovo issue [the Rambouillet ultimatum] would constitute a circumstance triggering an overwhelming humanitarian emergency." But events on the ground "relieved NATO of having to answer this point," he writes: namely, "the commencement of a massive and pre-planned campaign of forced deportation of what at one stage seemed to be almost the entire ethnic Albanian population of Kosovo just before the bombing campaign commenced."

There are two problems. First, the documentary record, including the volume he edited, provides no evidence for his crucial factual claim, and indeed refutes it (given the absence of evidence despite extensive efforts to unearth it). Second, even if it had been discovered later that the expulsion had commenced before the bombing, that could hardly justify the resort to force, by simple logic. Furthermore, as just discussed, even if the commencement of the expulsion had been known before the bombing (though mysteriously missing from the documentary record), it would have been far preferable to allow the expulsion to proceed, and then to initiate the bombing to ensure the return of those expelled: grotesque, but far less so than what was undertaken. But in the light of the evidence available, all of this is academic, merely an indication of the desperation of the efforts to justify the war.

Were less grotesque options available in March 1999? The burden of proof, of course, is on those who advocate state violence; it is a heavy burden, which there has been no serious attempt to meet. But let us put that aside and look into the range of options available.

An important question raised by Eric Rouleau is whether "Serbian atrocities had reached such proportions as to warrant breaking off the diplomatic process to save the Kosovars from genocide." He observes, "The OSCE's continuing refusal to release the report [on the observations of the KVM monitors from November until their withdrawal] can only strengthen doubts about the truth of that allegation." As noted earlier, the State Department and Tribunal indictments provide no meaningful support for the allegation—not an insignificant fact, since both sought to develop the strongest case. What about the OSCE report released since Rouleau wrote? As noted, the report makes no serious effort to support the allegation, indeed provides little information about the crucial period. Its references in fact confirm the testimony of French KVM member Jacques Prod'homme, which Rouleau cites, that "in the month leading up to the war, during which he moved freely throughout the Peć region, neither he nor his colleagues observed anything that could be described as systematic persecution, either collective or individual murders, burning of houses or deportations." The detailed reports of KVM and other observers omitted from the OSCE review undermine the allegation further, as already discussed.

The crucial allegation remains unsupported, though it is the central component of NATO's case, as even the most dedicated advocates recognize, Weller for example. Once again, it should be stressed that a heavy burden of proof lies on those who put it forth to justify the resort to violence. The discrepancy between what is required and the evidence presented is quite striking; the term "contradiction" would be more apt, particularly when we consider other pertinent evidence, such as the direct testimony of the military commander, General Clark.

Kosovo had been an extremely ugly place in the preceding year. About two thousand were killed according to NATO, mostly Albanians, in the course of a bitter struggle that began in February with KLA actions that the U.S. denounced as "terrorism" and a brutal Serb response. By summer the KLA had taken over about 40 percent of the province, eliciting a vicious reaction by Serb security forces and paramilitaries, targeting the civilian population. According to Albanian Kosovar legal adviser Marc Weller, "within a few days [after the withdrawal of the monitors on March 20], the number of displaced had again risen to over 200,000," figures that conform roughly to U.S. intelligence reports.

Suppose the monitors had not been withdrawn in preparation for the bombing and diplomatic efforts had been pursued. Were such options feasible? Would they have led to an even worse outcome, or perhaps a better one? Since NATO refused to entertain this possibility, we cannot know. But we can at least consider the known facts and ask what they suggest.

Could the KVM monitors have been left in place, preferably strengthened? That seems possible, particularly in the light of the immediate condemnation of the withdrawal by the Serb National Assembly. No argument has been advanced to suggest that the reported increase in atrocities after their withdrawal would have taken place even had they remained, let alone the vast escalation that was the predicted consequence of the bombing signaled by the withdrawal. NATO also made little effort to pursue other peaceful means; even an oil embargo, the core of any serious sanctions regime, was not considered until after the bombing.

The most important question, however, has to do with the diplomatic options. Two proposals were on the table on the eve of the bombing. One was the Rambouillet Accord, presented to Serbia as an ultimatum. The second was Serbia's position, formulated in its March 15 "Revised Draft Agreement" and the Serb National Assembly Resolution of March 23. A serious concern for protecting Kosovars might well have brought into consideration other options as well, including, perhaps, something like the 1992–93 proposal of the Serbian president of Yugoslavia, Dobrica Ćosić, that Kosovo be partitioned, separating itself from Serbia, apart from "a number of Serbian enclaves." At the time, the proposal was rejected by Ibrahim Rugova's Republic of Kosovo, which had declared independence and set up a parallel government; but it might have served as a basis for negotiation in the different circumstances of early 1999. Let us, however, keep to the two official positions of late March: the Rambouillet ultimatum and the Serb Resolution.

It is important and revealing that, with marginal exceptions, the essential contents of both positions were kept from the public eye, apart from dissident media that reach few people. The Serb National Assembly Resolution, though reported at once on the wire services, has remained a virtual secret. There has been little indication even of its existence, let alone its contents. The Resolution condemned the withdrawal of the OSCE monitors and called on the UN and OSCE to facilitate a diplomatic settlement through negotiations "toward the reaching of a political agreement on a wide-ranging autonomy for [Kosovo], with the securing of a full equality of all citizens and ethnic communities and with respect for the sovereignty and territorial integrity of the Republic of Serbia and the Federal Republic of Yugoslavia."

It raised the possibility of an "international presence" of a "size and character" to be determined to carry out the "political accord on the self-rule agreed and accepted by the representatives of all national communities living in [Kosovo]." FRY agreement "to discuss the scope and character of international presence in [Kosovo] to implement the agreement to be accepted in Rambouillet" had been formally conveyed to the negotiators on February 23 and announced by the FRY at a press conference the same day. Whether these proposals had any substance we cannot know, since they were never considered and remain unknown.

Perhaps even more striking is that the Rambouillet ultimatum, though universally described as the peace proposal, was also kept from the public, particularly the provisions that were apparently introduced in the final moments of the Paris peace talks in March after Serbia had expressed agreement with the main political proposals, and that virtually guaranteed rejection. Of particular importance are the terms of the implementation Appendices that accorded to NATO the right of "free and unrestricted passage and unimpeded access throughout the FRY including associated airspace and territorial waters," without limits or obligations or concern for the laws of the country or the jurisdiction of its authorities, who are, however, required to follow NATO orders "on a priority basis and with all appropriate means" (Appendix B).

The Annex was kept from journalists covering the Rambouillet and Paris talks, Robert Fisk reports. "The Serbs say they denounced it at their last Paris press conference—an ill-attended gathering at the Yugoslav Embassy at 11 PM on 18 March." Serb dissidents who took part in the negotiations allege that they were given these conditions on the last day of the Paris talks and that the Russians did not know about them. These provisions were not made available to the British House of Commons until April 1, the first day of the parliamentary recess, a week after the bombing started.

In the negotiations that began after the bombing, NATO abandoned these demands entirely, along with others to which Serbia had been opposed, and there is no mention of them in the final peace agreement. Reasonably, Fisk asks: "What was the real purpose of NATO's last minute demand? Was it a Trojan horse? To save the peace? Or to sabotage it?" Whatever the answer, if the NATO negotiators had been concerned with the fate of the Kosovar Albanians, they would have sought to determine whether diplomacy could succeed if NATO's most provocative, and evidently irrelevant, demands had been withdrawn; the monitoring enhanced, not terminated; and significant sanctions threatened.

When such questions have been raised, leaders of the U.S. and UK negotiating teams have claimed that they were willing to drop the exorbitant demands that they later withdrew, but that the Serbs refused. The claim is hardly credible. There would have been every reason for them to have made such facts public at once. It is interesting that they are not called to account for this startling performance.

Prominent advocates of the bombing have made similar claims. An important example is the commentary on Rambouillet by Marc Weller. Weller ridicules the "extravagant claims" about the implementation Appendices, which he claims were "published along with the agreement," meaning the Draft Agreement dated February 23. Where they were published he does not say, nor does he explain why reporters covering the Rambouillet and Paris talks were unaware of them. As was, it appears, the

British Parliament. The "famous Appendix B," he states, established "the standard terms of a status of forces agreement for KFOR [the planned NATO occupying forces]." He does not explain why the demand was dropped by NATO after the bombing began and is evidently not required by the forces that entered Kosovo under NATO command in June, which are far larger than what was contemplated at Rambouillet and, therefore, should be even more dependent on the status of forces agreement. Also unexplained is the March 15 FRY response to the February 23 Draft Agreement. The FRY response goes through the Draft Agreement in close detail, section by section, proposing extensive changes and deletions throughout, but includes no mention at all of the appendices—the implementation agreements, which, as Weller points out, were by far the most important part and were the subject of the Paris negotiations then underway. One can only view his account with some skepticism, even apart from his casual attitude toward crucial fact, already noted, and his clear commitments. For the moment, these important matters remain buried in obscurity.

Despite official efforts to prevent public awareness of what was happening, the documents were available to any news media that chose to pursue the matter. In the U.S., the extreme (and plainly irrelevant) demand for virtual NATO occupation of the FRY received its first mention at a NATO briefing of April 26, when a question was raised about it, but was quickly dismissed and not pursued. The facts were reported as soon as the demands had been formally withdrawn and had become irrelevant to democratic choice. Immediately after the announcement of the peace accords of June 3, the press quoted the crucial passages of the "take it or leave it" Rambouillet ultimatum, noting that they required that "a purely NATO force was to be given full permission to go anywhere it wanted in Yugoslavia, immune from any legal process," and that "NATO-led troops would have had virtually free access across Yugoslavia, not just Kosovo."[4]

Through the seventy-eight days of bombing, negotiations continued, each side making compromises—described in the U.S. as Serb deceit or capitulation under the bombs. The peace agreement of June 3 was a compromise between the two positions on the table in late March. NATO abandoned its most extreme demands, including those that had apparently undermined the negotiations at the last minute and the wording that had been interpreted as calling for a referendum on independence. Serbia agreed to an "international security presence with substantial NATO participation," the sole mention of NATO in the peace agreement or Security

Council Resolution 1244 affirming it. NATO had no intention of living up to the scraps of paper it had signed and moved at once to violate them, implementing a military occupation of Kosovo under NATO command. When Serbia and Russia insisted on the terms of the formal agreements, they were castigated for their deceit and bombing was renewed to bring them to heel. On June 7, NATO planes again bombed the oil refineries in Novi Sad and Pančevo, both centers of opposition to Milošević. The Pančevo refinery burst into flames, releasing a huge cloud of toxic fumes, shown in a photo accompanying a *New York Times* story of July 14, which discussed the severe economic and health effects. The bombing was not reported, though it was covered by wire services.

It has been argued that Milošević would have tried to evade the terms of an agreement had one been reached in March. The record strongly supports that conclusion, just as it supports the same conclusion about NATO—not only in this case, incidentally; forceful dismantling of formal agreements is the norm on the part of the great powers. As now belatedly recognized, the record also suggests that "it might have been possible [in March] to initiate a genuine set of negotiations—not the disastrous American diktat presented to Milošević at the Rambouillet conference—and to insert a large contingent of outside monitors capable of protecting Albanian and Serb civilians alike."

At least this much seems clear. NATO chose to reject diplomatic options that were not exhausted and to launch a military campaign that had terrible consequences for Kosovar Albanians, as anticipated. Other consequences are of little concern in the West, including the devastation of the civilian economy of Serbia by military operations that severely violate the laws of war. Though the matter was brought to the War Crimes Tribunal long ago, it is hard to imagine that it will be seriously addressed. For similar reasons, there is little likelihood that the Tribunal will pay attention to its 150-page "Indictment Operation Storm: A Prima Facie Case," reviewing the war crimes committed by Croatian forces that drove some two hundred thousand Serbs from Krajina in August 1995, with crucial U.S. involvement that elicited "almost total lack of interest in the US press and in the US Congress," *New York Times* Balkans correspondent David Binder observes.

The suffering of Kosovars did not end with the arrival of the NATO (KFOR) occupying army and the UN mission. Though billions of dollars were readily available for bombing, as of October the U.S. "has yet to pay any of the $37.9 million assessed for the start-up costs of the United Nations civilian operation in Kosovo." By November, "the US Office of Foreign Disaster Assistance has yet to distribute any heavy-duty kits and is only now bringing lumber" for the winter shelter program in Kosovo; the UNHCR and EU humanitarian agency ECHO have also "been dogged with criticism for delays and lack of foresight." The current shortfall for the UN mission is "the price of half a day's bombing," an embittered senior UN official said, and without it "this place will fail," to the great pleasure of Milošević. A November donors' conference of Western governments pledged only $88 million to cover the budget of the UN mission in Kosovo but pledged $1 billion in aid for reconstruction for the next year—public funds that will be transferred to the pockets of private contractors, if there is some resolution of the controversies within NATO about how the contracts are to be distributed. In mid-December the UN mission again pleaded for funds for teachers, police officers, and other civil servants, to little effect.

Despite the limited aid, the appeal of a disaster that can be attributed to an official enemy and exploited (on curious grounds) "to show why 78 days of airstrikes against Serbian forces and infrastructure were necessary" has been sufficient to bring severe cutbacks in aid elsewhere. The U.S. Senate is planning to cut tens of millions of dollars from Africa-related programs. Denmark has reduced non-Kosovo assistance by 26 percent. International Medical Corps is suspending its Angola program, having raised $5 million for Kosovo while it hunts, in vain, for $1.5 million for Angola, where 1.6 million displaced people face starvation. The World Food Program announced that it would have to curtail its programs for 2 million refugees in Sierra Leone, Liberia, and Guinea, having received less than 20 percent of requested funding. The same fate awaits 4 million starving people in Africa's Great Lakes region—whose circumstances are not unrelated to Western actions over many years and refusal to act at critical moments. UNHCR expenditures per refugee in the Balkans are eleven times as high as in Africa. "The hundreds of millions of dollars spent on Kosovo refugees and the crush of aid agencies eager to spend it 'was almost an obscenity,' said Randolph Kent," who moved from UN programs in the Balkans to East Africa. President Clinton held a meeting with leading aid agencies "to emphasize his own enthusiasm for aid to Kosovo."

All of this is against the background of very sharp reductions in aid in the U.S., now "at the height of its glory" (David Fromkin), the leadership basking in adulation for their historically unprecedented "altruism," as they virtually disappear from the list of donors to the poor and miserable.

The OSCE inquiry provides a detailed record of crimes committed under NATO military occupation. Though these do not begin to compare with the crimes committed by Serbia under NATO bombardment, they are not insignificant. The occupied province is filled with "lawlessness that has left violence unchecked," much of it attributed to the KLA, OSCE reports, while "impunity has reigned instead of justice." Albanian opponents of the "new order" under "KLA dominance," including officials of the "rebel group's principal political rival," have been kidnapped, murdered, targeted in grenade attacks, and otherwise harassed and ordered to withdraw from politics. The one selection from the OSCE reports in the *New York Times* concerns the town of Prizren, near the Albanian border. It was attacked by Serbs on March 28, but "the overall result is that far more damage has been caused . . . after the war than during it." British military police report involvement of the Albanian mafia in grenade attacks and other crimes, among such acts as murder of elderly women by "men describing themselves as KLA representatives."

The Serb minority has been largely expelled. Robert Fisk reports that "the number of Serbs killed in the five months since the war comes close to that of Albanians murdered by Serbs in the five months before NATO began its bombardment in March," so available evidence indicates; recall that the UN reported "65 violent deaths" of civilians (Albanian and Serb primarily) in the two months before the withdrawal of the monitors and the bombing. Murders are not investigated, even the murder of a Serb employee of the International Tribunal. The Croat community "left en masse" in October. In November, "the president of the tiny Jewish community in Priština, Cedra Prlincevic, left for Belgrade after denouncing 'a pogrom against the non-Albanian population.'" Amnesty International reported at the year's end that "Violence against Serbs, Roma, Muslim Slavs, and moderate Albanians in Kosovo has increased dramatically over the past month," including "murder, abductions, violent attacks, intimidation, and house burning . . . on a daily basis," as well as torture and rape, and attacks on independent Albanian media and political organizations in what appears to be "an organized campaign to silence moderate voices in ethnic Albanian society," all under the eyes of NATO forces.

KFOR officers report that their orders are to disregard crimes: "Of course it's mad," a French commander said, "but those are the orders, from NATO, from above." NATO forces also "seem completely indifferent" to attacks by "armed ethnic Albanian raiders" across the Serb-Kosovo border "to terrorize border settlements, steal wood or livestock, and, in some cases, to kill," leaving towns abandoned.

Current indications are that Kosovo under NATO occupation has reverted to what was developing in the early 1980s, after the death of Tito, when nationalist forces undertook to create an "ethnically clean Albanian republic," taking over Serb lands, attacking churches, and engaging in "protracted violence" to attain the goal of an "ethnically pure" Albanian region, with "almost weekly incidents of rape, arson, pillage and industrial sabotage, most seemingly designed to drive Kosovo's remaining indigenous Slavs . . . out of the province." This "seemingly intractable" problem, another phase in an ugly history of intercommunal violence, led to Milošević's characteristically brutal response, withdrawing Kosovo's autonomy and the heavy federal subsidies on which it depended and imposing an "Apartheid" regime. Kosovo may also come to resemble Bosnia, "a den of thieves and tax cheats" with no functioning economy, dominated by "a wealthy criminal class that wields enormous political influence and annually diverts hundreds of millions of dollars in potential tax revenue to itself." Much worse may be in store as independence for Kosovo becomes entangled in pressures for a "greater Albania," with dim portents.

The poorer countries of the region have incurred enormous losses from the blocking of the Danube by bombing at Novi Sad, another center of opposition to Milošević. They were already suffering from protectionist barriers that "prevent the ships from plying their trade in the EU," as well as "a barrage of Western quotas and tariffs on their exports." But "blockage of the [Danube] is actually a boon" for Western Europe, particularly Germany, which benefits from increased activity on the Rhine and at Atlantic ports.

There are other winners. At the war's end, the business press described "the real winners" as Western military industry, meaning high-tech industry generally. Moscow is looking forward to a "banner year for Russian weapons exports" as "the world is rearming apprehensively largely thanks to NATO's Balkans adventure," seeking a deterrent, as widely predicted during the war. More important, the U.S. was able to enforce its domination over the strategic Balkans region, displacing EU initiatives at least temporarily, a primary reason for the insistence that the operation be in the hands of NATO, a U.S. subsidiary. A destitute Serbia remains the last holdout, probably not for long.

A further consequence is another blow to the fragile principles of world order. The NATO action represents a threat to the "very core of the international security system" founded on the UN Charter, Secretary-General Kofi Annan observed in his annual report to the UN in September. That matters little to the rich and powerful, who will act as they please, rejecting World Court decisions and vetoing Security Council resolutions if that becomes necessary; it is useful to remember that, contrary to much mythology, the U.S. has been far in the lead in vetoing Security Council resolutions on a wide range of issues, including terror and aggression, ever since it lost control of the UN in the course of decolonization, with Britain second and France a distant third. But the traditional victims take these matters more seriously, as the global reaction to the Kosovo war indicated.

The essential point—not very obscure—is that the world faces two choices with regard to the use of force: (1) some semblance of world order, either the Charter or something better if it can gain a degree of legitimacy; or (2) the powerful states do as they wish unless constrained from within, guided by interests of power and profit, as in the past. It makes good sense to struggle for a better world, but not to indulge in pretense and illusion about the one in which we live.

Archival and other sources should provide a good deal more information about the latest Balkans war. Any conclusions reached today are at best partial and tentative. As of now, however, the "lessons learned" do not appear to be particularly attractive.

★ Originally published as: Noam Chomsky, "A Review of NATO's War over Kosovo," *Z Magazine*, April–May 2001.

Notes

1   For a detailed discussion of this issue, along with a discussion of East Timor in the broader context of "humanitarian intervention" see Noam Chomsky, *A New Generation Draws the Line: Kosovo, East Timor and the Standards of the West* (London: Verso, 2000).

2   BBC, *Panorama*, "War Room," April 19, 1999; quoted also in Noam Chomsky, "In Retrospect," *Z Magazine*, April 1, 2000, available also at https://zcomm.org/zmagazine/in-retrospect-by-noam-chomsky/.

3   Daniel Williams, "No Exit for the Chechens," *Washington Post*, October 30, 1999.

4   BBC Summary of World Broadcasts, March 25, 1999.

Humanitarian Imperialism: The New Doctrine of Imperial Right

Jean Bricmont's concept "humanitarian imperialism" succinctly captures a dilemma that has faced Western leaders and the Western intellectual community since the collapse of the Soviet Union. From the origins of the Cold War, there was a reflexive justification for every resort to force and terror, subversion and economic strangulation: the acts were undertaken in defense against what John F. Kennedy called "the monolithic and ruthless conspiracy" based in the Kremlin (or sometimes in Beijing), a force of unmitigated evil dedicated to extending its brutal sway over the entire world. The formula covered just about every imaginable case of intervention, no matter what the facts might be. But with the Soviet Union gone, either the policies would have to change or new justifications would have to be devised. It became clear very quickly which course would be followed, casting new light on what had come before and on the institutional basis of policy.

The end of the Cold War unleashed an impressive flow of rhetoric assuring the world that the West would now be free to pursue its traditional dedication to freedom, democracy, justice, and human rights unhampered by superpower rivalry, though there were some—called "realists" in international relations theory—who warned that in "granting idealism a near exclusive hold on our foreign policy," we may be going too far and might harm our interests.[1] Such notions as "humanitarian intervention" and "the responsibility to protect" soon came to be salient features of Western discourse on policy, commonly described as establishing a "new norm" in international affairs.

The millennium ended with an extraordinary display of self-congratulation on the part of Western intellectuals, awestruck at the sight of the "idealistic new world bent on ending inhumanity," which had entered a "noble phase" in its foreign policy with a "saintly glow" as for the first time in history a state is dedicated to "principles and values," acting from "altruism" and "moral fervor" alone as the leader of the "enlightened states," hence free to use force where its leaders "believe it to be just"—only a small sample of a deluge from respected liberal voices.[2]

Several questions immediately come to mind. First, how does the self-image conform to the historical record prior to the end of the Cold War? If it does not, then what reason would there be to expect a sudden dedication to "granting idealism a near exclusive hold on our foreign policy," or any hold at all? And how in fact did policies change with the superpower enemy gone? A prior question is whether such considerations should even arise.

There are two views about the significance of the historical record. The attitude of those who celebrate the "emerging norms" is expressed clearly by one of their most distinguished scholar/advocates, international relations professor Thomas Weiss: critical examination of the record, he writes, is nothing more than "sound-bites and invectives about Washington's historically evil foreign policy," hence "easy to ignore."[3]

A conflicting stance is that policy decisions substantially flow from institutional structures, and since these remain stable, examination of the record provides valuable insight into the "emerging norms" and the contemporary world. That is the stance that Bricmont adopts in his study of "the ideology of human rights" and that I will adopt here.

There is no space for a review of the record, but just to illustrate, let us keep to the Kennedy administration, the left-liberal extreme of the political spectrum, with an unusually large component of liberal intellectuals in policymaking positions. During these years, the standard formula was invoked to justify the invasion of South Vietnam in 1962, laying the basis for one of the great crimes of the twentieth century.

By then the U.S.-imposed client regime could no longer control the indigenous resistance evoked by massive state terror, which had killed tens of thousands of people. Kennedy therefore sent the U.S. Air Force to begin regular bombing of South Vietnam, authorized napalm and chemical warfare to destroy crops and ground cover, and initiated the programs that drove millions of South Vietnamese peasants to urban slums or to camps where they were surrounded by barbed wire to "protect" them from the South Vietnamese resistance forces that they were supporting, as Washington knew. All in defense against the two Great Satans, Russia and China, or the "Sino-Soviet axis."[4]

In the traditional domains of U.S. power, the same formula led to Kennedy's shift of the mission of the Latin American military from "hemispheric defense"—a holdover from the Second World War—to "internal security." The consequences were immediate. In the words of Charles Maechling—who led U.S. counterinsurgency and internal defense planning through the Kennedy and early Johnson years—U.S. policy shifted from toleration "of the rapacity and cruelty of the Latin American military" to "direct complicity" in their crimes, to U.S. support for "the methods of Heinrich Himmler's extermination squads."

One critical case was the Kennedy administration's preparation of the military coup in Brazil to overthrow the mildly social democratic Goulart government. The planned coup took place shortly after Kennedy's assassination, establishing the first of a series of vicious National Security States and setting off a plague of repression throughout the continent that lasted through Reagan's terrorist wars that devastated Central America in the 1980s. With the same justification, Kennedy's 1962 military mission to Colombia advised the government to resort to "paramilitary, sabotage and/or terrorist activities against known communist proponents," actions that "should be backed by the United States." In the Latin American context, the phrase "known communist proponents" referred to labor leaders, priests organizing peasants, human rights activists, in fact anyone committed to social change in violent and repressive societies.

These principles were quickly incorporated into the training and practices of the military. The respected president of the Colombian Permanent Committee for Human Rights, former minister of foreign affairs Alfredo Vásquez Carrizosa, wrote that the Kennedy administration "took great pains to transform our regular armies into counterinsurgency brigades, accepting the new strategy of the death squads," ushering in "what is known in Latin America as the National Security Doctrine . . . not defense against an external enemy, but a way to make the military establishment the masters of the game [with] the right to combat the internal enemy, as set forth in the Brazilian doctrine, the Argentine doctrine, the Uruguayan doctrine, and the Colombian doctrine: it is the right to fight and to exterminate social workers, trade unionists, men, and women who are not supportive of the establishment, and who are assumed to be communist extremists. And this could mean anyone, including human rights activists such as myself."

In 2002, an Amnesty International mission to protect human rights defenders worldwide began with a visit to Colombia, chosen because of its extreme record of state-backed violence against these courageous activists, as well as labor leaders, more of whom were killed in Colombia than in the rest of the world combined, not to speak of campesinos, indigenous people, and Afro-Colombians, the most tragic victims. As a member of the delegation, I was able to meet with a group of human rights activists in Vásquez Carrizosa's heavily guarded home in Bogotá, hearing their painful reports and later taking testimonials in the field, a shattering experience.

The same formula sufficed for the campaign of subversion and violence that placed newly independent Guyana under the rule of the cruel dictator Forbes Burnham. It was also invoked to justify Kennedy's campaigns against Cuba after the failed Bay of Pigs invasion. In his biography of Robert Kennedy, the eminent liberal historian and Kennedy advisor Arthur Schlesinger writes that the task of bringing "the terrors of the earth" to Cuba was assigned by the president to his brother, Robert Kennedy, who took it as his highest priority. The terrorist campaign continued at least through the 1990s, though in later years the U.S. government did not carry out the terrorist operations itself but only provided support for them and a haven for terrorists and their commanders, among them the notorious Orlando Bosch and, joining him recently, Luis Posada Carriles. Commentators have been polite enough not to remind us of the Bush Doctrine: "those who harbor terrorists are as guilty as the terrorists themselves" and must be treated accordingly, by bombing and invasion. This doctrine has "unilaterally revoked the sovereignty of states that provide sanctuary to terrorists," Harvard international affairs specialist Graham Allison observes, and has "already become a de facto rule of international relations"—with the usual exceptions.

Internal documents of the Kennedy-Johnson years reveal that a leading concern in the case of Cuba was its "successful defiance" of U.S. policies tracing back to the Monroe Doctrine of 1823, which declared (but could not yet implement) U.S. control over the hemisphere. It was feared that Cuba's "successful defiance," particularly if accompanied by successful independent development, might encourage others suffering from comparable conditions to pursue a similar path, the rational version of the domino theory that is a persistent feature of policy formation. For that reason, the documentary record reveals, it was necessary to punish the civilian population severely until they overthrew the offending government.

This is a bare sample of a few years of intervention under the most liberal U.S. administration, justified to the public in defensive terms. The broader record is much the same. With similar pretexts, the Russian dictatorship justified its harsh control of its Eastern European dungeon.

The reasons for intervention, subversion, terror, and repression are not obscure. They are summarized accurately by Patrice McSherry in the most careful scholarly study of Operation Condor, the international terrorist operation established with U.S. backing in Pinochet's Chile: "the Latin American militaries, normally acting with the support of the U.S. government, overthrew civilian governments and destroyed other centers of democratic power in their societies (parties, unions, universities, and constitutionalist sectors of the armed forces) precisely when the class orientation of the state was about to change or was in the process of change, shifting state power to non-elite social sectors. . . . Preventing such transformations of the state was a key objective of Latin American elites, and U.S. officials considered it a vital national security interest as well."[5]

It is easy to demonstrate that what are termed "national security interests" have only an incidental relation to the security of the nation, though they have a very close relation to the interests of dominant sectors within the imperial state and to the general state interest of ensuring obedience.

The U.S. is an unusually open society. Hence there is no difficulty documenting the leading principles of global strategy since the Second World War. Even before the U.S. entered the war, high-level planners and analysts concluded that in the postwar world the U.S. should seek "to hold unquestioned power," acting to ensure the "limitation of any exercise of sovereignty" by states that might interfere with its global designs. They recognized further that "the foremost requirement" to secure these ends was "the rapid fulfillment of a program of complete rearmament," then as now a central component of "an integrated policy to achieve military and economic supremacy for the United States." At the time, these ambitions were limited to "the non-German world," which was to be organized under the U.S. aegis as a "Grand Area," including the Western hemisphere, the former British Empire, and the Far East. As Russia beat back the Nazi armies after Stalingrad, and it became increasingly clear that Germany would be defeated, the plans were extended to include as much of Eurasia as possible.

A more extreme version of the largely invariant grand strategy is that no challenge can be tolerated to the "power, position, and prestige of the United States," so the American Society of International Law was instructed by the prominent liberal statesman Dean Acheson, one of the main architects of the postwar world. He was speaking in 1963, shortly after the missile crisis brought the world to the brink of nuclear war. There are few basic changes in the guiding conceptions as we proceed to the Bush II doctrine, which elicited unusual mainstream protest, not because of its basic content but because of its brazen style and arrogance, as was pointed out by Clinton's secretary of state Madeleine Albright, who was well aware of Clinton's similar doctrine.

The collapse of the "monolithic and ruthless conspiracy" led to a change of tactics but not fundamental policy. That was clearly understood by policy analysts. Dimitri Simes, senior associate at the Carnegie Endowment for International Peace, observed that Gorbachev's initiatives would "liberate American foreign policy from the straightjacket imposed by superpower hostility."[6] He identified three major components of "liberation." First, the U.S. would be able to shift NATO costs to its European competitors, one way to avert the traditional concern that Europe might seek an independent path. Second, the U.S. can end "the manipulation of America by third world nations." The manipulation of the rich by the undeserving poor has always been a serious problem, particularly acute with regard to Latin America, which in the preceding five years had transferred some $150 billion to the industrial West in addition to $100 billion of capital flight, amounting to twenty-five times the total value of the Alliance for Progress and fifteen times the Marshall Plan.

This huge hemorrhage is part of a complicated system whereby Western banks and Latin American elites enrich themselves at the expense of the general population of Latin America, who are then saddled with the "debt crisis" that results from these manipulations.

But thanks to Gorbachev's capitulation the U.S. can now resist "unwarranted third world demands for assistance" and take a stronger stand when confronting "defiant third world debtors."

The third and most significant component of "liberation," Simes continues, is that the decline in the "Soviet threat . . . makes military power more useful as a United States foreign policy instrument . . . against those who contemplate challenging important American interests." America's hands will now be "untied" and Washington can benefit from "greater reliance on military force in a crisis."

The Bush I administration, then in office, at once made clear its understanding of the end of the Soviet threat. A few months after the fall of the Berlin Wall, the administration released a new National Security Strategy. On the domestic front, it called for strengthening "the defense industrial base," creating incentives "to invest in new facilities and equipment as well as in research and development." The phrase "defense industrial base" is a euphemism referring to the high-tech economy, which relies crucially on the dynamic state sector to socialize cost and risk and eventually privatize profit—sometimes decades later, as in the case of computers and the internet. The government understands well that the U.S. economy is remote from the free market model that is hailed in doctrine and imposed on those who are too weak to resist, a traditional theme of economic history, recently reviewed insightfully by international economist Ha-Joon Chang.[7]

In the international domain, the Bush I National Security Strategy recognized that "the more likely demands for the use of our military forces may not involve the Soviet Union and may be in the Third World, where new capabilities and approaches may be required." The U.S. must concentrate attention on "lower-order threats like terrorism, subversion, insurgency, and drug trafficking [which] are menacing the United States, its citizenry, and its interests in new ways." "Forces will have to accommodate to the austere environment, immature basing structure, and significant ranges often encountered in the Third World." "Training and research and development" will have to be "better attuned to the needs of low-intensity conflict," crucially, counterinsurgency in the Third World. With the Soviet Union gone from the scene, the world "has now evolved from a 'weapon rich environment' [Russia] to a 'target rich environment' [the South]." The U.S. will face "increasingly capable Third World Threats," military planners elaborated.

Consequently, the National Security Strategy explained, the U.S. must maintain a huge military system and the ability to project power quickly worldwide, with primary reliance on nuclear weapons, which, Clinton planners explained, "cast a shadow over any crisis or conflict" and permit free use of conventional forces. The reason is no longer the vanished Soviet threat, but rather "the growing technological sophistication of Third World conflicts." That is particularly true in the Middle East, where the "threats to our interests" that have required direct military engagement "could not be laid at the Kremlin's door," contrary to decades of pretense, no longer useful with the Soviet Union gone. In reality, the "threat to our interests" had always been indigenous nationalism. The fact was sometimes acknowledged, as when Robert Komer, the architect of President Carter's Rapid Deployment Force (later Central Command), aimed primarily at the Middle East, testified before Congress in 1980 that its most likely role was not to resist a (highly implausible) Soviet attack but to deal with indigenous and regional unrest, in particular, the "radical nationalism" that has always been a primary concern, worldwide.

The term "radical" falls into the same category as "known Communist proponent." It does not mean radical. Rather, it means not under our control. Thus Iraq at the time was not radical. On the contrary, Saddam continued to be a favored friend and ally well after he had carried out his most horrendous atrocities (Halabja, al-Anfal, and others) and after the end of the war with Iran, for which he had received substantial support from the Reagan administration, among others. In keeping with these warm relations, in 1989, President Bush invited Iraqi nuclear engineers to the U.S. for advanced training in nuclear weapons development and in early 1990 sent a high-level Senate delegation to Iraq to convey his personal greetings to his friend Saddam. The delegation was led by Senate majority leader Bob Dole, later Republican presidential candidate, and included other prominent senators. They brought Bush's personal greetings, advised Saddam that he should disregard criticisms he might hear from some segments of the irresponsible American press, and assured him that the government would do what it could to end these unfortunate practices.

A few months later Saddam invaded Kuwait, disregarding orders, or perhaps misunderstanding ambiguous signals from the State Department. That was a real crime, and he instantly switched from respected friend to evil incarnate.

It is instructive to consider the reaction to Saddam's invasion of Kuwait, both the rhetorical outrage and the military response, a devastating blow to Iraqi civilian society that left the tyranny firmly in place. The events and their interpretation reveal a good deal about the continuities of policy after the collapse of the Soviet Union and about the intellectual and moral culture that sustains policy decisions.

Saddam's invasion of Kuwait in August 1990 was the second case of post–Cold War aggression. The first was Bush's invasion of Panama a few weeks after the fall of the Berlin Wall, in November 1989. The Panama invasion was scarcely more than a footnote to a long and sordid history, but it differed from earlier exercises in some respects.

A basic difference was explained by Elliott Abrams, then a high official responsible for Near East and North African Affairs, now charged with "promoting democracy" under Bush II, particularly in the Middle East. Echoing Simes, Abrams observed that "developments in Moscow have lessened the prospect for a small operation to escalate into a superpower conflict."[8] The resort to force, as in Panama, was more feasible than before, thanks to the disappearance of the Soviet deterrent. Similar reasoning applied to the reaction to Iraq's invasion of Kuwait. With the Soviet deterrent in place, the U.S. and Britain would have been unlikely to risk placing huge forces in the desert and carrying out the military operations in the manner they did.

The goal of the Panama invasion was to kidnap Manuel Noriega, a petty thug who was brought to Florida and sentenced for narcotrafficking and other crimes that were mostly committed when he was on the CIA payroll. But he had become disobedient—for example, failing to support Washington's terrorist war against Nicaragua with sufficient enthusiasm—so he had to go. The Soviet threat could no longer be invoked in the standard fashion, so the action was depicted as defense of the U.S. from Hispanic narcotrafficking, which was overwhelmingly in the domain of Washington's Colombian allies. While presiding over the invasion, President Bush announced new loans to Iraq to achieve the "goal of increasing U.S. exports and put us in a better position to deal with Iraq regarding its human rights record"—so the State Department replied to the few inquiries from Congress, apparently without irony. The media wisely chose silence.

Victorious aggressors do not investigate their crimes, so the toll of Bush's Panama invasion is not known with any precision. It appears, however, that it was considerably more deadly than Saddam's invasion of Kuwait a few months later. According to Panamanian human rights groups, the U.S. bombing of the El Chorillo slums and other civilian targets killed several thousand poor people, far more than the estimated toll of the invasion of Kuwait. The matter is of no interest in the West, but Panamanians have not forgotten. In December 2007, Panama once again declared a Day of Mourning to commemorate the U.S. invasion; it scarcely merited a flicker of an eyelid in the U.S.

Also gone from history is the fact that Washington's greatest fear when Saddam invaded Kuwait was that he would imitate the U.S. invasion of Panama. Colin Powell, then chairman of the Joint Chiefs of Staff, warned that Saddam "will withdraw, [putting] his puppet in. Everyone in the Arab world will be happy." In contrast, when Washington partially withdrew from Panama after putting its puppet in, Latin Americans were far from happy.

The invasion aroused great anger throughout the region, so much so that the new regime was expelled from the Group of Eight Latin American democracies as a country under military occupation. Washington was well aware, Latin American scholar Stephen Ropp observed, "that removing the mantle of United States protection would quickly result in a civilian or military overthrow of Endara and his supporters"—that is, the regime of bankers, businessmen, and narcotraffickers installed by Bush's invasion.

Even that government's own Human Rights Commission charged four years later that the right to self-determination and sovereignty of the Panamanian people continues to be violated by the "state of occupation by a foreign army." Fear that Saddam would mimic the invasion of Panama appears to be the main reason why Washington blocked diplomacy and insisted on war, with almost complete media cooperation—and, as is often the case, in violation of public opinion, which on the eve of the invasion, overwhelmingly supported a regional conference to settle the confrontation along with other outstanding Middle East issues. That was essentially Saddam's proposal at the time, though only those who read fringe dissident publications or conducted their own research projects could have been aware of that.

Washington's concern for human rights in Iraq was dramatically revealed, once again, shortly after the invasion, when Bush authorized Saddam to crush a Shi'ite rebellion in the South that would probably have overthrown him. Official reasoning was outlined by Thomas Friedman, then chief diplomatic correspondent of the *New York Times*. Washington hoped for "the best of all worlds," Friedman explained: "an iron-fisted Iraqi junta without Saddam Hussein" that would restore the status quo ante, when Saddam's "iron fist . . . held Iraq together, much to the satisfaction of the American allies Turkey and Saudi Arabia"—and, of course, the boss in Washington. But this happy outcome proved unfeasible, so the masters of the region had to settle for second best: the same "iron fist" they had been fortifying all along. Veteran *Times* Middle East correspondent Alan Cowell added that the rebels failed because "very few people outside Iraq wanted them to win": the U.S. and "its Arab coalition partners" came to "a strikingly unanimous view [that] whatever the sins of the Iraqi leader, he offered the West and the region a better hope for his country's stability than did those who have suffered his repression."

The term "stability" is used here in its standard technical meaning: subordination to Washington's will. There is no contradiction, for example, when liberal commentator James Chace, former editor of *Foreign Affairs*, explains that the U.S. sought to "destabilize a freely elected Marxist government in Chile" because "we were determined to seek stability" (under the Pinochet dictatorship).

With the Soviet pretext gone, the record of criminal intervention continued much as before. One useful index is military aid. As is well known in scholarship, U.S. aid "has tended to flow disproportionately to Latin American governments which torture their citizens . . . to the hemisphere's relatively egregious violators of fundamental human rights." That includes military aid, is independent of need, and runs through the Carter period.[9] More wide-ranging studies by economist Edward Herman found a similar correlation worldwide, also suggesting a plausible explanation. He found that aid, not surprisingly, is correlated with improvement in the investment climate.

Such improvement is often achieved by murdering priests and union leaders, massacring peasants trying to organize, blowing up the independent press, and so on. The result is a secondary correlation between aid and egregious violation of human rights. It would be wrong, then, to conclude that U.S. leaders (like their counterparts elsewhere) prefer torture; rather, it has little weight in comparison with more important values. These studies precede the Reagan years, when the questions were not worth posing because the correlations were so overwhelmingly obvious.

The pattern continued after the Cold War. Outside of Israel and Egypt, a separate category, the leading recipient of U.S. aid as the Cold War ended was El Salvador, which, along with Guatemala, was the site of the most extreme terrorist violence of the horrifying Reagan years in Central America, almost entirely attributable to the state terrorist forces armed and trained by Washington, as subsequent Truth Commissions documented. Washington was barred by Congress from providing aid directly to the Guatemalan murderers. They were effusively lauded by Reagan, but he had to turn to an international terror network of proxy states to fill the gap. In El Salvador, however, the U.S. could carry out the terrorist war unhampered by such annoyances.

One prime target was the Catholic Church, which had committed a grave sin: it began to take the Gospels seriously and adopted "the preferential option for the poor." It therefore had to be destroyed by U.S.-backed violence, with strong Vatican support. The decade opened with the 1980 assassination of Archbishop Romero while saying mass, a few days after he had sent a letter to President Carter pleading with him to cut off aid to the murderous junta, aid that "will surely increase injustice here and sharpen the repression that has been unleashed against the people's organizations fighting to defend their most fundamental human rights."

Aid soon flowed, paving the way for "a war of extermination and genocide against a defenseless civilian population," as the aftermath was described by Archbishop Romero's successor. The decade ended when the elite Atlacatl Brigade, armed and trained by Washington, blew out the brains of six leading Latin American intellectuals, Jesuit priests, after compiling a bloody record of the usual victims. None of this enters elite Western consciousness, by virtue of "wrong agency."

By the time Clinton took over, a political settlement had been reached in El Salvador, so it lost its position as leading recipient of U.S. military aid. It was replaced by Turkey, then conducting some of the worst atrocities of the 1990s, targeting its harshly oppressed Kurdish population. Tens of thousands were killed, 3,500 towns and villages were destroyed, huge numbers of refugees fled (three million, according to analyses by Kurdish human rights organizations), large areas were laid waste, dissidents were imprisoned, hideous torture and other atrocities were standard fare. Clinton provided 80 percent of the needed arms, including high-tech equipment used for savage crimes. In the single year 1997, Clinton sent more military aid to Turkey than in the entire Cold War period combined before the counterinsurgency campaign began. Media and commentary remained silent, with the rarest of exceptions.

By 1999, state terror had largely achieved its goals, so Turkey was replaced as leading recipient of military aid by Colombia, which had by far the worst human rights record in the hemisphere, as the programs of coordinated state-paramilitary terror inaugurated by Kennedy took a shocking toll.

Meanwhile other major atrocities continued to receive full support. One of the most extreme was the sanctions against Iraqi civilians after the large-scale demolition of Iraq in the bombing of 1991, which also destroyed power stations and sewage and water facilities, effectively a form of biological warfare. The horrific impact of the U.S.-UK sanctions, formally implemented by the UN, aroused so much public concern that in 1996 a humane modification was introduced: the "oil for food" program, which permitted Iraq to use profits from oil exports for the needs of its suffering people.

The first director of the program, the distinguished international diplomat Denis Halliday, resigned in protest after two years, declaring the program to be "genocidal." He was replaced by another distinguished international diplomat, Hans von Sponeck, who resigned two years later, charging that the program violated the Genocide Convention. Sponeck's resignation was followed immediately by that of Jutta Burghardt, in charge of the UN Food Program, who joined the declaration of protest by Halliday and Sponeck.

To mention only one figure, "During the years when the sanctions were imposed, from 1990 to 2003, there was a sharp increase in mortality from 56 per thousand children under five years of age in the early 1990s to 131 per thousand under five years of age at the beginning of the new century," and "everyone can easily understand that this was due to the economic sanctions" (Sponeck). Massacres of that scale are rare, and to acknowledge this one would be doctrinally difficult. Accordingly, great efforts were made to shift the blame to UN incompetence, "the largest fraud ever recorded in history" (*Wall Street Journal*). The fraudulent "fraud" was quickly exposed; it turned out that Washington and U.S. business were the major culprits. But the charges were too valuable to be allowed to vanish.

Halliday and Sponeck had numerous investigators all over Iraq, which enabled them to know more about the country than any other Westerners. They were barred from the U.S. media during the buildup to the war. The Clinton administration also prevented Sponeck from informing the UN Security Council, which was technically responsible, about the effects of the sanctions on the population. "This man in Baghdad is paid to work, not to speak," State Department spokesman James Rubin explained. U.S.-UK media evidently agree. Sponeck's carefully documented account of the impact of the U.S.-UK sanctions was published in 2006, to resounding silence.[10]

The sanctions devastated the civilian society, killing hundreds of thousands of people while strengthening the tyrant, compelling the population to rely on him for survival, and probably saving him from the fate of other mass murderers and torturers who were supported to the end of their bloody rule by the U.S., the United Kingdom, and their allies: Ceauşescu, Suharto, Mobutu, Marcos, and a rogues' gallery of others, to which new names are regularly added. The studied refusal to give Iraqis an opportunity to take their fate into their own hands by releasing the stranglehold of the sanctions, as Halliday and Sponeck recommended, eliminates whatever thin shred of justification for the invasion may be concocted by apologists for state violence.

Also continuing without change through the 1990s was strong U.S.-UK support for General Suharto of Indonesia—"our kind of guy," the Clinton administration happily announced when he was welcomed in Washington. Suharto had been a particular favorite of the West ever since he took power in 1965, presiding over a "staggering mass slaughter" that was "a gleam of light in Asia," the *New York Times* reported, while praising Washington for keeping its crucial role hidden so as not to embarrass the "Indonesian moderates" who took over.

The general reaction in the West was unconcealed euphoria after the mass slaughter, which the CIA compared to the crimes of Hitler, Stalin, and Mao. Suharto opened the country's wealth to Western exploitation, compiled one of the worst human rights records in the world, and also won the world record for corruption, far surpassing Mobutu and other Western favorites. On the side, he invaded the former Portuguese colony of East Timor in 1975, carrying out one of the worst crimes of the late twentieth century, leaving perhaps one-quarter of the population dead and the country ravaged.

From the first moment, he benefitted from decisive U.S. diplomatic and military support, joined by Britain as atrocities peaked in 1978, while other Western powers also sought to gain what they could by backing virtual genocide in East Timor. The U.S.-UK flow of arms and training of the most vicious counterinsurgency units continued without change through 1999, as Indonesian atrocities escalated once again, far beyond anything in Kosovo at the same time, before the NATO bombing. Australia, which had the most detailed information on the atrocities, also participated actively in training the most murderous elite units.

In April 1999, there was a series of particularly brutal massacres, as in Liquiçá, where at least sixty people were murdered when they took refuge in a church. The U.S. reacted at once. Admiral Dennis Blair, U.S. Pacific commander, met with Indonesian army chief general Wiranto, who supervised the atrocities, assuring him of U.S. support and assistance and proposing a new U.S. training mission, one of several such contacts at the time. Highly credible church sources estimated that three to five thousand were murdered from February through July.

In August 1999, in a UN-run referendum, the population voted overwhelmingly for independence, a remarkable act of courage. The Indonesian army and its paramilitary associates reacted by destroying the capital city of Dili and driving hundreds of thousands of the survivors into the hills. The U.S. and Britain were unimpressed. Washington lauded "the value of the years of training given to Indonesia's future military leaders in the U.S.

and the millions of dollars in military aid for Indonesia," the press reported, urging more of the same for Indonesia and throughout the world. A senior diplomat in Jakarta explained succinctly that "Indonesia matters and East Timor doesn't." While the remnants of Dili were smoldering and the expelled population were starving in the hills, Defense Secretary William Cohen, on September 9, reiterated the official U.S. position that occupied East Timor "is the responsibility of the Government of Indonesia, and we don't want to take that responsibility away from them."

A few days later, under intense international and domestic pressure (much of it from influential right-wing Catholics), Clinton quietly informed the Indonesian generals that the game was over, and they instantly withdrew, allowing an Australian-led UN peacekeeping force to enter the country unopposed. The lesson is crystal clear. To end the aggression and virtual genocide of the preceding quarter-century there was no need to bomb Jakarta, to impose sanctions, or in fact to do anything except to stop participating actively in the crimes. The lesson, however, cannot be drawn, for evident doctrinal reasons. Amazingly, the events have been reconstructed as a remarkable success of humanitarian intervention in September 1999, evidence of the enthralling "emerging norms" inaugurated by the "enlightened states." One can only wonder whether a totalitarian state could achieve anything comparable.

The British record was even more grotesque. The Labor government continued to deliver Hawk jets to Indonesia as late as September 23, 1999, two weeks after the European Union had imposed an embargo, three days after the Australian peacekeeping force had landed, well after it had been revealed that these aircraft had been deployed over East Timor once again, this time as part of the pre-referendum intimidation operation. Under New Labour, Britain became the leading supplier of arms to Indonesia, over the strong protests of Amnesty International, Indonesian dissidents, and Timorese victims. The reasons were explained by Foreign Secretary Robin Cook, the author of the new "ethical foreign policy."

The arms shipments were appropriate because "the government is committed to the maintenance of a strong defense industry, which is a strategic part of our industrial base," as in the U.S. and elsewhere. For similar reasons, Prime Minister Tony Blair later approved the sale of spare parts to Zimbabwe for British Hawk fighter jets being used by Mugabe in a civil war that cost tens of thousands of lives. Nonetheless, the new ethical policy was an improvement over Thatcher, whose defense procurement minister, Alan Clark, had announced, "My responsibility is to my own people. I don't really fill my mind much with what one set of foreigners is doing to another."[11]

It is against this background, barely sampled here, that the chorus of admired Western intellectuals praised themselves and their "enlightened states" for opening an inspiring new era of humanitarian intervention, guided by the "responsibility to protect," now solely dedicated to "principles and values," acting from "altruism" and "moral fervor" alone under the leadership of the "idealistic new world bent on ending inhumanity," now in a "noble phase" of its foreign policy with a "saintly glow."

The chorus of self-adulation also devised a new literary genre, castigating the West for its failure to respond adequately to the crimes of others (while scrupulously avoiding any reference to its own crimes). It was lauded as courageous and daring. Few allowed themselves to perceive that comparable work would have been warmly welcomed in the Kremlin, pre-Perestroika.

The most prominent example was the lavishly praised Pulitzer Prize–winning work *"A Problem from Hell": America and the Age of Genocide*, by Samantha Power, of the Carr Center for Human Rights Policy at the Kennedy School at Harvard University. It is unfair to say that Power avoids all U.S. crimes. A scattering are casually mentioned but explained away as derivative of other concerns.

Power does bring up one clear case: East Timor, where, she writes, Washington "looked away"—namely, by authorizing the invasion; immediately providing Indonesia with new counterinsurgency equipment; rendering the UN "utterly ineffective" in any effort to stop the aggression and slaughter, as UN ambassador Daniel Patrick Moynihan proudly recalled in his memoir of his UN service; and then continuing to provide decisive diplomatic and military support for the next quarter-century, in the manner briefly indicated.

Summarizing, after the fall of the Soviet Union, policies continued with little more than tactical modification. But new pretexts were needed. The new norm of humanitarian intervention fit the requirements very well. It was only necessary to put aside the shameful record of earlier crimes as somehow irrelevant to the understanding of societies and cultures that had scarcely changed and to disguise the fact that these crimes continued much as before. This is a difficulty that arises frequently, even if not as dramatically as it did after the collapse of the routine pretext for crimes. The standard reaction is to abide by a maxim of Tacitus: "Crime once exposed has no refuge but audacity." One does not deny the crimes of past and present; it would be a grave error to open that door. Rather, the past must be effaced and the present ignored as we march on to a glorious new future. That is, regrettably, a fair rendition of leading features of the intellectual culture in the post-Soviet era.

Nevertheless, it was imperative to find, or least to contrive, a few examples to illustrate the new magnificence. Some of the choices were truly astonishing. One, regularly invoked, is the humanitarian intervention of mid-September 1999 to rescue the East Timorese. The term "audacity" does not begin to capture this exercise, but it proceeded with little difficulty, testifying once again to what Hans Morgenthau, the founder of realist international relations theory, once called "our conformist subservience to those in power." There is no need to waste time on this achievement.

A few other examples were tried, also impressive in their audacity. One favorite was Clinton's military intervention in Haiti in 1995, which did in fact bring an end to the horrendous reign of terror that was unleashed when a military coup overthrew the first democratically elected president of Haiti, Jean-Bertrand Aristide, in 1991, a few months after he took office. To sustain the self-image, however, it has been necessary to suppress some inconvenient facts.

The Bush I administration devoted substantial effort to undermine the hated Aristide regime and prepare the grounds for the anticipated military coup. It then instantly turned to support for the military junta and its wealthy supporters, violating the OAS embargo—or as the *New York Times* preferred to describe the facts, "fine tuning" the embargo to exempt U.S. businesses, for the benefit of the Haitian people. Trade with the junta increased under Clinton, who also illegally authorized Texaco to supply oil to the junta. Texaco was a natural choice. It was Texaco that supplied oil to the Franco regime in the late 1930s, violating the embargo and U.S. law, while Washington pretended that it did not know what was being reported in the left press—later conceding quietly that it of course knew all along.

By 1995, Washington felt that the torture of Haitians had proceeded long enough, and Clinton sent the Marines in to topple the junta and restore the elected government—but on conditions that were sure to destroy what was left of the Haitian economy. The restored government was compelled to accept a harsh neoliberal program, with no barriers to U.S. export and investment. Haitian rice farmers are quite efficient but cannot compete with highly subsidized U.S. agribusiness, leading to the anticipated collapse. One small successful business in Haiti produced chicken parts. But Americans do not like dark meat, so the huge U.S. conglomerates that produce chicken parts wanted to dump the unwanted parts on others. They tried Mexico and Canada, but those are functioning societies that could prevent the illegal dumping. Haiti had been compelled to be defenseless, so even that small industry was destroyed. The story continues, declining to still further ugliness, unnecessary to review here.[12]

In brief, Haiti falls into the familiar pattern, a particularly disgraceful illustration in light of the way that Haitians have been tortured, first by France and then by the U.S., in part in punishment for having dared to be the first free country of free men in the hemisphere.

Other attempts at self-justification fared no better, until, at last, Kosovo came to the rescue in 1999, opening the floodgates. The torrent of self-congratulatory rhetoric became an uncontrollable deluge.

The Kosovo case is plainly of great significance in sustaining the self-glorification that reached a crescendo at the end of the millennium and in justifying the Western claim of a right of unilateral intervention. Not surprisingly, then, there is a strict party line on NATO's bombing of Kosovo.

The doctrine was articulated with eloquence by Vaclav Havel, as the bombing ended. The leading U.S. intellectual journal, the left-liberal *New York Review of Books*, turned to Havel for "a reasoned explanation" of why the NATO bombing must be supported, publishing his address to the Canadian Parliament, "Kosovo and the End of the Nation-State" (June 10, 1999). For Havel, the *Review* observed, "the war in Yugoslavia is a landmark in international relations: the first time that the human rights of a people—the Kosovo Albanians—have unequivocally come first."[13] Havel's address opened by stressing the extraordinary significance and import of the Kosovo intervention.

It shows that we may at last be entering an era of true enlightenment that will witness "the end of the nation-state," which will no longer be "the culmination of every national community's history and its highest earthly value," as has always been true in the past. The "enlightened efforts of generations of democrats, the terrible experience of two world wars . . . and the evolution of civilization have finally brought humanity to the recognition that human beings are more important than the state,"[14] so the Kosovo intervention reveals.

Havel's "reasoned explanation" of why the bombing was just reads as follows:

> There is one thing that no reasonable person can deny: this is probably the first war that has not been waged in the name of "national interests," but rather in the name of principles and values. . . . [NATO] is fighting out of concern for the fate of others. It is fighting because no decent person can stand by and watch the systematic state-directed murder of other people. . . . The alliance has acted out of respect for human rights, as both conscience and legal documents dictate. This is an important precedent for the future. It has been clearly said that it is simply not permissible to murder people, to drive them from their homes, to torture them, and to confiscate their property.[15]

Stirring words, though a few qualifications might be appropriate: to mention just one, it remains permissible, indeed obligatory, not only to tolerate such actions but to contribute massively to them, ensuring that they reach still greater peaks of fury—within NATO, for example—and of course to conduct them on one's own, when that is necessary.

Havel had been a particularly admired commentator on world affairs since 1990, when he addressed a joint session of Congress immediately after his fellow dissidents were brutally murdered in El Salvador (and the U.S. had invaded Panama, killing and destroying). He received a thunderous standing ovation for lauding the "defender of freedom" that had armed and trained the murderers of the six leading Jesuit intellectuals and tens of thousands of others, praising it for having "understood the responsibility that flowed" from power and urging it to continue to put "morality ahead of politics"—as it had done throughout Reagan's terrorist wars in Central America, in support for South Africa as it murdered some 1.5 million people in neighboring countries, and many other glorious deeds. The backbone of our actions must be "responsibility," Havel instructed Congress: "responsibility to something higher than my family, my country, my company, my success."

The performance was welcomed with rapture by liberal intellectuals. Capturing the general awe and acclaim, the editors of the *Washington Post* orated that Havel's praise for our nobility provided "stunning evidence" that his country is "a prime source" of "the European intellectual tradition" as his "voice of conscience" spoke "compellingly of the responsibilities that large and small powers owe each other." At the left-liberal extreme, Anthony

Lewis wrote that Havel's words remind us that "we live in a romantic age." A decade later, still at the outer limits of dissidence, Lewis was moved and persuaded by the argument that Havel had "eloquently stated" on the bombing of Serbia, which he thought eliminated all residual doubts about Washington's cause and signaled a "landmark in international relations."

The party line has been guarded with vigilance. To cite a few current examples, on the occasion of Kosovo's independence the *Wall Street Journal* wrote that Serbian police and troops were "driven from the province by the U.S.-led aerial bombing campaign of [1999], designed to halt dicta-tor Slobodan Milošević's brutal attempt to drive out the province's ethnic Albanian majority" (February 25, 2008). Francis Fukuyama urged in the *New York Times* (February 17, 2008) that "in the wake of the Iraq debacle," we must not forget the important lesson of the 1990s "that strong countries like the United States should use their power to defend human rights or promote democracy": crucial evidence is that "ethnic cleansing against the Albanians in Kosovo was stopped only through NATO bombing of Serbia itself."

The editors of the liberal *New Republic* wrote that Milošević "set out to pacify [Kosovo] using his favored tools: mass expulsion, systematic rape, and murder," but fortunately the West would not tolerate the crime "and so, in March 1999, NATO began a bombing campaign" to end the "slaughter and sadism." The "nightmare has a happy ending for one simple reason: because the West used its military might to save them" (March 12, 2008). The editors added that "You would need to have the heart of a Kremlin functionary to be unmoved by the scene that unfolded in Kosovo's capital Pristina," celebrating "a fitting and just epilogue to the last mass crime of the twentieth century." In less exalted but conventional terms, Samantha Power writes that "Serbia's atrocities had of course provoked NATO action."

Citing examples is misleading, because the doctrine is held with virtual unanimity and considerable passion, or perhaps "desperation" would be a more appropriate word. The reference to "Kremlin functionaries" by the editors of the *New Republic* is appropriate in ways they did not intend. The rare efforts to adduce the uncontroversial and well-documented record elicit impressive tantrums, when they are not simply ignored.

The record is unusually rich, and the facts presented in impeccable Western sources are explicit, consistent, and extensively documented. The sources include two major State Department compilations released to justify the bombing and a rich array of documents from the OSCE, NATO, the UN, and others. They also include a British parliamentary inquiry. And, notably, the very instructive reports of the monitors of the OSCE Kosovo Verification Mission established at the time of the October cease-fire nego-tiated by U.S. Ambassador Richard Holbrooke. The monitors reported reg-ularly on the ground from a few weeks later until March 19, when they were withdrawn (over Serbian objections) in preparation for the March 24 bombing.

The documentary record is treated with what anthropologists call "ritual avoidance." And there is a good reason. The evidence, which is une-quivocal, leaves the party line in tatters. The standard claim that "Serbia's atrocities had of course provoked NATO action" directly reverses the unequivocal facts: NATO's action provoked Serbia's atrocities, exactly as anticipated.[16]

Western documentation reveals that Kosovo was an ugly place prior to the bombing—though not, unfortunately, by international standards. Some two thousand are reported to have been killed in the year before the NATO bombing. Atrocities were distributed between the Kosovo Liberation Army (KLA) guerrillas attacking from Albania and Federal Republic of Yugoslav (FRY) security forces. An OSCE report accurately summarizes the record: the "cycle of confrontation can be generally described" as KLA attacks on Serb police and civilians, "a disproportionate response by the FRY authorities," and "renewed KLA activity."

The British government, the most hawkish element in the alliance, attributes most of the atrocities in the relevant period to the KLA, which in 1998 had been condemned by the U.S. as a "terrorist organization." On March 24, as the bombing began, British Defense Minister George Robertson, later NATO secretary-general, informed the House of Commons that until mid-January 1999, "the [Kosovo Liberation Army] were responsible for more deaths in Kosovo than the Serbian authorities had been." In citing Robertson's testimony in *A New Generation Draws the Line*, I wrote that he must be mistaken; given the distribution of force, the judgment was simply not credible. The British parliamentary inquiry, however, reveals that his judgment was confirmed by Foreign Secretary Robin Cook, who told the House on January 18, 1999, that the KLA "has committed more breaches of the ceasefire, and until this weekend was responsible for more deaths than the [Yugoslav] security forces."[17]

Robertson and Cook are referring to the Račak massacre of January 15, in which forty-five people were reported killed. Western documentation reveals no notable change in pattern from the Račak massacre until the withdrawal of the Kosovo Verification Mission monitors on March 19. So even factoring that massacre in (and overlooking questions about what happened), the conclusions of Robertson and Cook, if generally valid in mid-January, remained so until the announcement of the NATO bombing. One of the few serious scholarly studies even to consider these matters, a careful and judicious study by Nicholas Wheeler, estimates that Serbs were responsible for five hundred of the two thousand reported killed in the year before the bombing. For comparison, Robert Hayden, a specialist on the Balkans who is director of the Center for Russian and East European Studies of the University of Pittsburgh, observes that "the casualties among Serb civilians in the first three weeks of the war are higher than all of the casualties on both sides in Kosovo in the three months that led up to this war, and yet those three months were supposed to be a humanitarian catastrophe."[18]

U.S. intelligence reported that the KLA "intended to draw NATO into its fight for independence by provoking Serb atrocities." The KLA was arming and "taking very provocative steps in an effort to draw the west into the crisis," hoping for a brutal Serb reaction, Holbrooke commented. KLA leader Hashim Thaçi, now prime minister of Kosovo, informed BBC investigators that when the KLA killed Serb policemen, "We knew we were endangering civilian lives, too, a great number of lives," but the predictable Serb revenge made the actions worthwhile. The top KLA military commander, Agim Çeku, boasted that the KLA shared in the victory because "after all, the KLA brought NATO to Kosovo" by carrying out attacks in order to elicit violent retaliation.

So matters continued until NATO initiated the bombing, knowing that it was "entirely predictable" that the FRY would respond on the ground with violence, General Wesley Clark informed the press; earlier he had informed the highest U.S. government officials that the bombing would lead to major crimes, and that NATO could do nothing to prevent them. The details conform to Clark's predictions. The press reported that "The Serbs began attacking Kosovo Liberation Army strongholds on March 19," when the monitors were withdrawn in preparation for the bombing, "but their attack kicked into high gear on March 24, the night NATO began bombing Yugoslavia." The number of internally displaced, which had declined, rose again to two hundred thousand after the monitors were withdrawn. Prior to the bombing, and for two days following its onset, the United Nations

High Commissioner for Refugees (UNHCR) reported no data on refugees. A week after the bombing began, the UNHCR began to tabulate the daily flow.

In brief, it was well understood by the NATO leadership that the bombing was not a response to the huge atrocities in Kosovo but was their cause, exactly as anticipated. Furthermore, at the time the bombing was initiated, there were two diplomatic options on the table: the proposal of NATO and the proposal of the FRY (suppressed in the West, virtually without exception). After seventy-eight days of bombing, a compromise was reached between them, suggesting that a peaceful settlement might have been possible, avoiding the terrible crimes that were the anticipated reaction to the NATO bombing.

The Milošević indictment for war crimes in Kosovo, issued during the NATO bombing, makes no pretense to the contrary. The indictment, based on U.S.-UK intelligence, keeps to crimes committed during the NATO bombing. There is only one exception: the Račak massacre in January. "Senior officials in the Clinton administration were revolted and outraged," Samantha Power writes, repeating the conventional story. It is hardly credible that Clinton officials were revolted or outraged, or even cared. Even putting aside their past support for far worse crimes, it suffices to consider their reaction to the massacres in East Timor shortly after, for example, in Liquiçá, a far worse crime than Račak, which led the same Clinton officials to increase their participation in the ongoing slaughter.

Despite his conclusions on the distribution of killings, Wheeler supports the NATO bombing on the grounds that there would have been even worse atrocities had NATO not bombed. The argument is that by bombing with the anticipation that it would lead to atrocities, NATO was preventing atrocities. The fact that these are the strongest arguments that can be contrived by serious analysts tells us a good deal about the decision to bomb, particularly when we recall that there were diplomatic options and that the agreement reached after the bombing was a compromise between them.

Some have tried to support this line of argument by appealing to Operation Horseshoe, an alleged Serbian plan to expel Kosovar Albanians. The plan was unknown to the NATO command, as General Clark attested, and is irrelevant on those grounds alone: the criminal resort to violence cannot be justified by something discovered afterwards. The plan was exposed as a probable intelligence forgery, but that is of no relevance either. It is almost certain Serbia had such contingency plans, just as other states, including the U.S., have hair-raising contingency plans even for remote eventualities.

An even more astonishing effort to justify the NATO bombing is that the decision was taken under the shadow of Srebrenica and other atrocities of the early '90s. By that argument, it follows that NATO should have been calling for the bombing of Indonesia, the U.S., and the United Kingdom, under the shadow of the vastly worse atrocities they had carried out in East Timor and were escalating again when the decision to bomb Serbia was taken—for the U.S. and UK, only a small part of their criminal record. A last desperate effort to grasp at some straw is that Europe could not tolerate the pre-bombing atrocities right near its borders—though NATO not only tolerated but strongly supported far worse atrocities right within NATO in the same years, as already discussed.

Without running through the rest of the dismal record, it is hard to think of a case where the justification for the resort to criminal violence is so weak. But the pure justice and nobility of the actions has become a doctrine of religious faith, understandably: What else can justify the chorus of self-glorification that brought the millennium to an end? What else can be adduced to support the "emerging norms" that authorize the idealistic New World and its allies to use force where their leaders "believe it to be just"?

Some have speculated on the actual reasons for the NATO bombing. The highly regarded military historian Andrew Bacevich dismisses humanitarian claims and alleges that along with the Bosnia intervention, the bombing of Serbia was undertaken to ensure "the cohesion of NATO and the credibility of American power" and "to sustain American primacy" in Europe. Another respected analyst, Michael Lind, writes that "a major strategic goal of the Kosovo war was reassuring Germany so it would not develop a defense policy independent of the U.S.-dominated NATO alliance." Neither author presents any basis for the conclusions.[19]

Evidence does exist, however, from the highest level of the Clinton administration. Strobe Talbott, who was responsible for diplomacy during the war, wrote the foreword to a book on the war by his associate John Norris. Talbott writes that those who want to know "how events looked and felt at the time to those of us who were involved" in the war should turn to Norris's account, written with the "immediacy that can be provided only by someone who was an eyewitness to much of the action, who interviewed at length and in depth many of the participants while their memories were still fresh, and who has had access to much of the diplomatic record." Norris states that "it was Yugoslavia's resistance to the broader trends of political and economic reform—not the plight of Kosovar Albanians—that best explains NATO's war." That the motive for the NATO bombing could not have been "the plight of Kosovar Albanians" was already clear from the extensive Western documentary record. But it is interesting to hear from the highest level that the real reason for the bombing was that Yugoslavia was a lone holdout in Europe to the political and economic programs of the Clinton administration and its allies. Needless to say, this important revelation also is excluded from the canon.[20]

Though the "new norm of humanitarian intervention" collapses on examination, there is at least one residue: the "responsibility to protect." Applauding the declaration of independence of Kosovo, liberal commentator Roger Cohen writes that "at a deeper level, the story of little Kosovo is the story of changing notions of sovereignty and the prising open of the world" (*International Herald Tribune*, February 20, 2008). The NATO bombing of Kosovo demonstrated that "human rights transcended narrow claims of state sovereignty" (quoting Thomas Weiss).

The achievement, Cohen continues, was ratified by the 2005 World Summit, which adopted the "responsibility to protect," known as R2P, which "formalized the notion that when a state proves unable or unwilling to protect its people, and crimes against humanity are perpetrated, the international community has an obligation to intervene—if necessary, and as a last resort, with military force." Accordingly, "an independent Kosovo, recognized by major Western powers, is in effect the first major fruit of the ideas behind R2P." Cohen concludes: "The prising open of the world is slow work, but from Kosovo to Cuba it continues." The NATO bombing is vindicated, and the "idealistic new world bent on ending inhumanity" really has reached a "noble phase" in its foreign policy with a "saintly glow." In the words of international law professor Michael Glennon, "The crisis in Kosovo illustrates . . . America's new willingness to do what it thinks right—international law notwithstanding," though a few years later international law was brought into accord with the stance of the "enlightened states" by adopting R2P.

Again, there is a slight problem: those annoying facts. The UN World Summit of September 2005 explicitly rejected the claim of the NATO powers that they have the right to use force in alleged protection of human rights. Quite the contrary, the Summit reaffirmed "that the relevant provisions of the Charter [which explicitly bar the NATO actions] are sufficient to address the full range of threats to international peace and security." The Summit also reaffirmed "the authority of the Security Council to mandate coercive action to maintain and restore international peace and security . . . acting in accordance with the purposes and principles of the Charter," and the role of the General Assembly in this regard "in accordance with the relevant provisions of the Charter." Without Security Council authorization, then, NATO has no more right to bomb Serbia than Saddam Hussein had to "liberate" Kuwait. The Summit granted no new "right of intervention" to individual states or regional alliances, whether under humanitarian or other professed grounds.

The Summit endorsed the conclusions of a December 2004 high-level UN Panel, which included many prominent Western figures. The Panel reiterated the principles of the Charter concerning the use of force: it can be lawfully deployed only when authorized by the Security Council or under Article 51 in defense against armed attack until the Security Council acts. Any other resort to force is a war crime, in fact the "supreme international crime" encompassing all the evil that follows, in the words of the Nuremberg Tribunal. The Panel concluded that "Article 51 needs neither extension nor restriction of its long-understood scope . . . it should be neither rewritten nor reinterpreted." Presumably with the Kosovo war in mind, the Panel added that "For those impatient with such a response, the answer must be that, in a world full of perceived potential threats, the risk to the global order and the norm of nonintervention on which it continues to be based is simply too great for the legality of unilateral preventive action, as distinct from collectively endorsed action, to be accepted. Allowing one to so act is to allow all." There could hardly be a more explicit rejection of the stand of the self-declared "enlightened states."

Both the Panel and the World Summit endorsed the position of the non-Western world, which had firmly rejected "the so-called 'right' of humanitarian intervention" in the Declaration of the South Summit in 2000, surely with the recent NATO bombing of Serbia in mind. This was the highest-level meeting ever held by the former non-aligned movement, accounting for 80 percent of the world's population. It was almost entirely ignored, and the rare and brief references to their conclusions about humanitarian intervention elicited near hysteria. Thus Cambridge University international relations lecturer Brendan Simms, writing in the *Times Higher Education Supplement* (May 25, 2001), was infuriated by such "bizarre and uncritical reverence for the pronouncements of the so-called 'South Summit G-77'—in Havana!—an improvident rabble in whose ranks murderers, torturers and robbers are conspicuously represented"—so different from the civilized folk who have been their benefactors for the past centuries and can scarcely control their fury when there is a brief allusion, without comment, to the perception of the world by the traditional victims, a perception since strongly endorsed by the high-level UN Panel and the UN World Summit in explicit contradiction to the self-serving pronouncements of apologists for Western resort to violence.

We might ask finally whether humanitarian intervention even exists. There is no shortage of evidence that it does. The evidence falls into two categories. The first is declarations of leaders. It is all too easy to demonstrate that virtually every resort to force is justified by elevated rhetoric about noble humanitarian intentions. Japanese counterinsurgency documents eloquently proclaim Japan's intention to create an "earthly paradise" in independent Manchukuo and North China, where Japan is selflessly sacrificing blood and treasure to defend the population from the "Chinese bandits" who terrorize them.

Since these are internal documents, we have no reason to doubt the sincerity of the mass murderers and torturers who produced them. Perhaps we may even entertain the possibility that Japanese emperor Hirohito was sincere in his surrender declaration in August 1945, when he told his people that "We declared war on America and Britain out of Our sincere desire to ensure Japan's self-preservation and the stabilization of East Asia, it being far from Our thought either to infringe upon the sovereignty of other nations or to embark upon territorial aggrandizement." Hitler's pronouncements were no less noble when he dismembered Czechoslovakia and were accepted at face value by Western leaders. President Roosevelt's close confidant Sumner Welles informed him that the Munich settlement "presented the opportunity for the establishment by the nations of the world of a new world order based upon justice and upon law," in which the Nazi "moderates" would play a leading role. It would be hard to find an exception to professions of virtuous intent, even among the worst monsters.

The second category of evidence consists of military intervention that had benign effects, whatever its motives: not quite humanitarian intervention, but at least partially approaching it. Here too there are illustrations. The most significant ones by far during the post–Second World War era are in the 1970s: India's invasion of East Pakistan (now Bangladesh), ending a huge massacre; and Vietnam's invasion of Cambodia in December 1978, driving out the Khmer Rouge just as their atrocities were peaking. But these two cases are excluded from the canon on principled grounds. The invasions were not carried out by the West, hence do not serve the cause of establishing the West's right to use force in violation of the UN Charter. Even more decisively, both interventions were vigorously opposed by the "idealistic new world bent on ending inhumanity." The U.S. sent an aircraft carrier to Indian waters to threaten the miscreants. Washington supported a Chinese invasion to punish Vietnam for the crime of ending Pol Pot's atrocities and, along with Britain, immediately turned to diplomatic and military support for the Khmer Rouge.

The State Department even explained to Congress why it was supporting both the remnants of the Pol Pot regime (Democratic Kampuchea) and the Indonesian aggressors who were engaged in crimes in East Timor that were comparable to Pol Pot's. The reason for this remarkable decision was that the "continuity" of Democratic Kampuchea with the Khmer Rouge regime "unquestionably" makes it "more representative of the Cambodian people than the Fretilin [the East Timorese resistance] is of the Timorese people." The explanation was not reported and has been effaced from properly sanitized history.

Perhaps a few genuine cases of humanitarian intervention can be discovered. There is, however, good reason to take seriously the stand of the "improvident rabble," reaffirmed by the authentic international community at the highest level. The essential insight was articulated by the unanimous vote of the International Court of Justice in one of its earliest rulings, in 1949: "The Court can only regard the alleged right of intervention as the manifestation of a policy of force, such as has, in the past, given rise to most serious abuses and such as cannot, whatever be the defects in international organization, find a place in international law . . . ; from the nature of things, [intervention] would be reserved for the most powerful states, and might easily lead to perverting the administration of justice itself."[21] The judgment does not bar "the responsibility to protect," as long as it is interpreted in the manner of the South, the high-level UN Panel, and the UN World Summit.

Sixty years later, there is little reason to question the court's judgment. The UN system doubtless suffers from severe defects. The most critical defect is the overwhelming role of the leading violators of Security Council resolutions. The most effective way to violate them is to veto them, a privilege of the permanent members. Since the UN fell out of its control forty years ago the U.S. is far in the lead in vetoing resolutions on a wide range of issues, its British ally is second, and no one else is even close. Nevertheless, despite these and other serious defects of the UN system, the current world order offers no preferable alternative than to vest the "responsibility to protect" in the United Nations. In the real world, the only alternative, as Bricmont eloquently explains, is the "humanitarian imperialism" of the powerful states that claim the right to use force because they "believe it to be just," all too regularly and predictably "perverting the administration of justice itself."

★ Originally published as: Noam Chomsky, "Humanitarian Imperialism: The New Doctrine of Imperial Right," *Monthly Review*, September 2008.

Notes

1   Thomas L. Friedman, "A New U.S. Problem: Freely Elected Tyrants," *New York Times*, January 12, 1992, available at http://www.nytimes.com/1992/01/12/weekinreview/the-world-a-new-us-problem-freely-elected-tyrants.html.
2   For more, including sources, see Chomsky, *The New Military Humanism* (Monroe, ME: Common Courage Press, 1999).
3   Thomas G. Weiss, "Letter to the Editor," *Boston Review*, February–March 1994.
4   For detailed examination of the role assigned to China in the "virulence and pervasiveness of American visionary globalism underlying Washington's strategic policy" in Asia, see James Peck, *Washington's China* (Amherst: University of Massachusetts Press, 2006).
5   J. Patrice McSherry, *Predatory States* (Boulder, CO: Rowman & Littlefield, 2005).
6   Dimitri Simes, "If the Cold War Is Over, Then What?," *New York Times*, December 27, 1988.
7   Ha-Joon Chang, *Bad Samaritans* (New York: Bloomsbury, 2007).
8   Reporters' paraphrase; Stephen Kurkjian and Adam Pertman, "Unsettling Questions amid the High Spirits," *Boston Globe*, January 5, 1990, available at https://www.highbeam.com/doc/1P2-8154732.html.
9   Lars Schoultz, *Human Rights and United States Policy toward Latin America* (Princeton, NJ: Princeton University Press, 1981).
10   Hans C. Von Sponeck, *A Different Kind of War* (New York: Berghahn, 2006). On the oil for food program fraud, see Chomsky, *Failed States* (New York: Metropolitan Books, 2006), 58–59, 61–63.
11   For a review of the miserable denouement, see Chomsky, *A New Generation Draws the Line* (London: Verso, 2000).
12   See Peter Hallward, *Damming the Flood* (New York: Verso, 2007), for an expert and penetrating study of what followed, through the 2004 military coup that overthrew the elected government once again, backed by the traditional torturers, France and the U.S.; and the resilience of the Haitian people as they sought to rise again from the ruins.
13   Paul Wilson, introducing Havel's address to the Canadian Parliament: "Kosovo and the End of the Nation-State," *New York Review of Books*, June 10, 1999, available at http://www.nybooks.com/articles/1999/06/10/kosovo-and-the-end-of-the-nation-state/.

14 "Speech: Tony Blair—A New Generation Draws the Line," *Newsweek*, April 19, 1999, available at https://newimperialism.wordpress.com/2010/03/01/speech-tony-blair-a-new-generation-draws-the-line/; Vaclav Havel, "Kosovo and the End of the Nation-State," *New York Review of Books*, June 10, 1999, available at http://www.nybooks.com/articles/1999/06/10/kosovo-and-the-end-of-the-nation-state/.

15 Quoted in Chomsky, *New Military Humanism*, 88.

16 Chomsky, *A New Generation Draws the Line*. On what was known at once, see Chomsky, *New Military Humanism*.

17 Chomsky, *New Generation*, 106–7; Cook, House of Commons Session 1999–2000, Defence Committee Publications, Part II, 35.

18 Nicholas Wheeler, *Saving Strangers: Humanitarian Intervention and International Society* (Oxford: Oxford University Press, 2000). "A Very European War," Robert Hayden interview by Doug Henwood, WBAI, New York, reprinted in *Left Business Observer*, no. 89 (April 27, 1999), available at http://www.leftbusinessobserver.com/Hayden.html.

19 Andrew J. Bacevich, *American Empire* (Cambridge, MA: Harvard, 2003); Michael Lind, "Beyond American Hegemony," *National Interest*, no. 152 (May–June 2007), available at http://nationalinterest.org/article/beyond-american-hegemony-1558.

20 John Norris, *Collision Course* (Westport, CT: Praeger, 2005).

21 Norris, *Collision Course*, 154.

Comments on Milošević Ouster

A number of people in the *ZNet* forum system and elsewhere have raised questions about the prominent role they see assigned to U.S.-NATO in the flood of commentary on recent events in Yugoslavia, "gloating over the victory of the opposition in Yugoslavia—as if that affirms the NATO bombing" (as one puts it). Others have noticed a similar focus with an opposite emphasis: denunciations of U.S. violence and subversion for the overthrow of an independent Serb government in favor of Western clients. I've been asked for my own reaction. What follows is an amalgam of several responses.

It's surely right that publicly the Clinton-Blair administrations are "gloating" over the outcome, and that the usual cheerleaders are doing their duty as well. That is commonly the case whatever the outcome. But we should not overlook the fact that more serious observers—as anti-Milošević as you can find—are telling quite a different story. For example, the senior news analyst of United Press International (UPI), Martin Sieff, described the outcome of the election as "an unpleasant shock to both incumbent Slobodan Milošević and the Clinton administration" (September 25), pointing out that (Vojislav) Koštunica "regularly denounces the NATO bombing of Yugoslavia last year as 'criminal,'" "implacably opposes having Milosevic or any other prominent Serb tried as a war criminal," and worse still from the Clinton-Blair point of view, "does appear to accurately express the democratic aspirations of the Serbian people."

That's correct across the board, and Sieff is not alone in reporting it. In his campaign throughout the country and on state TV, Koštunica condemned "NATO's criminal bombing of Yugoslavia" and denounced the International Criminal Tribunal on Yugoslavia (ICTY) as "an American tribunal—not a court, but a political instrument" (Steven Erlanger and

Carlotta Gall, *New York Times*, September 21). Speaking on state TV after taking office, he reiterated that while he sought normalization of relations with the West, neither "the crimes during the NATO aggression, nor the war damages, could not be forgotten," and he again described the ICTY as a "tool of political pressure of the US administration" (October 5, 6).

In the British press, some prominent (and bitterly anti-Milošević) correspondents have pointed out that "The West's self-satisfaction cannot disguise the reality of the Balkans. . . . It was not the bombing, the sanctions and the posturing of NATO politicians" that got rid of Milošević. Rather "he was toppled by a self-inflicted, democratic miscalculation," and if anything his fall was impeded by Western intervention: the rotten situation in the Balkans "has been made worse by intervention. . . . NATO's actions escalated the nastiness, prolonged the resolution and increased the cost." "At the very least, outsiders such as [British Foreign Secretary] Mr. Cook should stop rewriting history to their own gain. They did not topple Mr. Milošević. They did not bomb democracy into the last Communist dictatorship in Europe. They merely blocked the Danube and sent Serb politics back to the Dark Ages of autocracy. It was not sanctions that induced the army to switch sides; generals did well from the black market. The fall of Mr. Milošević began with an election that he called and then denied, spurring the electors to demand that the army respect their decision and protect their sovereignty. For that, Yugoslavia's democracy deserves the credit, not NATO's Tomahawk missiles" (Simon Jenkins, *London Times*, October 7). "The kind of people who made last Thursday's revolution" were those who were "depressed in equal measure by the careless savagery of the Nato bombing and the sheer nastiness of the Milošević regime" (John Simpson, world affairs editor of BBC, *Sunday Telegraph*, October 8).

Serb dissidents, to the extent that their voices are heard here, are saying pretty much the same thing. In a fairly typical comment on BBC, a Belgrade university student said: "We did it on our own. Please do not help us again with your bombs." Reaffirming these conclusions, a correspondent for the opposition daily *Blic* writes that "Serbs felt oppressed by their regime from the inside and by the West from the outside"; she condemns the U.S. for having "ignored the democratic movement in Yugoslavia and failing to aid numerous Serbian refugees"—by far the largest refugee population in the region. A prominent dissident scholar, in a letter of remembrance for a leading human rights activist who recently died, asks whether "the ones who said they imposed sanctions 'against Milošević' knew or cared how they impoverished you and the other people like you, and turned our lives into misery while helping him and his smuggling allies to become richer and richer," enabling him to "do whatever he wanted"; and instead of realizing "the stupidity of isolating a whole nation, of tarring all the people with the same broad brush under the pretense that they are striking a blow against a tyrannical leader," are now saying—self-righteously and absurdly—"that all that is happening in Serbia today was the result of their wise policy, and their help" (Ana Trbovich and Jasmina Teodosijević, *Boston Globe*, October 8).

These comments, I think, are on target. What happened was a very impressive demonstration of popular mobilization and courage. The removal of the brutal and corrupt regimes of Serbia and Croatia (Milošević and Tuđman were partners in crime throughout) is an important step forward for the region, and the mass movements in Serbia—miners, students, innumerable others—merit great admiration and provide an inspiring example of what united and dedicated people can achieve. Right now, workers' committees are taking control of many companies and state institutions, "revolting against their Milošević-era managers and taking over the directors' suites," as "workers took full advantage of Yugoslav's social ownership traditions." "With Milošević's rule crumbling, the workers have taken the communist rhetoric literally and taken charge of their enterprises," instituting various forms of "worker management" (London *Financial Times*, October 11). What has taken place and where it will go is in the hands of the people of Serbia, though, as always, international solidarity and support—not least in the U.S.—can make a substantial difference.

On the elections themselves, there is plenty of valid criticism: there was extensive interference by the West and by Milošević's harshly repressive (but by no means "totalitarian") apparatus. But I think the Belgrade student is right: they did it on their own and deserve plenty of credit for that. It's an outcome that the left should welcome and applaud, in my opinion.

It could have happened before. There is good reason to take seriously the judgment of Balkans historian Miranda Vickers (again, as anti-Milošević as they come) that Milošević would have been ousted years earlier if the Kosovar Albanians had voted against him in 1992 (they were hoping he would win, just as they did this September). And the mass popular demonstrations after opposition victories in local elections in 1996 might have toppled him if the opposition hadn't fractured. Milošević was bad enough but nothing like the rulers of totalitarian states or the murderous gangsters the U.S. has been placing and keeping in power for years all over the world.

But ridding the country of Milošević doesn't in itself herald a final victory for the people of Serbia, who are responsible for the achievement. There's plenty of historical evidence to the contrary, including very recent evidence. It's hard to think of a more spectacular recent achievement than the overthrow of South Africa's Apartheid horror, but the outcome is far from delightful, as Patrick Bond has been documenting impressively on *ZNet*, and as is obvious even to the observer or visitor with limited information. The U.S. and Europe will doubtless continue their (to an extent, competing) efforts to incorporate Serbia along with the rest of the Balkans into the Western-run neoliberal system, with the cooperation of elite elements that will benefit by linkage to Western power, and with the likely effects of undermining independent economic development and functioning democracy and harming a good part (probably considerable majority) of the population, with the countries expected to provide cheap human and material resources and markets and investment opportunities, subordinated to Western power interests. Serious struggles are barely beginning, as elsewhere.

★ Originally published as: Noam Chomsky, "Chomsky Comments on Milosevic Ouster, Etc," *ZNet*, October 12, 2000, https://zcomm.org/zcommentary/chomsky-comments-on-milosevic-ouster-etc-by-noam-chomsky/.

On the NATO Bombing of Yugoslavia

Danilo Mandić: *Last month marked the seventh anniversary of the beginning of the bombing of Yugoslavia. Why did NATO wage that war? Or, rather, why did the U.S. wage that war?*

Noam Chomsky: We have, for the first time, a very authoritative comment on that from the highest level of the Clinton administration, which is something that one could have surmised before, but now it is asserted. This is from Strobe Talbott, who was in the State Department during the entire affair, including the bombing. That is the very top of the Clinton administration. He recently wrote the foreword to a book by his director of communications, John Norris. In the foreword, he says that if you really want to understand what the thinking was of the top of the Clinton administration, this is the book you should read. He says that the real purpose of the war had nothing to do with any concern for Kosovar Albanians. It was because Serbia was not carrying out the required social and economic reforms, meaning it was the last corner of Europe that had not subordinated itself to the U.S.-led neoliberal programs. Therefore, it had to be eliminated. That's from the highest level.

Again, we could have guessed that it wasn't because of the Kosovo Albanians, but I've never seen it said before. This is a point of religious fanaticism that the West can't talk about for interesting reasons having to do with Western culture.

DM: *Given this clear documentary record, I want to ask you about the elite intellectual opinion in the U.S. and in the West in general. It seems that every critic of the NATO intervention was one of two things—either a "Milošević sympathizer" or someone who doesn't care about genocide.*

NC: First of all, that's a common feature of intellectual culture. One good U.S. critic, Harold Rosenberg, once described intellectuals as a "herd of independent minds," and that's true. They think they are very independent but they are a stampede in a herd. When there is a party line, you have to adhere to it, and the party line is systematic. The party line is subordination to state power and to state violence. Now you are allowed to criticize it but on very narrow grounds. You can criticize it because it is not working or for some mistake or benign intentions that went astray.

This can be seen right now in the Iraq War and in the tone of the debate about the Iraq War. It's very similar to the debate in the Soviet *Pravda* during the invasion of Afghanistan. Actually, I brought this up to a Polish reporter recently, and I asked him if he had been reading *Pravda*. He just laughed and said, "Yeah, it's the same." Now you read *Pravda* in the 1980s, it's as such: "the travail of the Russian soldiers that are going to get killed, and now there are these terrorists who prevent us from bringing justice and peace to the Afghans." Of course, "we did not invade them," we intervened and "helped them at the request of the legitimate government," and "the terrorists are preventing us from doing all the good things we wanted to do."

I have read Japanese counterinsurgency documents from the 1930s and 1940s, which were similar: "We tried to bring them an earthly paradise, but the Chinese bandits are preventing it." British imperialism was the same. In fact, I don't know of any exception in history. Even people of the highest moral integrity like John Stuart Mill were talking about how to intervene in India and conquer India because the barbarians couldn't control themselves; there were atrocities, but they were going to bring them the benefits of British rule, civilization, and so on.

Now it's the same in the U.S. Take the bombing of Kosovo. That was an incredibly important event for American intellectuals. The 1990s were probably the lowest point for Western intellectual history, not just in the U.S. but also in France and Britain. It was like a comic strip mimicking a satire of Stalinism. If you take a look at the *New York Times* or read the French or the British press, it was full of talk about how there was a "normative revolution" that had swept through the West. For "the first time in history," a state, namely the U.S., "the leader of the free world," was acting because of "pure altruism." Following the same accounts, Clinton's policy had entered into a "noble phase," with a "saintly glow," and so on and on. I am quoting here from the liberal media.

DM: *Among other reasons that were offered to justify NATO intervention was the claim that the intervention was necessary to prevent a genocide. In an interview, around the time of the NATO bombing, you said that "the term 'genocide' as applied to Kosovo is an insult to the victims of Hitler. In fact, it's revisionist to an extreme." What did you mean by that?*

NC: They needed some event to justify this massive self-adulation. Kosovo came along fortunately, so now they had to stop a "genocide." What was the genocide in Kosovo? We know from the Western documentation what it was. In the year prior to the bombing, according to Western sources, about two thousand people were killed. According to the British government, which was the most hawkish element of the Alliance, up until January 1999, the majority of the killings came from the KLA guerrillas who were coming in to try to incite a harsh Serbian response, which they got, in order to appeal to Western humanitarians to bomb the Serbs. We know from the Western records that nothing changed between January and March. On March 20, the sources indicated an increase in KLA attacks. It was ugly. However, by international standards, it was almost invisible and very dispersed.

DM: *As it turned out later, the KLA was also receiving financial and military support.*

NC: They were being supported by the CIA in those months. To call that genocide is to really insult the victims of the Holocaust. If that's genocide, then the whole world is covered with genocide. In fact, it's kind of striking. At the same time the Western intellectuals were praising themselves for their magnificent humanitarianism, much worse atrocities were going on right across the border in Turkey. That's inside NATO, not at the borders of NATO. "How can we allow this on the borders of NATO?" was a standard argument for the NATO bombing of FRY, but how about much worse crimes happening inside NATO, where Turkey had driven probably several million Kurds out of their homes, destroyed about 3,500 villages, laid waste to the whole place with every conceivable form of torture and massacre you can imagine, and killed nobody knows how many people? We don't count victims of our own military campaigns, which in this case was tens of thousands of people. How were they able to do that? The reason is because they were getting 80 percent of their arms from Clinton, and as the atrocities increased, the arms flow increased. In one single year, 1997, Clinton sent more arms to Turkey than in the entire Cold War period combined, up until the counterinsurgency. That was not reported in the West. You do not report your own crimes.

And right in the midst of all of this, there's the question of "how can we tolerate a couple of thousand people being killed in Kosovo?" The answer can probably be found in the fiftieth anniversary of NATO, which took place right in the middle of all of this. There were lamentations about what was going on right across NATO's border. Not a word about the much worse things going on inside NATO's borders, thanks to the massive flow of arms from the U.S. Now that's only one case. Comparable things were going on all over the world where the U.S. was supportive of much worse—another topic for the "herd of independent minds." NATO bombing played a crucial role in their self-image, because they had been going through a period of praising themselves for their magnificence in their "normative revolution" and the "noble phase" and so on and so forth. It was a godsend, and therefore you couldn't ask any questions about it. Incidentally, the same happened in the earlier phase of the Balkan wars. It was awful. However, if you look at the coverage for example, there was one famous incident that completely reshaped the Western opinion—the photograph of the thin man behind the barbed wire.

DM: *A fraudulent photograph, as it turned out.*
NC: The photo of the thin man behind the barbed wire was presented in the Western media as a "new Auschwitz," and, of course, "we can't have Auschwitz again." The intellectuals went crazy. The French were posturing on television with their usual antics. It was carefully investigated by the leading Western specialist on the topic, Phillip Knightley, who is a highly respected media analyst. He did a detailed analysis of it and determined that it was probably the reporters who were behind the barbed wire. The place was ugly, but it was a refugee camp, so people could leave if they wanted. Near the thin man was a fat man. There was one tiny newspaper in England, probably three people, called *LM* that ran a critique of this. Then ITN, a big media corporation, sued the tiny newspaper for libel. Following the absolutely atrocious British libel laws, the persons accused have to prove that what they are reporting is not done in malice. Now, when you have a huge corporation with batteries of lawyers carrying out a suit against three people in the office, who probably don't have the pocket money, it's obvious what is going to happen, especially under these grotesque libel laws. The little newspaper couldn't prove it wasn't done out of malice, so they were put out of business. The left-liberal British press was euphoric. After they put the newspaper out of business under this utterly grotesque

legal case, the left-liberal newspapers like the *Guardian* were in a state of euphoria about this wonderful achievement. They had managed to destroy a tiny newspaper because it questioned some image that they had presented and they were very proud of themselves for it. Phillip Knightley wrote a very harsh critique of the British media for behaving in this way and tried to teach them an elementary lesson about freedom of speech. He also added that the photograph probably was misinterpreted but couldn't get published. That's when Kosovo came along; it was the same thing—that you couldn't tell the truth about it.

DM: *We also witnessed a selective coverage of the NATO bombing in the mainstream Western media. Amnesty International, among others, reported about NATO committing "serious violations of the rules of war" during the bombing. Why were these crimes completely unreported in the mainstream media, and is there any prospect, in your view, of any responsibility being taken for these crimes?*

NC: I'd say the crimes were reported but they were cheered. It's not that they were unknown, like the bombing of the Serbian television station.[1] Yes, it was reported, but it was considered fine because the TV station was described as a propaganda outlet, so therefore it was right to bomb it. That happens all the time. It just happened last year, in November 2004 in Fallujah.

The invasion of Fallujah was similar to Srebrenica. The first thing the invading U.S. troops did was to take over the general hospital and throw the patients on the floor. Patients were taken out of their beds, put on the floor, hands tied behind their backs, doctors thrown on the floor, hands behind their backs. There was a picture of it on the front page of the *New York Times*—they said it was wonderful. Of course, it's a grave breach of the Geneva Conventions. George Bush should be facing the death penalty for that, even under U.S. law. But it was presented as a wonderful thing, without any mention of the Geneva Conventions. The Fallujah General Hospital was labeled as a "propaganda center," namely because it was releasing casualty figures, so therefore it was correct to carry out a massive war crime.

The bombing of the TV station was presented the same way. There was an offer from NATO, who said that they would not bomb if they agreed to broadcast six hours of NATO propaganda. This is considered quite right.

A group of international lawyers did appeal to the ICTY. They presented a case, saying they should look into NATO war crimes. What they cited was reports from Human Rights Watch, Amnesty International, and admissions by the NATO command. The prosecutor responded that they would not look into it because they "had faith in NATO." And that was the answer.

Something else interesting happened after that. Yugoslavia brought the case to the World Court. The court accepted it and deliberated for a couple of years, but what is interesting is that the U.S. excused itself from the case, and the court accepted the excuse. Why? Because Yugoslavia had mentioned the Genocide Convention, and the U.S. did sign the Genocide Convention (after forty years). It ratified it, but with a reservation, saying it was "inapplicable to the United States." In other words, the U.S. is entitled to commit genocide. That was the case that the U.S. Justice Department of President Clinton brought to the World Court, and the court had to agree. If a country does not accept World Court jurisdiction, it has to be excluded, so the U.S. was excluded from the trial on the grounds that it grants itself the right to commit genocide. Do you think this was reported here? Does any of this get reported?

We are lucky that we do not have censorship, but although it's a free society, the self-censorship is overwhelming. Orwell once wrote about this in *Animal Farm*, however almost nobody has read the introduction to *Animal Farm*. In it, he said *Animal Farm* is a satire of a totalitarian state. He said free England is not very different. In free England, unpopular ideas can be suppressed without the use of force, and he gave examples. It's very similar here. It does not matter how extreme they are. The Iraq invasion is a perfect example. You cannot find anywhere in the mainstream a suggestion that it is wrong to invade another country. If you invade another country, you have to pay reparations; you have to withdraw, and the leadership has to be punished.

There was a so-called Independent Commission of Inquiry on the Kosovo bombing led by a very respected South African jurist, Justice Goldstone. They concluded that the bombing was "illegal but legitimate." Illegal makes it a war crime, but they said it was legitimate because it was necessary to stop genocide. Then comes the usual inversion of the history. Justice Goldstone later recognized that the atrocities came after the bombing, and that they were furthermore the anticipated consequence. He did recognize that in a lecture in New York a few years ago. He said something like "well, nevertheless we can take some comfort in the fact that Serbia was planning it anyway." Furthermore, even if that was true, it was a contingency plan. Now, Israel has contingency plans to drive all the Palestinians out of the West Bank if there is a conflict, so does that mean that Iran has the right to bomb Israel? The U.S. has contingency plans to invade Canada, so does that mean that everybody has a right to bomb the U.S.? That's the last straw of justification on the part of a respectable person. But for the "herd of independent minds," it does not matter.

DM: *I want to ask you about some of the present developments. Slobodan Milošević died last month. What is the significance of his death in your view?*
NC: Milošević was a terrible person. He committed many crimes, but the ICTY charges against him would never have held up. He was originally indicted on the Kosovo charges. The indictment was issued right in the middle of the bombing which already nullified it. It used British and U.S. intelligence reports during the bombing, so it can't possibly be taken seriously. However, if you look at the indictment, it was for crimes committed after the bombing had started. There was one exception—Račak. No evidence that he was involved. Almost the entire indictment was for after the beginning of the bombing. How are those charges going to stand up unless you put Bill Clinton and Tony Blair on the dock alongside him? Then they realized that it was a weak case, so they added the earlier Yugoslav wars. Lots of horrible things happened there. But the worst crime, the one that they were really going to charge him for, was Srebrenica.

Now, there is a little problem with that. There was an extensive, detailed inquiry into it by the Dutch government, which was the responsible government. There were Dutch forces there, so that's hundreds of pages of inquiry. Their conclusion is that Milošević did not know anything about it, and that when it was discovered in Belgrade, they were horrified. Well, suppose that had entered into the testimony?

DM: *Does this mean that you are a "Milošević sympathizer"?*
NC: No, he was terrible. In fact, he should have been thrown out. He probably would have been thrown out in the early 1990s, if the Albanians had voted. He did all sorts of terrible things, but it wasn't quite a totalitarian state. There were elections with the opposition. There were a lot of rotten things, but there are rotten things everywhere. I certainly wouldn't have wanted to have dinner with him or talk to him, and he deserved to be tried for his crimes, but the trial in The Hague was never going to hold up if it was even semi-honest. It was a farce. They were lucky that he died.

DM: *In what sense?*

NC: Because they did not have to go through the whole trial. Now they can build up an image about how he would have been convicted as another Hitler.

DM: *I just want to bring you back to the bombing of the Serbian TV station. Some have argued that this particular act of NATO in 1999 set precedents for targeting media and labeling them as propaganda in order for the U.S. to bomb—as in the wars in Afghanistan and Iraq. Do you make any connection there?*

NC: Well, the chronology is correct, but I don't think they need excuses. The point is: they can bomb anybody they want to. Let's take 1998, so it was before the bombing of FRY. I'll say here another thing you're not allowed to say in the U.S. and the West more generally, as it leads to hysteria. In 1998, Clinton bombed the major pharmaceutical plant in the Sudan. The plant was using most of its pharmaceuticals and veterinary medicines for a poor African country that was under embargo. What's that going to do? Obviously they killed unknown numbers of people. The U.S. barred an investigation by the UN, so we don't know. Of course you don't want to investigate your own crimes, but there was some evidence. The German ambassador, who is a fellow at Harvard University, wrote an article in the *Harvard International Review* in which he estimated the casualties to be in the tens of thousands. The head of the Near East Foundation, a very respectable foundation, and their regional director, who had completed fieldwork in Sudan, did a study. They came out with the same conclusions, including that there were tens of thousands of dead.

Within weeks following the bombing, Human Rights Watch issued a warning that it was going to be a humanitarian catastrophe and gave examples of aid workers being pulled out from areas where people were dying. You cannot mention this. Any mention of this brings the same hysteria as criticizing the bombing of the TV station does. It is a Western crime and therefore it was legitimate.

Let's just suppose that Al Qaida blew up half the pharmaceutical supplies in the U.S., or England, or Israel, or any country in which people lived, human beings—not ants—people. Can you imagine the reaction? We'd probably have a nuclear war! But when we do it to a poor African country, it's not discussed. In fact, the only issue that is debated, if there is a discussion at all, is whether the intelligence was correct when it claimed that it was also producing chemical weapons. That is the only question. Mention anything else and the usual hysteria and tirades ensue. Western intellectual culture is extremely disciplined and rigid. You cannot go beyond fixed bounds. It's not censored, it's all voluntary. The Third World countries are different.

So take Turkey, a half Third World country. In Turkey, the leading intellectuals, now best-known writers, academics, journalists, and artists, not only protest atrocities relating to the Kurdish massacre, they protest them constantly. They were also constant in carrying out civil disobedience against them. I also participated with them sometimes. They publish banned writings, and their opposition presented them to the Prosecutor's Office, demanding that they be prosecuted. It's not a joke. Sometimes they are sent to prison. There's nothing like that in the West. When I am in Western Europe, I hear them telling me Turkey is not civilized enough to enter the European Union, I burst out laughing!

DM: *You mentioned the democratic movements in various countries. There was a promising democratic movement in Serbia before and during the bombing. People like Wesley Clark had claimed that this bombing would be of benefit to the anti-Milošević forces. Of course, it turned out to be a disaster. Was this a sincere evaluation on behalf of NATO?*

NC: Well, I can't look into their minds. When you commit a crime it is extremely easy to find a justification for it. That's true of personal life and it's true of international affairs. So yes, maybe they believed it. I think there's convincing evidence that the Japanese fascists believed that they were doing good in World War II. John Stuart Mill surely believed he was being honorable and noble when he was calling for the conquest of India right after some of the worst atrocities which he didn't mention. You can easily believe you are noble. It was obvious that it was going to harm the democratic movement. It's happening right now in Iran. There is a democratic movement in Iran. They are pleading with the U.S. not to maintain a harsh embargo, certainly not to attack. It is harming them, and it strengthens the most reactionary violent elements in the society, of course.

DM: *Let me ask you one final question about the future. Negotiations over Kosovo's final status are under way right now. The U.S. is backing Agim Çeku, who was someone involved in ethnic cleansing, not only in Kosovo.*

NC: Not "someone"—he was a war criminal.

DM: *What do you see as an appropriate, realistic solution for the final status of Kosovo, and how does that differ from what the U.S. is now promoting?*

NC: My feeling has been for a long time that the only realistic solution is the one proposed by Dobrica Ćosić, around 1993, namely some kind of partition, with the Serbian areas being part of Serbia and the rest of what they called "independent" joining Albania.

★ Based on: "On the NATO Bombing of Yugoslavia: Noam Chomsky interviewed by Danilo Mandić," *RTS Online*, April 25, 2006.

Notes

1   Chomsky refers here to the NATO bombing of the central building of the Radio-Television of Serbia (RTS) in downtown Belgrade, during the night of April 23–24, 1999, when sixteen staff members were killed. See Noam Chomsky, "We Are All . . . Fill in the Blank," January 10, 2015, available at https://chomsky.info/20150110/.

Perspectives

Davor Džalto: *How do you see the future of the ex-Yugoslav region? How do you see the EU integration process?*
Noam Chomsky: Despite all the challenges that the European continent has been facing, a lot of good things have happened with EU integrations. The steps toward the EU are, I think, very sensible. Europe has become quite a civilized place by comparative standards. Of course, there is the struggle about the influence, power, and policies of the EU and so on, and that is something to be anticipated. Germany has done very respectably in many ways. I mean, it has become kind of what it was like in the 1920s. At that time Germany was a peak of Western civilization—in the sciences and the arts, for instance. It was also regarded as a model of democracy. In many ways Germany is a very civilized place now. The economy, again, by comparative standards is doing quite well. It's the one Western society that has maintained a real, well-functioning manufacturing base and export economy; it's shifting, more than most other countries, to sustainable energy, so plenty of favorable things to say.

However, Germany does want to maintain the domination of the German financial and industrial sector over Europe as much as possible, and I think that's what drives the economic policies. It's a policy that will probably soon be worsened, producing a crisis in Europe. You can't pursue austerity in the midst of a recession, when you need growth. It can only get harder to get out of the recession, harder to pay the debt. We can already see that happening. What you need is a stimulus. Europe has plenty of resources to stimulate its economies, so for them to be borrowing from China or Russia is kind of comical. Europe has far greater resources, but they have to want to use them, and that has to be the decision of the European Central Bank and the political leaders. But they are stuck, they have kind of a mantra that "you have to keep inflation below 2 percent," because "remember what happened in 1923," as if that has any relevance. And keeping inflation (meaning potential inflation) low becomes a priority, since inflation is not good for bankers, investment firms, and so on. However, moderate inflation is good for debtors and manufacturers, but we don't care much about them. So we'll keep that policy, we'll impose greater austerity, we'll reduce the likelihood of the poorer countries growing out of the recession, which is exactly what's happening.

There are, of course, differences among the poor European countries. Greece is a difficult problem, but take Spain for instance. Its financial situation was quite decent before the collapse of the bubble, and it has a manufacturing industry; it's in fact pretty advanced in many respects. Spain is one of the leaders of technological innovation and development. However, it'll be probably crushed by these austerity measures. All of this is, I think, part of the effort of, basically, the German financial sectors to expand German influence but also, and probably more significantly, to fight a class war. The rich never liked the welfare state measures. They don't like the power of labor such as it is. Consequently, the policies that are applied are perfect ways to undermine them.

DDž: *Do you think that this economic crisis, ongoing since 2008, can lead, as some people have pointed out, to some sort of United States of Europe in which there will be a stronger central European government, diminishing the sovereignty of national states?*

NC: Well, that's in fact happened to an extent. The Schengen Agreements reduced the sovereignty of individual states and led to a more civilized society. It's quite nice to be able to go from, you know, Belgium to Austria without crossing borders. There have been many other forms of integration, like educational, cultural, commercial, etc., which have been very successful. If it were to move in that direction, I think it would probably be a good idea. However, it could be the opposite. In fact, some very unpleasant things are happening in Europe. Let's not forget what happened in Germany in the early twentieth century. I said that in the 1920s it was probably the peak of Western civilization, but by the 1930s it was kind of the depths of human history. Same individuals. Same culture. Europe has a lot of conflicting strains and some of the uglier ones are coming out: dramatically in Hungary, pretty seriously in Austria, and to an extent in the rest of the countries, even countries like Denmark where you wouldn't expect it. It's not an attractive prospect.

★ Noam Chomsky interviewed by Davor Džalto, January 6, 2012, Cambridge, MA.

About the authors

Noam Chomsky is a laureate professor at the University of Arizona and institute professor emeritus in the MIT Department of Linguistics and Philosophy. His work is widely credited with having revolutionized the field of modern linguistics and Chomsky is one of the foremost critics of U.S. foreign policy. He has published numerous groundbreaking books, articles, and essays on global politics, history, and linguistics. His recent books include *Who Rules the World?* and *Hopes and Prospects*.

Davor Džalto is associate professor and program director at the American University of Rome and president of the Institute for the Study of Culture and Christianity. His research interests include the fields of history and politics of the Balkans, political theology, and religious philosophy.

Andrej Grubačić is the chair of the Anthropology and Social Change department at the California Institute of Integral Studies. His books include *Don't Mourn, Balkanize: Essays after Yugoslavia*. Andrej is a member of the International Council of the World Social Forum, the Industrial Workers of the World, and the Global Balkans Network.

Index

"Passim" (literally "scattered") indicates intermittent discussion of a topic over a cluster of pages.

PM Press is an independent, radical publisher of books and media to educate, entertain, and inspire. Founded in 2007 by a small group of people with decades of publishing, media, and organizing experience, PM Press amplifies the voices of radical authors, artists, and activists. Our aim is to deliver bold political ideas and vital stories to all walks of life and arm the dreamers to demand the impossible. We have sold millions of copies of our books, most often one at a time, face to face. We're old enough to know what we're doing and young enough to know what's at stake. Join us to create a better world.

PM Press
PO Box 23912
Oakland CA 94623
510-658-3906
www.pmpress.org

PM Press in Europe
europe@pmpress.org
www.pmpress.org.uk

FRIENDS OF PM

These are indisputably momentous times—the financial system is melting down globally and the Empire is stumbling. Now more than ever there is a vital need for radical ideas.

In the many years since its founding—and on a mere shoestring—PM Press has risen to the formidable challenge of publishing and distributing knowledge and entertainment for the struggles ahead. With hundreds of releases to date, we have published an impressive and stimulating array of literature, art, music, politics, and culture. Using every available medium, we've succeeded in connecting those hungry for ideas and information to those putting them into practice.

Friends of PM allows you to directly help impact, amplify, and revitalize the discourse and actions of radical writers, filmmakers, and artists. It provides us with a stable foundation from which we can build upon our early successes and provides a much-needed subsidy for the materials that can't necessarily pay their own way. You can help make that happen—and receive every new title automatically delivered to your door once a month—by joining as a Friend of PM Press. And, we'll throw in a free T-shirt when you sign up.

Here are your options:
- **$30 a month** Get all books and pamphlets plus 50% discount on all webstore purchases
- **$40 a month** Get all PM Press releases (including CDs and DVDs) plus 50% discount on all webstore purchases
- **$100 a month** Superstar—Everything plus PM merchandise, free downloads, and 50% discount on all webstore purchases

For those who can't afford $30 or more a month, we have **Sustainer Rates** at $15, $10, and $5. Sustainers get a free PM Press T-shirt and a 50% discount on all purchases from our website.

Your Visa or Mastercard will be billed once a month, until you tell us to stop. Or until our efforts succeed in bringing the revolution around. Or the financial meltdown of Capital makes plastic redundant. Whichever comes first.

Don't Mourn, Balkanize!
Essays After Yugoslavia

Andrej Grubačić with an introduction by
Roxanne Dunbar-Ortiz

ISBN: 978-1-60486-302-4
$20.00   272 pages

Don't Mourn, Balkanize! is the first book written from the
radical left perspective on the topic of Yugoslav space
after the dismantling of the country. In this collection of
essays, commentaries and interviews, written between
2002 and 2010, Andrej Grubačić speaks about the politics of balkanization—
about the trial of Slobodan Milošević, the assassination of Prime Minister Zoran
Djindjic, neoliberal structural adjustment, humanitarian intervention, supervised
independence of Kosovo, occupation of Bosnia, and other episodes of Power which
he situates in the long historical context of colonialism, conquest and intervention.

But he also tells the story of the balkanization of politics, of the Balkans seen from
below. A space of bogumils—those medieval heretics who fought against Crusades
and churches—and a place of anti-Ottoman resistance; a home to hajduks and
klefti, pirates and rebels; a refuge of feminists and socialists, of anti-fascists
and partisans; of new social movements of occupied and recovered factories; a
place of dreamers of all sorts struggling both against provincial "peninsularity"
as well as against occupations, foreign interventions and that process which is
now, in a strange inversion of history, often described by that fashionable term,
"balkanization."

For Grubačić, political activist and radical sociologist, Yugoslavia was never just
a country—it was an idea. Like the Balkans itself, it was a project of inter-ethnic
co-existence, a trans-ethnic and pluricultural space of many diverse worlds.
Political ideas of inter-ethnic cooperation and mutual aid as we had known them
in Yugoslavia were destroyed by the beginning of the 1990s—disappeared in the
combined madness of ethno-nationalist hysteria and humanitarian imperialism.
This remarkable collection chronicles political experiences of the author who is
himself a Yugoslav, a man without a country; but also, as an anarchist, a man
without a state. This book is an important reading for those on the Left who are
struggling to understand the intertwined legacy of inter-ethnic conflict and inter-
ethnic solidarity in contemporary, post-Yugoslav history.

*"These thoughtful essays offer us a vivid picture of the Balkans experience from the
inside, with its richness and complexity, tragedy and hope, and lessons from which we
can all draw inspiration and insight."*
—Noam Chomsky

Theory and Practice: Conversations with Noam Chomsky and Howard Zinn (DVD)

Noam Chomsky, Howard Zinn, Sasha Lilley

ISBN: 978-1-60486-305-5
$19.95   105 minutes

Two of the most venerable figures on the American Left—Howard Zinn and Noam Chomsky—converse with Sasha Lilley about their lives and political philosophies, looking back at eight decades of struggle and theoretical debate. Howard Zinn, interviewed shortly before his death, reflects on the genesis of his politics, from the civil rights and anti-Vietnam War movements to opposing empire today, as well as history, art and activism. Noam Chomsky discusses the evolution of his libertarian socialist ideals since childhood, his vision for a future postcapitalist society, and his views on the state, science, the Enlightenment, and the future of the planet.

Noam Chomsky is one of the world's leading intellectuals, the father of modern linguistics, and an outspoken media and foreign policy critic. He is Institute Professor emeritus of linguistics at MIT and the author of numerous books and DVDs including *Hegemony and Survival: America's Quest for Global Dominance*, *Chomsky on Anarchism*, *The Essential Chomsky*, and *Crisis and Hope: Theirs and Ours* published by PM Press

Howard Zinn was one of the country's most beloved and respected historians, the author of numerous books and plays including *Marx in Soho*, *You Can't Be Neutral on a Moving Train*, and the best-selling *A People's History of the United States*, and a passionate activist for radical change.

Sasha Lilley (interviewer) is a writer and radio broadcaster. She is the co-founder and host of the critically acclaimed program of radical ideas *Against the Grain*. As program director of KPFA Radio, the flagship station of the Pacifica Network, she headed up such award-winning national broadcasts as *Winter Soldier: Iraq and Afghanistan*. Lilley is the series editor of PM Press's political economy imprint, Spectre.

"Chomsky is a global phenomenon... perhaps the most widely read voice on foreign policy on the planet."
—*The New York Times Book Review*

"What can I say that will in any way convey the love, respect, and admiration I feel for this unassuming hero who was my teacher and mentor; this radical historian and people-loving 'troublemaker,' this man who stood with us and suffered with us? Howard Zinn was the best teacher I ever had, and the funniest."
—Alice Walker, author of *The Color Purple*

Crisis and Hope:
Theirs and Ours (DVD)

Noam Chomsky with an introduction by
Amy Goodman and interview conducted
by Big Noise Films

ISBN: 978-1-60486-210-2
$19.95   80 minutes

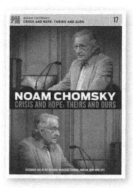

On June 12, 2009, Noam Chomsky gave a historic
address at the Riverside Church in New York City.

The talk was sponsored by the Brecht Forum and co-sponsors included
the Education Ministry of the Riverside Church, Mission and Social Justice
Commission of the Riverside Church, Theatre of the Oppressed at the Riverside
Church, the Theater of the Oppressed Laboratory & Bluestockings Books.

More than 2,000 people attended the lecture captured here, in which Chomsky
offered a powerful analysis of the current economic crisis and its structural roots;
the continuity in U.S. foreign policy under the Barack Obama administration; and
the class interests driving U.S. domestic and foreign policy. He also speaks here
at length about the tradition of worker self-management as a concrete alternative
to the business-as-usual approach of corporations and the government during the
current crisis. The DVD also features an introduction by Amy Goodman and an
exclusive one-on-one interview with Noam Chomsky.

*"Chomsky is a global phenomenon... perhaps the most widely read voice on foreign
policy on the planet."*
—*The New York Times Book Review*

"The conscience of the American people."
—*New Statesman*

Crisis and Hope:
Theirs and Ours (CD)

Noam Chomsky with an introduction by
Amy Goodman

ISBN: 978-1-60486-211-9
$14.95   80 minutes

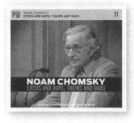

On June 12, 2009, Noam Chomsky gave a historic address at the Riverside Church
in New York City where he offered a powerful analysis of the current economic
crisis and its structural roots; the continuity in U.S. foreign policy under the Barack
Obama administration; and the class interests driving U.S. domestic and foreign
policy.

The Mafia Principle of Global
Hegemony: The Middle East,
Empire, and Activism (CD)

Noam Chomsky

ISBN: 978-1-60486-304-8
$14.95   70 minutes

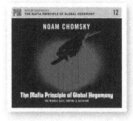

The world's most influential living intellectual holds forth on the root causes of the
conflicts in the Middle East, and talks about hopes for future social change. The
renowned foreign policy critic and linguist brings the full force of his rapier-like
mind and deadpan wit to bear in slicing through mainstream misconceptions—
many of them intentional—about the internal and external politics of Iran and
Israel/Palestine.

Iraq: The Forever War (CD)

Noam Chomsky

ISBN: 978-1-60486-100-6
$14.95   60 minutes

Presenting an arresting analysis of U.S. foreign policy
and the war on terror, this original recording delivers a
provocative lecture on the nation's past and present use of force. Demonstrating
how imperial powers have historically invented fantastic reasons to sell their wars
to their people, this powerful examination illustrates the attack on Iraq as not just a
mistake but also a crime, proposing that the criminals behind it should be brought
to justice.

Capital and Its Discontents: Conversations with Radical Thinkers in a Time of Tumult

Sasha Lilley

ISBN: 978-1-60486-334-5
$20.00   320 pages

Capitalism is stumbling, empire is faltering, and the planet is thawing. Yet many people are still grasping to understand these multiple crises and to find a way forward to a just future. Into the breach come the essential insights of *Capital and Its Discontents*, which cut through the gristle to get to the heart of the matter about the nature of capitalism and imperialism, capitalism's vulnerabilities at this conjuncture—and what can we do to hasten its demise. Through a series of incisive conversations with some of the most eminent thinkers and political economists on the Left—including David Harvey, Ellen Meiksins Wood, Mike Davis, Leo Panitch, Tariq Ali, and Noam Chomsky—*Capital and Its Discontents* illuminates the dynamic contradictions undergirding capitalism and the potential for its dethroning. At a moment when capitalism as a system is more reviled than ever, here is an indispensable toolbox of ideas for action by some of the most brilliant thinkers of our times.

"These conversations illuminate the current world situation in ways that are very useful for those hoping to orient themselves and find a way forward to effective individual and collective action. Highly recommended."
—Kim Stanley Robinson, *New York Times* bestselling author of the *Mars Trilogy* and *The Years of Rice and Salt*

"In this fine set of interviews, an A-list of radical political economists demonstrate why their skills are indispensable to understanding today's multiple economic and ecological crises."
—Raj Patel, author of *Stuffed and Starved* and *The Value of Nothing*

"This is an extremely important book. It is the most detailed, comprehensive, and best study yet published on the most recent capitalist crisis and its discontents. Sasha Lilley sets each interview in its context, writing with style, scholarship, and wit about ideas and philosophies."
—Andrej Grubačić, radical sociologist and social critic, co-author of *Wobblies and Zapatistas*

Wobblies and Zapatistas: Conversations on Anarchism, Marxism and Radical History

Staughton Lynd and Andrej Grubačić

ISBN: 978-1-60486-041-2
$20.00   300 pages

Wobblies and Zapatistas offers the reader an encounter between two generations and two traditions. Andrej Grubačić is an anarchist from the Balkans. Staughton Lynd is a lifelong pacifist, influenced by Marxism. They meet in dialogue in an effort to bring together the anarchist and Marxist traditions, to discuss the writing of history by those who make it, and to remind us of the idea that "my country is the world." Encompassing a Left libertarian perspective and an emphatically activist standpoint, these conversations are meant to be read in the clubs and affinity groups of the new Movement.

The authors accompany us on a journey through modern revolutions, direct actions, anti-globalist counter summits, Freedom Schools, Zapatista cooperatives, Haymarket and Petrograd, Hanoi and Belgrade, 'intentional' communities, wildcat strikes, early Protestant communities, Native American democratic practices, the Workers' Solidarity Club of Youngstown, occupied factories, self-organized councils and soviets, the lives of forgotten revolutionaries, Quaker meetings, antiwar movements, and prison rebellions. Neglected and forgotten moments of interracial self-activity are brought to light. The book invites the attention of readers who believe that a better world, on the other side of capitalism and state bureaucracy, may indeed be possible.

"There's no doubt that we've lost much of our history. It's also very clear that those in power in this country like it that way. Here's a book that shows us why. It demonstrates not only that another world is possible, but that it already exists, has existed, and shows an endless potential to burst through the artificial walls and divisions that currently imprison us. An exquisite contribution to the literature of human freedom, and coming not a moment too soon."
—David Graeber, author of *Fragments of an Anarchist Anthropology* and *Direct Action: An Ethnography*

"I have been in regular contact with Andrej Grubačić for many years, and have been most impressed by his searching intelligence, broad knowledge, lucid judgment, and penetrating commentary on contemporary affairs and their historical roots. He is an original thinker and dedicated activist, who brings deep understanding and outstanding personal qualities to everything he does."
—Noam Chomsky

Practical Utopia: Strategies for a Desirable Society

Michael Albert with a preface by Noam Chomsky

ISBN: 978-1-62963-381-7
$20.00   288 pages

Michael Albert's latest work, *Practical Utopia* is a succinct and thoughtful discussion of ambitious goals and practical principles for creating a desirable society. It presents concepts and their connections to current society; visions of what can be in a preferred, participatory future; and an examination of the ends and means required for developing a just society. Neither shying away from the complexity of human issues, nor reeking of dogmatism, *Practical Utopia* presupposes only concern for humanity.

Part one offers conceptual tools for understanding society and history, for discerning the nature of the oppressions people suffer and the potentials they harbor. Part two promotes a vision for a better way of organizing economy, polity, kinship, culture, ecology, and international relations. It is not a blueprint, of course, but does address the key institutions needed if people are to be free to determine their own circumstances. Part three investigates the means of seeking change using a variety of tactics and programs.

"*Practical Utopia immediately struck me because it is written by a leftist who is interested in the people winning and defeating oppression. The book is an excellent jumping off point for debates on the framework to look at actually existing capitalism, strategy for change, and what we need to do about moving forward. It speaks to many of the questions faced by grassroots activists who want to get beyond demanding change but who, instead, want to create a dynamic movement that can bring a just world into existence. As someone who comes out of a different part of the Left than does Michael Albert, I was nevertheless excited by the challenges he threw in front of the readers of this book. Many a discussion will be sparked by the arguments of this work.*"
—Bill Fletcher Jr., author of *"They're Bankrupting Us!" And 20 Other Myths about Unions*

"*Albert mulls over the better society that we may create after capitalism, provoking much thought and offering a generous, hopeful vision of the future. Albert's prescriptions for action in the present are modest and wise, his suggestions for building the future are ambitious and humane.*"
—Milan Rai

William Morris: Romantic to Revolutionary

E.P. Thompson
with a foreword by Peter Linebaugh

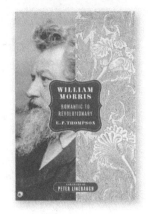

ISBN: 978-1-60486-243-0
$32.95   880 pages

William Morris—the great 19th century craftsman, architect, designer, poet and writer—remains a monumental figure whose influence resonates powerfully today. As an intellectual (and author of the seminal utopian *News from Nowhere*), his concern with artistic and human values led him to cross what he called the 'river of fire' and become a committed socialist—committed not to some theoretical formula but to the day by day struggle of working women and men in Britain and to the evolution of his ideas about art, about work and about how life should be lived.

Many of his ideas accorded none too well with the reforming tendencies dominant in the Labour movement, nor with those of 'orthodox' Marxism, which has looked elsewhere for inspiration. Both sides have been inclined to venerate Morris rather than to pay attention to what he said.

Originally written less than a decade before his groundbreaking *The Making of the English Working Class*, E.P. Thompson brought to this biography his now trademark historical mastery, passion, wit, and essential sympathy. It remains unsurpassed as the definitive work on this remarkable figure, by the major British historian of the 20th century.

"*Two impressive figures, William Morris as subject and E. P. Thompson as author, are conjoined in this immense biographical-historical-critical study, and both of them have gained in stature since the first edition of the book was published... The book that was ignored in 1955 has meanwhile become something of an underground classic—almost impossible to locate in second-hand bookstores, pored over in libraries, required reading for anyone interested in Morris and, increasingly, for anyone interested in one of the most important of contemporary British historians... Thompson has the distinguishing characteristic of a great historian: he has transformed the nature of the past, it will never look the same again; and whoever works in the area of his concerns in the future must come to terms with what Thompson has written. So too with his study of William Morris.*"
—Peter Stansky, *The New York Times Book Review*

"*An absorbing biographical study... A glittering quarry of marvelous quotes from Morris and others, many taken from heretofore inaccessible or unpublished sources.*"
—Walter Arnold, *Saturday Review*